Towards Ada 9X

edited by

A. Burns
University of York

IOS Press
1992
Amsterdam • Oxford • Washington, DC • Tokyo

ISBN 90 5199 075 8

Publisher:

IOS Press
Van Diemenstraat 94
1013 CN Amsterdam
Netherlands

Sole distributor in the UK and Ireland:

IOS Press/Lavis Marketing
73 Lime Walk
Headington
Oxford OX3 7AD
England

Distributor in the USA and Canada:

IOS Press, Inc.
P.O. Box 10558
Burke, VA 22009-0558
USA

Sole distributor in Japan:

IOS Japan Dept.
Highway Development Co. Ltd.
1st Golden Bldg, 8-2-9 Ginza
104 Tokyo - Chuoku
Japan

PRINTED IN THE NETHERLANDS

Preface

As we progress into the 1990s the Ada language is at a crucial milestone. The 1983 version is now well understood and good quality compilers and run-time systems are available. Many successful Ada-based systems have been built and many more are in the pipeline. The technology is maturing but the language itself is not stationary; all Ada users will have to become familiar with the 9X version in the coming months and years. When Ada was standardised, by ANSI in 1983, before compilers were built and substantial experience of using the language was obtained, it soon became clear that the review in 1993 was going to be a significant activity. Some of the difficulties with the 1983 reference manual have been removed by producing binding interpretations. Other difficulties require language changes. The award of an international standard (ISO) in 1987 also left some language issues to be addressed by the next revision.

This book is aimed at both reviewing current Ada-based technology and appraising the 9X process. It contains some eleven technical papers which are extended versions of talks given during the 1991 International Ada UK conference. This conference took as its main theme the Ada 9X activity. Topics covered include CIFO (the catalogue of run-time features and options), proposed 9X mappings, asynchronous transfer of control in the tasking model, the design method HOOD and proposed extensions for hard real-time systems, applicable formal methods (LOTUS and Z), secondary bindings (including POSIX), multi-transputer applications, and recent initiatives of the AJPO. The authors are drawn from Europe and the US, and from industry, government agencies and academia. They include the Chair of ARTEWG, an Ada 9X distinguished reviewer, a member of the Ada 9X mapping team, and the director of the AJPO.

The book's contents should be of interest to anyone concerned with Ada based technology. An introduction to the Ada 9X activity is given, but also included are details of the current proposals. In addition to the papers directly addressing Ada 9X, others cover a range of Ada related issues.

Alan Burns
University of York
December 1991

Contents

Towards Ada 9X
A. Burns, Ed.
IOS Press, 1992

1

TOWARDS ADA 9X

EDITORIAL

Alan Burns
Department of Computer Science
University of York, UK

1. INTRODUCTION

Has Ada generated more debate and controversy than any other computer language? At times this certainly seems to be the case. The enthusiasm of the early 1980's was soon displaced by the seemingly interminable wait for first any compilers and subsequently good compilers. And now just when mature tools seem to be coming available, and sizable Ada based systems are being commissioned, it is time to review the language itself!

When Ada was standardised, by ANSI in 1983, before compilers were built and substantial experience of using the language was obtained, it was clear that the review in 1993 was going to be a significant activity. Some of the difficulties with the 1983 reference manual have been removed by producing binding interpretations — a group of Ada Elders being charged with this responsibility. Other difficulties require language changes. These are predominantly concerned with the use of Ada for real-time embedded system, which one must remember is the primary target area for Ada. The award of an international standard (ISO) in 1987 also left some language issues to be addressed by Ada 93 (or Ada 9X as the sceptics call it!). These are mainly concerned with the use of an international character set.

Even if Ada 83 had been perfect, ten years of advancement is bound to bring new requirements for a general purpose programming language (which most people believe Ada is). The two most important of these are the support for applications being implemented on distributed hardware, and the support of programming abstractions of the object oriented kind.

Against this background, the Ada revision exercise commenced in 1988. To attempt to limit the scope of the activity it was said that the changes should have *minimum negative impact and maximum positive impact*. Emphasis was place on language *revision* not *redesign*. The first stage of this revision process was an open invitation for members of the Ada community to send in Revision Requests. This generated over 770 such comments. These were then distilled down to 150 Revision Issues, which were then reduced to 49 User Needs, 41 actual requirements plus 22 study topics[3]. A study topic could be interpreted as a requirement that should be satisfied if the benefits clearly outweighed the cost.

A number of teams were set up to conduct the revision exercise. The mappings themselves (i.e. the specific language changes that are needed to meet the requirements) are being developed by a group from Intermetrics. Their proposals are then vetted by a collection of Distinguished Reviewers. Eventually the proposed language changes will need to be agreed by ANSI (and ISO).

2. THE ADA 9X LANGUAGE

The first major public (i.e. Ada community) review of the proposals took place in March 1991 during a Mapping Workshop held in Florida. At that time the proposals could be discussed under ten major language enhancements:

- Increased Data Abstraction — user defined initialisation, copy, conversion and finalisation.
- Type Inheritance — extending the notion of derived types.
- Run-Time Polymorphism — introduction of the notion of *class*.
- Indirect Access to Data and Subprograms — pointers to static objects.
- Data-Oriented Synchronisation — a new *protected record* abstraction.
- Asynchronous Interactions Between Tasks — asynchronous message passing and asynchronous transfer of control.
- Hierarchical Library Support — introduction of *child* units.
- Distributed Programming — introduction of *active* and *passive* partitions.
- Hierarchical Grouping of Exceptions — introduction of exception classes.
- More Flexible Generic Parameterisation — integration of the notion of class into generic parameters.

Since that time there has been a general reduction of the scope of the changes. Many feel that the mapping team's ideas are too ambitious; they go beyond minimal change and could require substantial modification to existing compilers. Others feel that this is exactly what most Ada compilers need!

The original aim of the mappings was to simplify the language by generalising a number of the concepts contained in Ada 83 and by reducing the number of special cases. Unfortunately this lead to an excessive number of language changes, and hence the pressure to reduce scope. The following gives an outline of some of the proposed language changes[1,2]. It should however be emphasised that the definition of Ada 9X is not yet fixed and that the final language will inevitably be different, perhaps in significant ways.

Subprogram Issues

Introducing true *first-class* subprograms was considered too complex whilst having only subprogram parameters would be too restrictive. It is proposed that Ada 9X will have allow access types to be defined that point at subprograms. Access types themselves will be classified as either *limited* or *non-limited*. The new limited category forces an access instance to always point to the same object; it must therefore be initialised on declaration.

Reduced Recompilation and Library Support

The notion of a hierarchical library structure is to be introduced. Packages may be extended without recompilation by using a child unit. If another package *withs* a child unit it also gets the parent. A child unit may be private or visible, it has access to the private part of the parent.

Programming by Adaptation

Although not a directly defined requirement (it was actually a study topic) the mapping team has proposed a fundamental change to the type model in order to simplify the existing model and to directly support Object Oriented Programming (OOP). The proposal allows any record type to be extended by the "derived type" mechanism. For example given the type:

```
type Points is
record
   X, Y : Float;
end record
```

a new type with an added field can be derived:

```
type Spatial_Points is new Points with
record
   Z : Float;
end record
```

A *root* type and all its derivatives form a *class* in Ada 9X. Operators can be defined to work on a class rather than a specific type and hence a form of polymorphism is supported. It is claimed by the mapping team that this inheritance method can be efficiently implemented. Moreover if a program does not use the facility there will be no run-time cost.

Storage Management

There is a clear need to eliminate storage leaks. The mapping team have addressed this issue in two ways. First it has reduced the number of circumstances that require dynamic allocation (by the introduction of protected records and limited access types), secondly it has a proposal for allowing finalisation code to be associated with each object. Finalisation is however one of the proposals that is liable to be lost during scope reduction.

Fast Mutual Exclusion for Tasking

One of the major extensions to Ada comes in the form a new synchronisation primitive — the *protected record*. Its semantics are close to that of a monitor (or conditional critical region) for it does not require a thread of control of its own. Three kinds of operation can be defined in the specification part of a protected record; procedures which are guaranteed not to be blocked (inside the protected record), entries which have guards (and hence can block), and functions which can facilitate multiple read operations. For example the following sketch code implements a buffer in which the writer does not block (it over-writes if the buffer is full):

```
protected buffer is
   procedure PUT(I : ITEM);
   entry GET(I : out ITEM);
private record
   BUFF : array ...
   TOP, BASE : ...
   FULL, EMPTY : BOOLEAN;
end buffer;
```

```
protected body buffer is

   procedure PUT(I : ITEM) is
   begin
      BUFF[TOP] := I;
      if not FULL then -- increment TOP end if;
      -- assign to FULL and EMPTY
   end PUT;

   entry GET(I : out ITEM) when not EMPTY is
   begin
      I := BUFF[BASE];
      ...
   end GET;

end buffer;
```

The protected record also has a *requeue* facility that will allow a call to be requeued on another (possible private) entry. This facility significantly simplifies the coding of resource controllers.

Asynchronous Transfer of Control

After consideration of many alternatives a *select-in* construct is being proposed. This will allow a sequence of statement to be abandoned if an outstanding call is accepted. For example in the following if the call to STOP in object CONTROL is taken, a "local" abort is effected (note that CONTROL could be either a task or a protected record):

```
select
   CONTROL.STOP
in
   ...
   -- sequence of statements
   ...
end select;
```

The rules concerning the situations in which the sequence of statement can be immediately abandoned are similar to those enforced for the abort in Ada 83.

Asynchronous Message Passing

The protected record could clearly be used to hold data passed asynchronously between tasks. However to allow a task to wait for more than one source of asynchronous message the select call structure is generalised to allow an arbitrary number of calls to be made:

TOWARDS ADA 9X

Studies in
Computer and Communications Systems

Volume 2

Editors
Arvind (MIT)
Ulrich Herzog (Universität Erlangen)
Richard Muntz (UCLA)
Brigitte Plateau (IMAG, Grenoble)
Ken Sevcik (University of Toronto)
Satish Tripathi (University of Maryland)

```
select
   O1.A
or
   O2.B
or
   O3.C
or
   . . .
end select;
```

Note that a fully symmetric select that could have call outs and accepts was rejected because of inefficiencies in implementation. The objects O1, O2, O3, etc in the above could be either protected records or tasks; hence a task can wait for the arrival or either synchronous or asynchronous messages.

Unsigned Integers

These will now be supported as will *wraparound* operations. For example

type unsigned **is base range** 0 .. 2**32-1;

TOP : **cyclic range** 0 .. MAX;

Data Interoperability

Two predefined attributes 'WRITE and 'READ will be introduced to allow an object to be flattened (into a bit structure) and re-assembled. Other minor changes will be made to Size and Alignment Rep-Clauses for types, subtypes and objects.

Interrupts

The use of protected record procedures allows data to pass out of an interrupt handler without a context switch away from the handler. Indeed it will be possible to bind a handler directly to such a procedure. Dynamic interrupt binding will also be supported.

Dynamic References to Global Objects

This is achieved via the use of limited access types; see earlier discussion.

Shared Memory

The effect of pragma SHARED will now be obtained by a modifier that will designate a variable as *atomic*. Variables may also be designated *volatile*, if it can change arbitrarily, or *independent*. An independent variable is required to be stored in memory that is independent of that for neighbouring objects. This will allow true parallel tasks to not block each other by assessing neighbouring objects.

Task Scheduling

There is a need to allow alternative scheduling algorithms and to support common real-time paradigms. This will be facilitated by a *Real-Time Annex*. In this annex there will be, for example, subprograms for manipulating dynamic priorities. Note that the introduction of protected records will significantly help the generation of programs that meet timing requirements.

Time and Timers

A need to delay for either absolute or relative time has been recognised by extending the delay primitive to allow for delay DURATION or delay_until CLOCK. The real-time annex will specify a method of detecting CPU budget exhaustion.

Distribution

Here the mapping team have chosen an approach of facilitating distribution rather than directly supporting it. Library units will be designated as either *passive* or *active* partitions. Active partitions will only be able to communicate with each other via a defined communications package that will support remote procedure calls. Remore rendezvous will not be allowed. Configuration and reconfiguration is deemed to be outside the language and will not be supported; there may however be a distribution annex.

Predictability of Execution

This is needed for safety critical applications that require traceability through to the assembler. There will be pragmas to limit optimisation and to ensure a canonical program form is maintained. It will be possible to define pragmas that will cause compile-time rejection or run-time exceptions. Assertions may be introduced and be applicable at all points in the program text (e.g. on procedure parameters).

3. OVERVIEW OF THE BOOK

The 1991 International Ada UK conference took Ada 9X as its main theme. Tutorials on the current state of the proposals were given, and the management stream of the conference considered issues of transition. Ada is specifically aimed at large embedded systems. Such systems require modifications throughout their lifetime; which is typically over 30 years. Hence, not only is the transition to 9X an issue but also future revisions.

The papers contained in this book are extended versions of talks given during the technical sessions of the above conference. Although most are concerned with 9X issues directly, these are not the only topics that are relevant to Ada in the middle to late 1990's. Three others concerns are specifically covered:

(1) Formal Methods

(2) Bindings to other standards (e.g. POSIX and GKS)

(3) Multiprocessor Implementations

The first paper, by Mike Kamrad, discusses the latest release of the CIFO (Catalogue of Interface Features and Options) which is produced by ARTEWG (ACM Ada Run-Time Environments Working Group). Mike Kamrad is chair of ARTEWG. This group has been working for some years to try and define and standardise means by which Ada's expressive power, in the real-time domain, can by enhanced. Many of the features introduced by ARTEWG as extensions and options will be directly supported in Ada 9X. Hence this latest version of CIFO helps to explain some of the rationale behind Ada 9X, and can be used as a bridge to the new language. Ada 83 with CIFO brings one close to Ada 9X in terms of the needs of real-time programmers.

The second and third paper directly discuss Ada 9X. Bill Taylor, one of the Distinguished Reviewers, presents a description of the three main language modifications: protected records, hierarchical library units and type extensions. Offer Pazy, who is one of the Intermetrics mapping team, discusses the topic of asynchronous transfer of control. For many years the lack of this provision has been seen as one of the major draw backs of the Tasking Model. In real-time systems there is often a need to gain the attention (quickly) of a task. But it is very inefficient for this task to be constantly checking to see if it should respond to such a call. What is required is some asynchronous means of making a task stop what it is going and respond to a new situation. Ada 9X will (probably!) support such a feature.

There is, of course, no real experience with using Ada 9X. Some groups are however attempting to apply the new language in paper studies and to relate their findings to the mapping team. The paper by Andy Wellings and myself looks at how Ada 9X should be used for programming hard real-time systems. Extensive use is made of protected records, asynchronous transfer of control and multi-way (and nested) selective calls. We consider Ada 9X to be the implementation language of a design method that directly support abstractions such as periodic objects and deadlines; and which restricts a design to one that can be analysed for worst case execution time and schedulability. The proposed design method is called HRT-HOOD (Hard Real-Time HOOD). A case study is included in this paper.

The next two papers are concerned with formal methods. Tim Read addresses the issue of using formal specifications for defining reusable Ada packages. He applies the formal notation, Z. This is becoming an increasingly popular notation and is now supported by tools. Examples of Z are given in the paper but prior knowledge of the method on the part of the reader is not required. The second of the pair of pages on formal notations comes from the Technical University of Madrid and concerns LOTUS. LOTUS is a formal description technique based on the temporal ordering of observations. It is unique amongst formal techniques in having its own ISO standard. The paper describes the design and implementation of a tool, LOTAda, that translates LOTUS specifications into Ada.

One of the truisms that the Ada community often ignores is that Ada systems do not live in isolation. The idealistic model, that views all systems as consisting of a single Ada program running on a bare processor, is rarely achievable. Indeed it is becoming increasingly the case that Ada code must be interfaced to external systems that are themselves standardised. Two papers touch on this issue. Daniel Juttelstad and James Oblinger, from the US Navy Next Generation Computer Resources (NGCR) program, consider the role of POSIX and Ada in future Navy Systems. It is clear that considerable advantages will accrue if it becomes possible to execute (efficiently) Ada 9X programs on top of real-time POSIX. This will continue to be an issue while Ada 9X and real-time POSIX evolve. The paper by Edwards, Atkinson and Griffiths looks at the opposite issue of calling up from an Ada program to some existing utility. They use, as an example, calls to a GKS system and X windows. One of the questions addressed in whether to use a new Ada binding to these routines, or get at the routines via calls to C code (via a C language interface).

Issues of multiprocessor and distributed execution of Ada programs have long been debated. The paper from King's College, London, looks at a particular set of experiments concerned with a multi-transputer implementation of a Kinematics algorithm coded in Ada. They are motivated by the needs to program adaptive robots undertaking real-time tasks in an environment which is not fully deterministic. The task is taken as the unit of distribution but as often is the case performance enhancements are not as great as one would like.

The final paper comes from John Solomond, the Director of the Ada Joint Program Office (AJPO). In addition to enforcing the mandate for Ada within the US

Department of Defence, the AJPO has instituted a number of initiatives that are important to the whole of the Ada community. Four such initiatives are outlined in this paper: the Portable Common Interface Set (PCIS) program; the merger of the Ada Compiler Evaluation Capability (ACEC) and the Ada Evaluation System (AES); the Ada Technology Insertion Program (ATIP); and the Ada Style Guide.

Taken together these papers address many of the key aspects of Ada Technology as the language moves towards revision. Although there is pressure to reduce the scope of the changes it is to be hoped that the key modifications will not be sacrificed. It is particularly important that the new real-time features remain. If they do then the future of Ada looks extremely encouraging.

References

1.   Intermetrics, ''Draft Mapping Document'', Ada 9X Project Report (August 1991).
2.   Intermetrics, ''Draft Mapping Rationale Document'', Ada 9X Project Report (August 1991).
3.   Ada 9X Project Office, *Ada 9X Requirements Document*, December 1990.

Towards Ada 9X
A. Burns, Ed.
IOS Press, 1992

The Catalogue of Interface Features and Options: Bridge to the Future for Real-Time Ada Applications

Mike Kamrad, ARTEWG Chair

Unisys Electronic and Information Systems Group
M/S U2F13
PO Box 64525
St Paul MN 55164-0525
612-456-7315
mkamrad@ajpo.sei.cmu.edu

Abstract

Ada programs require a sophisticated runtime environment to support its execution. Real-time embedded applications in Ada are sensitive to the behavior of the Ada runtime environment. Builders of real-time applications in Ada seek mechanisms from Ada implementations that will control that behavior to the benefit of the real-time application.

The Ada RunTime Environment Working Group (ARTEWG) of the ACM Special Interest Group on Ada (SIGAda) has just released version 3.0 of the Catalogue of Interface Features and Options (CIFO) which describes an inventory of proposals for these mechanisms in the following areas:

- Scheduling Control
- Asynchronous Cooperation Mechanisms
- Interrupt Support
- Miscellaneous Services

The goal of CIFO has been to seek commonality of Ada runtime environments with these proposals to enhance portability of real-time applications across Ada implementations. This newest release is a significant improvement of the previous release by providing additional mechanisms, cleaner and clearer semantics, and detailed description of interactions among all the mechanisms.

This paper begins with a brief description of the basics of an Ada runtime environment. From this foundation, the presentation will explain how mechanisms of CIFO fit into the Ada runtime environment and then present an overview of the mechanisms themselves. CIFO is not meant be a monolithic interface to runtime environment but rather it is meant to be an inventory of loosely coupled entries from which an application selects an appropriate set that supports the application and then seeks to find in an Ada application. The presentation will describe how applications should use CIFO and choose the appropriate mechanisms from CIFO and procure them from Ada vendors. Finally, the presentation will examine the future status of CIFO in light of the development of Ada9X and standardization efforts for features to support real-time application.

1   A Framework for Ada Runtime Environments

In order to gain a better understanding of the purpose and function of the Catalogue of Interface Features and Options release 3.0 (CIFO 3.0), it is useful to put it into the context of Ada runtime environments. This section gives brief overview of the major elements of Ada runtime environments and show several important compositions of them.

The **runtime environment (RTE)** for Ada consists of three elements: abstract data structures, code sequences, and predefined subroutines. These are the same elements that other languages and executives provide. The **compilation system** for Ada selects the appropriate elements as directed by the **source Ada program** and as dictated by the **underlying computing resource** (which could be one or more computers, with or without an executive or operating system). The result, as Figure 1 shows, is a **translated Ada program**, which is similar to the translated program produced by other language compilers.

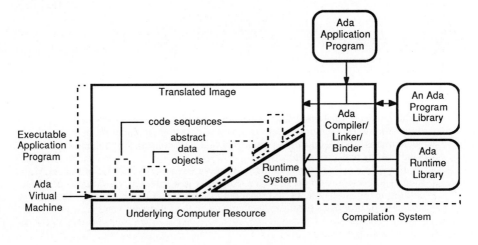

Figure 1.   Elements of Ada Compilation Process

The code of the generated Ada program adheres to conventions for data structures and code that the Ada implementors have selected for representing abstract data types and program structures in the Ada language. In addition, the generated Ada program may use predefined subroutines to support features of the Ada language that the Ada implementor has chosen not to directly represent in generated code. The set of predefined subroutines for any generated Ada program is called the **runtime system (RTS)** for that program. These predefined subroutines are chosen from the **runtime library (RTL)** for that Ada compilation system. Altogether, the data structures, the code conventions, and the runtime system selected by the Ada implementation for a generated Ada program provide an **Ada virtual machine** on which the translated Ada program executes.

One of the important compositions of an Ada runtime environment is one targeted to a computer system that has an existing operating system or executive. Unlike many other languages, Ada includes high level abstractions for concurrent programming, exception handling, and resource allocation. The Ada compilation system is expected to provide the runtime environment that supports these sophisticated features. An Ada compilation system can not assume that translated Ada programs will be supported by a specific executive or operating system. This means that the Ada implementation must be tailored directly to the capabilities of the underlying computing resource that includes an existing executive or operating system as shown in Figure 2. The Ada compilation process may choose to have the runtime environment take advantage of some subset of the executive so that the runtime system of subroutines that is created by the Ada compilation system shares the support of the translated Ada program with the executive.

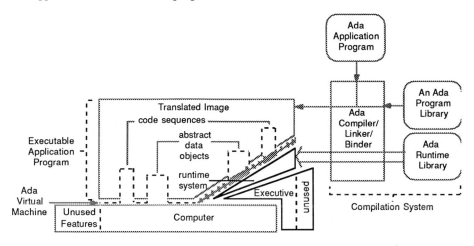

Figure 2. Ada Compilation Process Targeted to an Executive

This means that the capability needed to support a feature of the translated Ada program, such as tasking, may be provided directly by some combination of the bare computer and the executive or by the runtime system selected for the translated Ada program. In turn, the runtime system may either provide all the requested capability itself or it may require assistance from the existing executive of the underlying computing resource. Finally, some features of the executive of the underlying computing resource, like some features of the bare computer, may never be used by the runtime environment, as they may be inconsistent or unnecessary to the execution of any translated Ada program.

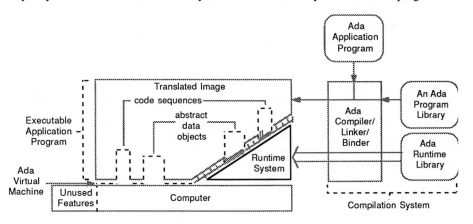

Figure 3. Ada Compilation Process for Bare Machine

The other important composition of an Ada runtime environment is one targeted to a bare computer without the support of an existing operating system or executive. Ada blurs the separation of the responsibilities of runtime environment support between executives and programming language compilers because Ada includes features for concurrent programming and storage management, and Ada demands no specific supporting executive. All capabilities required by a translated Ada program that are not directly supported by the bare computer must be supplied by the runtime system for that translated Ada program, as shown in Figure 3. Consequently, Ada compilation systems are responsible for providing all the elements of the runtime environment to support applications written in Ada.

It is apparent that the runtime system has all the aspects of an executive, which has caught the attention of those who are concerned about performance. It would be straightforward to build a fixed Ada runtime system executive that supports all translated Ada programs, as Figure 4 shows. But it does not need to be that way. Ideally, the Ada compilation system can configure the runtime system of subroutines from the runtime library to exactly fit the needs of the application written in Ada, just as software engineers have custom built executives for applications in the past. The result would be the smallest runtime system for that translated Ada program. This configuration process could potentially generate a unique runtime system for each application written in Ada.

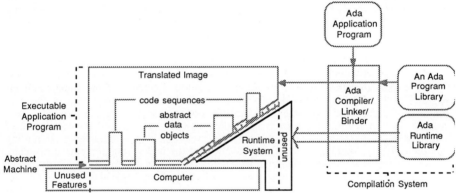

Figure 4. Ada Compilation Process with Fixed Ada Runtime System

The runtime environment of the Ada compilation system must always comply with the rules of the Ada language as defined by the Ada Reference Manual. Yet the Ada Reference Manual provides significant flexibility in how the runtime environments support the language definition. The runtime environment is thus allowed to exhibit different performance characteristics (that may reflect the needs of the application) for the same features or combination of features of Ada. In fact, the Ada Reference Manual provides the pragma construct as one method to help the Ada compilation system determine the performance characteristics that the runtime environment should provide for an application. Thus, the runtime environment of an Ada compilation system may be able to accommodate many interpretations of an application in Ada that comply with the Ada language standard. These interpretations can be guided by the pragma construct or by other mechanisms provided by the Ada compilation system. This provides the appropriate context to explain the function and purpose of CIFO 3.0.

2 An Overview of the Catalogue of Interface Features and Options

The Ada Reference Manual intentionally (necessarily) leaves the details of many important capabilities of the Ada runtime system to the individual implementation, such as scheduling discipline, interrupt, control, storage management, and so on. In many applications, these capabilities and services are essential to the success of a project, and will of necessity be provided. Since the user's interface to these capabilities is often not specified in great detail, implementations will differ as they emerge.

The objective of the "Catalogue of Interface Features and Options" (CIFO) is to propose and describe a common set of user accessible runtime environment (user-RTE, for short) interfaces, with which a programmer can both request services of the runtime environment (RTE) and tailor the RTE to meet application-specific requirements. These interfaces are described as Entries in the CIFO and their descriptions represent "contracts" provided to the application builders. By "common", implementations are intended to provide the capabilities expressed by the language-oriented interface descriptions of CIFO Entries in such a way that programmers need not learn a new interface when using a different Ada implementation.

The declarations for these interfaces are intended to be available to users via an Ada program library. The implementations are logically unit entries in the runtime library of an Ada compilation system, but may be implemented by compiler-emitted code, or by combinations of both. The effect of the CIFO features (See Figure 5) is to create an "extended runtime library" ("**Ext. Ada Runtime Library**") to supplement the original runtime library. From both libraries, the Ada compilation draws the necessary routines as directed by the users in their code. The result is extending the implemented runtime system with extensions ("**XRTS**") from the "extended runtime library".

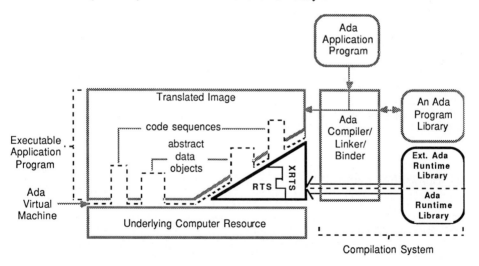

Figure 5. Impact of CIFO on Ada Compilation Process

It should be emphasized that presence of CIFO does not mean that the language is viewed as being deficient in all of the areas addressed (although implementations may be). Highly application-dependent requirements are not appropriately found in a language reference manual. However, in keeping with the concept of "extensibility", implementations should be expected to extend the language, in the RM-prescribed manner, to meet application-specific requirements. Thus, many "language deficiencies" are more correctly expressed as "procurement issues".

The primary mechanisms for specifying the capabilities in the CIFO Entries are packages and subprograms. The use of pragmas has been minimized for a number of reasons, primarily because a compiler can ignore them without informing the user if it does not support them. In contrast, packages, generics, and subprograms which are not supported must be rejected. Furthermore, the proposed features, expressed as packages and subprograms, could, at least, be conceivably implemented entirely via RTE modules. Pragmas and attributes would absolutely require the mediation of a cognizant compiler. However, when the semantics of pragmas are truly appropriate, they may be used.

It should be noted that these proposed interfaces are not changes to the language. On the contrary, they represent "legal enhancements" in the sense that the Ada Reference Manual (ARM) prescribes various means of providing additional functionality at the language level (packages, pragmas, attributes, etc.). They do not alter the semantics of existing ARM-defined constructs, since such alterations would be "illegal". Instead, the Entries in CIFO are to be used to tailor a set of Ada resources for differing application environments.

3   Descriptions of CIFO Entries

The Entries are divided into four categories: Scheduling Control, Asynchronous Cooperation Mechanisms, Interrupt Support, and Miscellaneous Services. The categories define capabilities that support various abstract levels of control and behavior in the runtime environment in support of application execution. Scheduling Control Entries propose abstract functions and capabilities that directly control the time and extent of task execution. On the other hand, the Asynchronous Cooperation Mechanisms Entries propose abstract communication and synchronization structures that indirectly control the time and execution of task execution. To illustrate, the Scheduling Control Category contains several Task Suspend/Resumption Entries that control the execution of tasks in a very direct manner, while the Asynchronous Cooperation Mechanisms Category contains Event and Signal Entries that indirectly control task execution by synchronization and communication. The Interrupt Support Category contains Entries that provide much needed services and abstractions for fast and effective interrupts and interrupt management. The last category, Miscellaneous Services, provides support for other Entries and a set of capabilities that control not only the behavior of the runtime system but also the translated code of an applications, namely abstractions such shared variables and passive tasks.

Detailed descriptions of all CIFO Entries can be found in Appendix A.

3.1   Scheduling Control.

This collection of Entries is designed to implicitly control the execution of tasks in an application by manipulating the properties of tasks, or explicitly control execution by directly specifying the scheduling or dispatching decisions. The Entries are grouped as follows:

a.   Synchronization Discipline, Priority Inheritance Discipline, and Dynamic Priorities.
b.   Time Critical Sections
c.   Task Suspension, Two Stage Task Suspension, and Asynchronous Task Suspension
d.   Synchronous and Asynchronous Task Scheduling and Time Slicing
e.   Abort Via Task Identifiers.

The first group controls scheduling and dispatching by manipulating the priorities of tasks and how the priorities of those are used for dispatching executable programs, selection of waiting callers in task entry queues, and selection of alternatives in selective wait statements. Time Critical Sections are used to guarantee uninterrupted execution for a time critical sequence of statements. Group C Entries are designed to directly control the suspension and resumption of specific tasks for simple blocking for services like I/O, intertask communication and synchronization, and asynchronous suspension and resumption. The fourth group of Entries are designed to control the scheduling of tasks by defining the events or time these tasks will execute or terminate. Finally the Abort Via Task Identifiers is designed to provide the same semantics of the abort statement for tasks specified by their Task Identifiers.

Obviously these Entries provide semantics that have very pervasive effects on the execution of the application. Despite this they have been included in the CIFO because of the well founded requests for them from application builders and the unsafe and non-portable mechanisms that would be used in their place. They should be used judiciously, especially when several of them are used within the same application.

3.2 Asynchronous Cooperation Mechanisms.

The Asynchronous Cooperation Mechanisms Entries propose abstract structures that indirectly control the time and execution of task execution. These Entries propose familiar asynchronous and synchronous communication and signaling objects. The first set of these Entries (for Resources, Events, Pulses, Buffers, Blackboards, Broadcasts, and Barriers) have been developed and recommended by the French consortium of avionics vendors, who created a set of CIFO-like extensions, called Extensions des services Temps Reels Ada (ExTRA)[1]. All of these Entries share the concept of a "common reference memory model", where the cooperation objects, very similar to Ada access type, proposed by these Entries are defined to permit either static or dynamic memory management implementation techniques. All objects must be created and destroyed by the application software.

The remaining Entries (Mutual Exclusive Access to Shared Data, Shared Locks, Signals, and Asynchronous Transfer of Control) propose asynchronous communication and cooperation mechanisms described do formally define the memory management model used to implement the underlying resource (where appropriate). Some of the Entries in this section do not imply any underlying resource that must be concerned with such issues as dangling references (for instance, Signals). Two of the Entries in this section, Shared Locks and Mutually Exclusive Access to Shared Data, may at first appear very similar. In fact, Shared Locks could be used to create mutually exclusive access to shared data. However, Shared Locks is better used to ensure mutually exclusive access to objects other than data.

3.3 Interrupt Support.

This section provides facilities for the control of interrupt- oriented hardware (as opposed to control of preemption) and for the specification of additional information to the runtime system in order to significantly enhance performance of interrupt handling. Specifically, there are three Entries:

- Interrupt Management, which provides for the low-level management of interrupts directly enabling and disabling them and masking and unmasking them.
- Trivial Task Entries, which identifies the special case where the task entry has no formal part and no associated accept statements has any sequence of statements and thereby promotes optimization of task synchronization between "interrupt" tasks and "non interrupt" tasks.
- Fast Interrupt Pragmas, which provides two means of improving the performances of tasks that service interrupts.

3.4 Miscellaneous Services.

This section provides facilities which furnish the compiler with additional information about the application in order to increase performance, reduce executable image size, support shared data, and support additional functionality (such as referencing a static object via an access value) as follows:

- Pre-elaboration, which identifies all objects to be pre-elaborated, thereby requiring no runtime elaboration and making them eligible for storage in ROMs.
- Access Values to Designate Static Objects, which provides the means to create pointers to non-heap objects.
- Passive Task, which provides means to define tasks which have no thread of control of their own but executed with the thread of control from the caller.
- Unchecked Subprogram Invocation, which permits calling subprograms by the use of their addresses.
- Data Synchronization, which improves upon the SHARED variable feature of the Ada language.
- Dynamic Storage Management, which facilities for storage management that executes safely in multitasking environment and in a (small) bounded time.

This category also contains two CIFO entries that are used by many of the other CIFO entries. Neither of these two entries is very useful by itself. However, both supply a standard way for other CIFO entries to perform two important functions:

- Tasks Identifiers, which specify tasks, where Ada typing rules would not permit it.
- Queuing Discipline, which specify queueing disciplines that can be applied to callers to several other CIFO Entries.

4   Changes in CIFO from Previous Release

For those of you familiar with the previous release of CIFO 2.0 released in December 1987, this section describes the differences between the two releases.

The changes in CIFO 3.0 reflect the impact of four activities since the release of CIFO 2.0:

- Refinements provided by feedback from actual implementations and applications of previous releases which recommend some new Entries and that semantics be tightened and clarified.
- Convergence with proposals found in Extensions des services Temps Reels Ada (ExTRA). ExTRA was produced by French consortium of avionics vendors under the sponsorship of the French Armament Board, and proposes set of CIFO-like extensions. ARTEWG worked closely with the ExTRA group in merging Entries from both documents.
- Participation in the Ada9X Project, which provided insights into wide spectrum of real-time application needs requested for Ada9X.
- Requirements from major airframe programs for the US Air Force and Army that were published by the Joint Integrated Avionics Working Group (JIAWG).

As a result of these activities, the reader will find the following changes:

- New Entries have been added: Queuing Discipline, Priority Inheritance Discipline, Two Stage Task Suspension, Asynchronous Task Suspension, Synchronization Discipline, Resources, Events, Pulses, Buffers, Blackboards, Broadcasts, Farriers,

Asynchronous Transfer of Control, Shared Locks, Access Values That Designate Static Objects, Passive Task Pragma, Unchecked Subprogram Invocation, Data Synchronization Pragma, and Dynamic Storage Management.

* Several Entries were deleted: Special Delays and Transmitting Task Identifiers between Tasks.
* The remaining Entries were revised with cleaner and clearer semantics. More uniformity was also introduced in the presentation of all Entries. All revised Entries describe the significant differences from CIFO 2.0
* All Entries describe the interactions that each Entry may have with all other Entries when those Entries are used in the same application. Additionally a matrix of all interactions is found in the appendix of CIFO 3.0.

5 Choice and Use of CIFO Entries.

For the implementation of Entries in CIFO, all readers of CIFO must understand that **CIFO is not a monolithic runtime system or operating system interface.** CIFO is a loosely coupled set of Entries from which an application builder selects an appropriate subset of Entries that support the application and then seeks to find those Entries in an Ada implementation. In fact, **application builders are encouraged to select subsets of CIFO Entries.** Ada vendors are in the process of providing significant subsets of CIFO Entries and actually have many of them in place. Both application builders and Ada vendors should analyze carefully the cost-benefit of the extent of the subset of CIFO Entries they demand for application or provide in their implementations. Rather than dictate or suggest subsets, ARTEWG expects the marketplace to converge on these subsets.

Because CIFO is a collection of loosely couple Entries, many Entries have overlapping capabilities and, in some cases, conflicting capabilities. To assist both application builders and Ada vendors on the appropriate choices of Entries for their subsets, CIFO has defined the interactions among Entries. These interactions are guidance on the impact and cost of one Entry to other Entries. Those Entries, that do not interact well or not at all, are not expected to be combined and therefore should not be included in the selected subset of Entries that an application needs or an Ada implementation supports. Each Entry has a list of all interactions with all the other Entries and all interactions are summarized in a matrix at the end of the CIFO.

CIFO "conformance" always refers to each specific Entries and should never refer to the CIFO as a whole. Conformance to an Entry by an implementation means that the implementation fully supports the required semantics described in the CIFO Entry. This includes any restrictions implied by the interactions with other Entries. By the same token, an implementation that includes "more" Entries from this catalogue should not automatically be judged a "better" implementation. Once again, **subsets of CIFO Entries are welcomed and encouraged!**

6 The Future of CIFO

ARTEWG believes that CIFO 3.0 is a bridge to the future for real-time embedded applications in several important areas: Ada9X, ISO standards, and POSIX.

The definitions of these Entries exist now considerably in advance of the Ada9X standard. This benefits developments that need these capabilities before similar capabilities are available in Ada9X. Several projects has recognized this, most notably the JIAWG Common Ada Run-Time Working Group and F16 Mission Management Computer Upgrade, and have endorsed the use of CIFO 3.0 on those programs. Many of the Entries have been defined with the anticipation of Ada9X standard in mind. In fact, a preliminary analysis of CIFO Entries (as compared to Ada9X Mapping Document Version 3.0) shows that most of them can be replaced in a straight-forward manner with proposed Ada9X features. Soon after the release of Ada9X, a subsequent release of CIFO will reflect significant changes made possible by the standardization of the Ada9X. Finally, there was always be a need for a document such as CIFO, even in light of the anticipated improvements with Ada9X, because the needs of critical, embedded applications may not be possible or appropriate to completely satisfy in Ada9X or subsequent language revisions. ARTEWG will continue to examine these needs and propose new Entries to meet those needs.

A new Rapporteur Group for Real-Time Ada (RTARG) has been formed under the direction of Working Group 9 (on Ada standards) within the ISO. The goal of the RTARG is to define standards for extensions to Ada to support real-time applications and they have proposed CIFO 3.0 as their baseline document. The Chair of the RTARG, Dominique Chandesris, has contacted the ARTEWG to obtain ARTEWG cooperation in meeting the goals of the RTARG.

The POSIX initiative represents a significant development in operating system interface standardization. Within the POSIX organization, there is a group (P1003.4) which is defining the extensions to POSIX to support real-time applications. This group has shown an interest in CIFO 3.0 and have meet with ARTEWG leadership to discuss how to include appropriate Entries from CIFO 3.0.

References

[1] Dominique CHANDESRIS et al, *Extension Temps Reel Ada (ExTRA),* French Armament Board, 1990.

Appendix A Detailed Descriptions of CIFO 3.0 Entries

The proposals presented in this paper only summarize the proposal by providing the issue the proposal addresses and a brief description of the proposal. Detailed description of each proposal are found in the Catalogue of Interface Features and Options Version 3.0. This can be obtained directly from the ARTEWG (by sending a self-addressed large envelope **with US$4 in postage** to the author) or from SIGAda as one of their Special Issues of *AdaLetters.*

A.1 Scheduling Control.

Synchronization Discipline

Issue. The Reference Manual has left undefined the criteria for selecting waiting callers on entry queues or for selecting among open alternatives in a select statement. For many applications, it is important to be able to specify that criteria in order to meet performance requirements. One such criteria is the priority of tasks.

Proposal. Two alternative mechanisms are proposed for specifying criteria for queuing entry calls and selection criteria for selective waits: the packages COMPLEX_DISCIPLINE and SYNCHRONIZATION_DISCIPLINE or the set of four pragmas:

```
with QUEUING_DISCIPLINE;
use QUEUING_DISCIPLINE;
package COMPLEX_DISCIPLINE is
   type TIEBREAK is ( ARBITRARY, FIFO, LEXICAL );

   type SELECT_DISCIPLINE( QD : DISCIPLINE := ARBITRARY_QUEUING ) is
      record
         case QD is
            when QUEUING_DISCIPLINE.PRIORITY_QUEUING => T : TIEBREAK;
            when others => null;
         end case;
      end record;

   type SELECT_CRITERIA( LEXICAL_ORDER : BOOLEAN := FALSE ) is
      record
         case LEXICAL_ORDER is
            when TRUE =>       null;
            when FALSE =>      DISCIPLINE : SELECT_DISCIPLINE;
         end case;
      end record;

   ELECTION_ERROR : exception;
end COMPLEX_DISCIPLINE;

with TASK_IDS;
with QUEUING_DISCIPLINE;
with COMPLEX_DISCIPLINE;
package SYNCHRONIZATION_DISCIPLINE is

   procedure SET_ENTRY_CRITERIA
             (OF_TASK : in TASK_IDS.TASK_ID;
              TO : in QUEUING_DISCIPLINE.DISCIPLINE );

   procedure SET_GLOBAL_ENTRY_CRITERIA
             ( TO : in QUEUING_DISCIPLINE.DISCIPLINE);

   procedure SET_SELECT_CRITERIA
             (OF_TASK : in TASK_IDS.TASK_ID;
              TO : in COMPLEX_DISCIPLINE.SELECT_CRITERIA );

   procedure SET_GLOBAL_SELECT_CRITERIA
             (TO : in COMPLEX_DISCIPLINE.SELECT_CRITERIA );
end SYNCHRONIZATION_DISCIPLINE;
```

An alternative implementation of these features takes the form of pragmas, as described below.

```
pragma SET_ENTRY_CRITERIA
             ( TO : in QUEUING_DISCIPLINE.DISCIPLINE );

pragma SET_GLOBAL_ENTRY_CRITERIA
             ( TO : in QUEUING_DISCIPLINE.DISCIPLINE );

pragma SET_SELECT_CRITERIA
             ( TO : in COMPLEX_DISCIPLINE.SELECT_CRITERIA );

pragma SET_GLOBAL_SELECT_CRITERIA
             ( TO : in COMPLEX_DISCIPLINE.SELECT_CRITERIA );
```

The package COMPLEX_DISCIPLINE specifies the record type that encapsulate the arbitration policy to be used in selective wait statements.

The subprograms and pragmas with GLOBAL in their name apply the criteria to entries and select statements throughout the program. The other subprograms and pragmas apply their criteria to all the entries and select statements in a specific task.

When the criteria is specified for entries and the discipline specifies "PRIORITY" queuing, then the queues are managed such that processing entry queues has the effect that queued tasks are serviced in priority order. It may happen that an entry queue contains more than one task whose priority is "highest", i.e. at least as high as that of any other task currently in the entry queue. In this case, the "PRIORITY" discipline chooses the task that has been in the queue at this priority level longest. Note that through priority inheritance, a task that is already waiting in the entry queue may be given a different (higher or lower) priority.

For the subprograms or pragmas that specify select criteria, whenever a task is executing a select statement for which more than one accept alternative is open, the alternative will be chosen according to the specified discipline. If the discriminant LEXICAL_ORDER is TRUE, the decision among several eligible accept alternatives will be made according to the lexical order in which the accept alternatives appear in the source text. The first eligible alternative will be chosen.

If the discriminant is FALSE, the user can specify any discipline from QUEUING_DISCIPLINE in the field DISCIPLINE. When FIFO discipline is chosen, the task at the head of the relevant entry queues that has been in the queue longest is chosen. When queuing discipline PRIORITY_QUEUING is specified, there may be more than one task at the head of a relevant entry queue such that that task's priority is highest. The user needs to specify(in the component T of type TIEBREAK) how this situation should be resolved. For the tie-breaking criteria, the value LEXICAL indicates a policy like the one described earlier: eligible alternatives are considered in the lexical order in which they appear in the program text. The value ARBITRARY leaves the policy to the implementation. The value FIFO indicates that among the eligible "highest priority" tasks at the heads of the different entry queues, the one will be chosen that has been waiting at its current priority longest.

An implementation does not need to support all criteria; the only value required is ARBITRARY_QUEUING. An implementation of this CIFO Entry must document the options that are supported.

Priority Inheritance Discipline

Issue. Many applications can benefit from software technology methods that can be used to achieve analyzable and predictable system behavior. One such method, Rate Monotonic Scheduling (RMS) uses the dynamic preemptive nature of the Ada tasking and task communication model and requires certain behavior of specific implementation dependent portions of the Ada language. Namely, all unbounded priority inversion (i.e., unbounded blocking of a high priority task by the execution of a lower priority task) must be eliminated. This may occur in implementation dependent areas of the language; in open alternatives of the select statement, in entry calls to an accept body that may result in FIFO queuing, and when a server task is executing outside its rendezvous and is blocking a higher priority task.

Proposal. Two mechanisms are proposed for specifying priority inheritance discipline:

```
package PRIORITY_INHERITANCE_DISCIPLINE is
      procedure SET_PRIORITY_INHERITANCE_CRITERIA;
      procedure RESET_PRIORITY_INHERITANCE_CRITERIA;
end PRIORITY_INHERITANCE_DISCIPLINE;
```

or

```
pragma SET_PRIORITY_INHERITANCE_CRITERIA;
```

When the procedure SET_PRIORITY_INHERITANCE_CRITERIA or the pragma SET_PRIORITY_INHERITANCE_CRITERIA is in effect, all tasks in the program have the following properties:

1. A task's (active) priority is at least as high as the highest priority among all the tasks currently suspended in ANY of its entry queues (including closed alternatives).
2. A rendezvous is executed at the higher of the two (active) priorities of the tasks engaged in the rendezvous as specified by the LRM. If the priority of one or both of these tasks change while the rendezvous is in progress, the priority of the rendezvous is adjusted accordingly, if necessary.
3. Any newly created task executes its activation at a priority not lower than that of the task whose execution created the new task.
4. Whenever a master completes, all the tasks that depend directly or indirectly on this master have their priorities elevated to at least the level of the task under whose control the completing master executes.
5. Whenever the priority of a task changes, either through the SET_PRIORITY procedure of the DYNAMIC_PRIORITIES package or as a consequence of the rules 1-4 above, the priorities of other tasks are adjusted to satisfy rules 1-4.
6. Priority inheritance (i.e., Rules 1, 2, and 5) is also applied when tasks are competing for other resources and it is sensible to do so. If a task is waiting for a shared lock (see the Shared Locks CIFO Entry) held by a lower priority task then the task holding the lock has its priority elevated to that of the waiting task.

Unbounded priority inversion, that may be caused when no priority discipline is in effect on open alternatives of the select statement and on entry queues, can be eliminated using the Synchronization Discipline CIFO Entry to select the appropriate queuing discipline. Note that though a global priority discipline is intended for both entry queues and open select alternatives when the PRIORITY_INHERITANCE_DISCIPLINE is in effect, it is not necessary but the effect of priority inheritance will be extremely limited.

Dynamic Priorities

Issue. The minimal priority scheme defined by the LRM provides static priorities only. Many applications require a more dynamic priority assignment capability. For instance, degraded operation implies that the work performed in some task may be much less important than in normal operation, and should be assigned a less urgent priority (if retained at all).

Proposal. This proposal consists of a package and an associated pragma:

```
with TASK_IDS;
package DYNAMIC_PRIORITIES is
    subtype DYNAMIC_PRIORITY is INTEGER range 0 .. <31 or greater>;

    procedure SET_DYNAMIC_PRIORITY
              (  OF_TASK     : in TASK_IDS.TASK_ID;
                 TO          : in DYNAMIC_PRIORITY );
    function DYNAMIC_PRIORITY_OF( THE_TASK : TASK_IDS.TASK_ID )
       return DYNAMIC_PRIORITY;

    PRIORITY_CHANGE_NOT_ALLOWED : exception;
end DYNAMIC_PRIORITIES;


pragma INITIAL_PRIORITY( <static_expression> );
```

The package DYNAMIC_PRIORITIES provides a capability to assign priorities to tasks dynamically. The DYNAMIC_PRIORITY subtype is defined independently of the static Ada priority. If a task specification contains pragma PRIORITY, then this package cannot be used to modify its priority. A new pragma, INITIAL_PRIORITY, may be provided by the compiler to allow the user to specify an initial priority for the task. If neither pragma is included, then the priority is initially undefined but can be set using this package.

The semantics of this proposal are defined in terms of base and active priorities. Courtesy of the Ada 9X Project, the concept of "base" and "active" priority is used to explain the impact of priority on the execution of tasks. The base priority is given to a task at task creation or changed by the use of this CIFO Entry. The active priority is used by the runtime environment for dispatching and resource allocation. Generally speaking, the active priority is determined by the runtime environment and is the maximum of the base priority of the task and the active priorities of all tasks "waiting" on it.

The SET_DYNAMIC_PRIORITY procedure sets the new base priority of the task specified by OF_TASK, which may be the task performing the call or any other task whose task ID is known. Priority changes affect every place in which priorities are considered, namely:

1. Changing a target task's priority affects its position in the run queue
2. If the target task is the caller in a rendezvous, the active priority of the acceptor task is set to the maximum of the caller's new priority and acceptor's old priority.
3. If the target task is the acceptor in a rendezvous, the priority of the caller is not affected.
4. If Priority Inheritance Discipline is in effect (see Priority Inheritance Discipline CIFO Entry), the active priority of a task is always the maximum of its own base priority and the active priorities of all the tasks that are currently "waiting for it".

The DYNAMIC_PRIORITY_OF function returns the base priority of the specified task regardless of how it was last set.

Time Critical Sections

Issue. Certain time-critical sections of code must be guaranteed to be executed to completion without preemption and with minimal interruption. In particular, there may be a timing constraint on the section. Minimal standard Ada provides no way of ensuring that the processor is not preempted by the RTE from a task at any time. Moreover, it is difficult to even ensure against preemption by other Ada tasks of the same priority, since the RTE is permitted to use time-slicing to interleave execution of such tasks. In some applications it could be catastrophic to switch tasks during such a section.

Proposal. This Entry proposes this package:

```
package TIME_CRITICAL_SECTIONS is
      procedure BEGIN_TIME_CRITICAL_SECTION;
      procedure END_TIME_CRITICAL_SECTION;
      function TIME_CRITICAL return BOOLEAN;
end TIME_CRITICAL_SECTIONS;
```

or a generic procedure:

```
generic
      with procedure TIME_CRITICAL_SECTION;
procedure CALL_TIME_CRITICAL_SECTION;
```

The effect of calling procedure BEGIN_TIME_CRITICAL_SECTION is to guarantee that the processor is not preempted from the calling task, until it next calls END_TIME_CRITICAL_SECTION. The intention is that the timing of execution between such calls should be predictable from examination of the intervening code.

The effect of calling an instance of the generic procedure is to guarantee that the procedure parameter is executed without preemption. The effect is the same as if BEGIN_TIME_CRITICAL_SECTION is called followed by a call to the procedure NON_PREEMPTIBLE_SECTION followed by a call to END_TIME_CRITICAL_SECTION (see the example). In particular, any exception raised within a call to an instance of CALL_TIME_CRITICAL_SECTION ends the time critical section and re-raises the exception.

Task Suspension

Issue. Real-time systems need efficient mechanisms to allow a task to temporarily block itself from executing. For example, the implementation of a messaging system needs to suspend a task awaiting the arrival of a message, and resume the task when the bus interrupt indicates that a message has arrived.

Proposal. This proposal consists of the following package:

```
with TASK_IDS;
package TASK_SUSPENSION is
     procedure ENABLE_DISPATCHING;
     procedure DISABLE_DISPATCHING;
     function DISPATCHING_ENABLED return BOOLEAN;
     procedure SUSPEND_SELF;
     procedure RESUME_TASK( T : in TASK_IDS.TASK_ID );
end TASK_SUSPENSION;
```

This package provides a means for a task to control its own execution and protection against pre-emption in order to release resources. However it does not provide protection against "race" conditions, that is provided by the Two Stage Task Suspension Entry.
The SUSPEND_SELF service suspends the current task.
The RESUME_TASK service resumes the specified task if the task has called SUSPEND_SELF. If the specified task has not performed SUSPEND_SELF, the RESUME_TASK call has no effect. Furthermore resuming a task that is not yet activated or is abnormal, completed, or terminated has no effect.
The DISABLE_DISPATCHING and ENABLE_DISPATCHING operations provide a mechanism whereby a task can define specific regions of code in which the processor can not be involuntarily reassigned to another task. The DISABLE_DISPATCHING service guarantees that the processor will not be involuntarily relinquished from the calling task.
The ENABLE_DISPATCHING service allows the processor to be reassigned to another task. All tasks are activated with dispatching enabled.

Two Stage Task Suspension

Issue. Real-time systems need efficient mechanisms for building intertask communication and synchronization constructs that allow tasks to be temporarily blocked from executing. Such tasks must be able to specify their intention to suspend before unlocking a shared resource and then suspending. This is necessary in order to avoid race conditions if a task waiting on the shared resource will resume the task that is suspending itself.

Proposal. This proposal consists of the following package:

```
with TASK_IDS;
package TWO_STAGE_TASK_SUSPENSION is
     SUSPENSION_ERROR : exception;
     procedure WILL_SUSPEND;
     procedure SUSPEND_SELF;
     procedure RESUME_TASK( T : in TASK_IDS.TASK_ID );
end TWO_STAGE_TASK_SUSPENSION;
```

This package provides a means for a task to safely suspend its own execution. The suspended task must be subsequently resumed by some other task. This allows the calling task to unlock any locks or semaphores it may be holding and suspend itself safely, without entering into a race condition with another task that may be contending for the lock and calling RESUME_TASK.

The WILL_SUSPEND and SUSPEND_SELF procedures are used to implement a "two-stage" suspend operation. The WILL_SUSPEND procedure notifies the implementation that the task is about to suspend itself.

The SUSPEND_SELF service suspends the current task if that task has called WILL_SUSPEND, unless some other task has called RESUME_TASK on it since the last time the current task called WILL_SUSPEND. In that case the task is not suspended (the resume was "latched") and the SUSPEND_SELF has no effect.

The RESUME_TASK procedure resumes the specified task if the task has called both WILL_SUSPEND and SUSPEND_SELF. If the specified task has called WILL_SUSPEND but not SUSPEND_SELF, the RESUME_TASK is "latched" by the implementation and will have the effect of immediately resuming the task when it next calls SUSPEND_SELF. The call to RESUME_TASK before that task has called a WILL_SUSPEND has no effect.

These operations are probably most useful when used to build blocking synchronization constructs. They can be combined with non-blocking lock operations (e.g. test-and-set on uniprocessors, spin locks on multiprocessors) to build a wide range of blocking task synchronization and communication primitives.

The services in this package are designed to be used in conjunction with low level locking primitives (see example below). If simple task suspension is all that is required, the TASK_SUSPENSION package can be used instead.

Asynchronous Task Suspension

Issue. Some Real-time systems require that one task have the ability to prevent the further execution of another. This capability is inherently dangerous, but in some instances unavoidable. It is hoped that most applications will not require the use of this package, and that other packages defined in this catalogue can be used in its place, e.g. the TASK_SUSPENSION package that provides the SUSPEND_SELF operation.

However, there are applications that require this capability. For example, some applications may implement a mode change by holding and releasing groups of tasks. Fault-tolerant applications might use HOLD_TASK to aid in recovering CPU resources from tasks caught in infinite loops.

Proposal. This proposal consists of the following package:

```
with TASK_IDS;
package ASYNCHRONOUS_TASK_HOLDING is
     HOLDING_ERROR : exception;
     procedure ENABLE_HOLDING;
     procedure DISABLE_HOLDING;
     function HOLDING_ENABLED return BOOLEAN;
     procedure HOLD_TASK (T : in TASK_IDS.TASK_ID);
     procedure HOLD_TASK
          (T : in TASK_IDS.TASK_ID; HOLDING : out BOOLEAN);
     procedure RELEASE_TASK (T: in TASK_IDS.TASK_ID);
end ASYNCHRONOUS_TASK_HOLDING;
```

This package provides a means for a task to temporarily prevent the further execution of any other task (i.e., to "hold" the task). The task may be subsequently released to continue its execution.

Tasks are created and activated with holding enabled. The DISABLE_HOLDING procedure cancels the effects of the ENABLE_HOLDING procedure and the calling task is no longer eligible for holding via the HOLD_TASK procedure. Once disabled (e.g., by a call to DISABLE_HOLDING), the ENABLE_HOLDING procedure must be called by a task before it can again be held by HOLD_TASK.

The HOLDING_ENABLED function returns TRUE if the calling task has made itself holdable via a call to ENABLE_HOLDING.

The HOLD_TASK procedures asynchronously hold the execution of the specified task if that task is currently eligible for holding. HOLD_TASK is provided in two overloaded forms. The first procedure contains a single parameter of type TASK_IDS.TASK_ID. If the specified task has not made itself eligible for holding via a call to ENABLE_HOLDING the exception HOLDING_ERROR is raised in the calling task. The second form provides a parameter, HOLDING, of type BOOLEAN. If the specified task has not made itself eligible for holding via a call to ENABLE_HOLDING, the value of the HOLDING parameter will be FALSE. Conversely, if the specified task has made itself eligible to be held via a call to ENABLE_HOLDING, the value of the HOLDING parameter will be TRUE. A call to HOLD_TASK designating a task that is already held has no effect.

The RELEASE_TASK procedure cancels the effect of a previous HOLD_TASK call. If the task id specified is not held via a previous call to HOLD_TASK this operation has no effect. If a task is otherwise eligible for execution when it is released, it will be considered for execution at the time of the RELEASE_TASK call. If the task is not otherwise eligible for execution (e.g. it has a pending delay, or is waiting for a rendezvous) a RELEASE_TASK call has no effect other than to remove the hold.

Synchronous and Asynchronous Task Scheduling

Issue. The common mode of task scheduling in real-time systems is via explicit synchronous (cyclic) and asynchronous scheduling.

The Ada language definition does not support explicit task scheduling. Rather, it defines only the most rudimentary level of task control, leaving it up to the user to devise his own methodology for implementing higher abstractions of task scheduling. This proposal defines a scheduling package to implement a synchronous and asynchronous scheduling capability. The proposal is based on the process scheduling paradigm used with the HAL/S language currently in use in the Shuttle avionics software.

Proposal. The package supports the explicit assertion of scheduling requirements for each task via a procedure call to the runtime environment. The procedure calls would be legal from within the task to be scheduled and from outside the task from anywhere that the task id could be obtained through the TASK_IDS package defined elsewhere. The schedule package would be defined as follows:

```
with TASK_IDS, DYNAMIC_PRIORITIES, EVENTS, CALENDAR;
package SCHEDULER is
    TASK_OVERRUN : constant EVENTS.EVENT := EVENTS.CREATE;
    type TASK_PRIORITIES is (CURRENT, ALTERED);
    type TASK_OVERRUNS is (IGNORE, REPORT);
    type TASK_INITIATIONS is
            (IMMEDIATELY, AT_TIME, AFTER_DELAY, ON_EVENT_SET,
            ON_EVENT_RESET);
    type TASK_REPETITIONS is
        (NONE, REPEAT_EVERY, REPEAT_AFTER);
    type TASK_COMPLETIONS is
        ( NONE, AT_TIME, ON_EVENT_SET, ON_EVENT_RESET);
```

```
type INITIATION_INFO
   ( INITIATION : TASK_INITIATIONS := IMMEDIATELY ) is
   record
      case INITIATION is
         when IMMEDIATELY => null;
         when AT_TIME => T : CALENDAR.TIME;
         when AFTER_DELAY => D : DURATION;
         when ON_EVENT_SET | ON_EVENT_RESET =>
            E : EVENTS.EVENT := EVENTS.CREATE;
      end case;
   end record;

type REPETITION_INFO
   ( REPETITION : TASK_REPETITIONS := NONE ) is
   record
      case REPETITION is
         when NONE => null;
         when REPEAT_EVERY | REPEAT_AFTER => D : DURATION;
      end case;
   end record;

type COMPLETION_INFO
   ( COMPLETION : TASK_COMPLETIONS := NONE ) is
   record
      case COMPLETION is
         when NONE => null;
         when AT_TIME => T : CALENDAR.TIME;
         when ON_EVENT_SET | ON_EVENT_RESET =>
            E : EVENTS.EVENT := EVENTS.CREATE;
      end case;
   end record;

type PRIORITY_INFO( PRIO : TASK_PRIORITIES := CURRENT ) is
   record
      case PRIO is
         when CURRENT => null;
         when ALTERED => P :
            DYNAMIC_PRIORITIES.DYNAMIC_PRIORITY;
      end case;
   end record;

type OVERRUN_INFO( OVERRUN : TASK_OVERRUNS := IGNORE ) is
   record
      case OVERRUN is
         when IGNORE => null;
         when REPORT =>
            OVERRUN_EVENT : EVENTS.EVENT := EVENTS.CREATE;
      end case;
   end record;

IMMEDIATE: constant INITIATION_INFO := (INITIATION => IMMEDIATELY);
NO_REPETITION    : constant REPETITION_INFO := (REPETITION => NONE);
NO_COMPLETION    : constant COMPLETION_INFO := (COMPLETION => NONE);
CURRENT_PRIORITY : constant PRIORITY_INFO := (PRIO => CURRENT);
IGNORE_OVERRUNS  : constant OVERRUN_INFO := (OVERRUN => IGNORE);

procedure SCHEDULE
      ( SCHEDULED_TASK : in TASK_IDS.TASK_ID;
        INITIATION          : in INITIATION_INFO;
        REPETITION      : in REPETITION_INFO;
        COMPLETION      : in COMPLETION_INFO := NO_COMPLETION;
        PRIORITY        : in PRIORITY_INFO := CURRENT_PRIORITY;
        OVERRUNS        : in OVERRUN_INFO := IGNORE_OVERRUNS );
```

```
procedure WAIT_FOR_SCHEDULE
     (  RELEASE_AFTER_DESCHEDULE       : in BOOLEAN := False;
        DESCHEDULED                    : out BOOLEAN );

procedure DESCHEDULE
     (  SCHEDULED_TASK : in TASK_IDS.TASK_ID;
        STOP_TASK              : in BOOLEAN := False );

function IS_DESCHEDULED( SCHEDULED_TASK : in TASK_IDS.TASK_ID )
     return BOOLEAN;

INVALID_SCHEDULE : exception;

end SCHEDULER;
```

The types in the package describe enumerations and records that encapsulate the attributes that are desired of all the tasks that will be controlled by this Entry.

The SCHEDULE procedure submits to the runtime system the attributes that determine when the referenced task is to execute. The task referenced by the SCHEDULE call is permitted to return from a call to WAIT_FOR_SCHEDULE whenever the conditions expressed by its parameters are met. That is, whenever a task calls WAIT_FOR_SCHEDULE, it begins to wait; it will be released, so that it is eligible for execution and can return from the call, as soon as the conditions expressed by the last call to SCHEDULE for that task have been met. In addition, any number of calls may be made to SCHEDULE. The scheduling attributes provided by the last call to SCHEDULE supersede all previous calls.

A task is descheduled in one of two ways: when the criteria for the task to complete (as specified in a call to SCHEDULE) have become true or the task becomes descheduled via a call to procedure DESCHEDULE.

Time Slicing

Issue. The minimal scheduling rules defined in the LRM do not provide for setting time slices, nor do they provide a way to dynamically assign or change slices for tasks.

Proposal. This proposal consists of the following package:

```
with TASK_IDS;
package TIME_SLICING is
     subtype SLICE is DURATION <implementation-defined>;
     procedure SET_TIME_SLICE(OF_TASK : in TASK_IDS.TASK_ID;
                              TO : in SLICE );
     procedure TURN_OFF_TIME_SLICE( OF_TASK : in TASK_IDS.TASK_ID );
end TIME_SLICING;
```

Time slicing is defined to be preemptive round-robin dispatching with a fixed amount of time allocated to each task. In the absence of a call to SET_TIME_SLICE for a particular task, that task is not subject to time slicing. Such a task, once it begins execution, continues until it blocks itself (e.g. for a delay or rendezvous), or until it is preempted by a higher priority task.

In contrast, once SET_TIME_SLICE(OF_TASK => T, TO => D) is called, task T is dispatched preemptively, with time slice D and executes for at most D units of time (or until blocked), before yielding its place to any other tasks of equal priority. The time slice of a task can be changed by calling SET_TIME_SLICE dynamically. The implementation shall document the precision with which time accounting is done. If a task's time slice is dynamically set while it is executing, the new value takes effect immediately.

The procedure TURN_OFF_TIME_SLICE is used to eliminate any time slicing on a specified task. If the specified task has no time slice, the procedure TURN_OFF_TIME_SLICE has no effect.

Abortion via Task Identifier

Issue. It is sometimes necessary to abort a task that is not visible. This capability partially addresses the problem of writing reusable executives and failure-recovery tasks. If such a component is reusable, it cannot have visibility of those other tasks which it manages, since these are different for each application. Furthermore, even if visible, a given task may be one of many visible tasks, and thus may not be discernible at the point at which abortion is necessary, such as within an accept body or while traversing a list of task identifiers.

Proposal. This proposal consists of one library procedure:

```
with TASK_IDS;
procedure ABORT_TASK( I : in TASK_IDS.TASK_ID);
```

Calling this procedure would request the RTE to abort the task corresponding to identifier I. If a null TASK_ID is passed to ABORT_TASK then the exception TASK_ID_ERROR is raised.

The semantics of this procedure are intended to be the same as that of LRM 9.10. It does, however, extend the capability to those task objects that are never accessible except via their TASK_ID (i.e., the main subprogram).

A.2 Asynchronous Cooperation Mechanisms.

Resources

Issue. Real-time applications need a synchronization object to efficiently control access to a shared hardware resource.

Proposal. The interface is a generic package defining the private RESOURCE type and importing the queuing discipline, which is used to manage the queue of waiting tasks associated with each resource object.

```
with QUEUING_DISCIPLINE;
use QUEUING_DISCIPLINE;
generic
   RESOURCE_QUEUING_DISCIPLINE : DISCIPLINE := FIFO_QUEUING;
package RESOURCES is
   type RESOURCE is private;

   NULL_ACCESSOR: constant RESOURCE;
   IMMEDIATELY: constant DURATION := 0.0;

   NON_EXISTENT_RESOURCE: exception;
   INVALID_RESOURCE_NAME: exception;
   RESOURCE_CAPACITY_OVERFLOW: exception;
   RESOURCE_DESTROYED: exception;

   MAX_CAPACITY : constant POSITIVE := <implementation defined>;
   MAX_WAITING_TASKS : constant POSITIVE :=<implementation defined>;
   type CAPACITY_RANGE is range 1..MAX_CAPACITY;
   type COUNTER_RANGE is range -MAX_WAITING_TASKS..MAX_CAPACITY;
   type WAITING_RANGE is range 0..MAX_WAITING_TASKS;
```

```
function CREATE
            (  INITIAL : in CAPACITY_RANGE := CAPACITY_RANGE'FIRST;
               CAPACITY: in CAPACITY_RANGE := CAPACITY_RANGE'LAST;
               NAME: in STRING := "" ) return RESOURCE;
   function CAPACITY (R: in RESOURCE) return CAPACITY_RANGE;
   procedure GET (R: in RESOURCE);
   procedure GET( R: in RESOURCE;
               PASSED: out BOOLEAN;
               TIME_OUT: in DURATION := IMMEDIATELY);
   procedure RELEASE (R: in RESOURCE);
   procedure DESTROY (R: in out RESOURCE);
   function COUNT (R: in RESOURCE) return WAITING_RANGE;
   function VALUE (R: in RESOURCE) return COUNTER_RANGE;
private
   type RESOURCE is <implementation defined>;
   NULL_ACCESSOR : constant RESOURCE := <implementation defined>;
end RESOURCES;
```

Conceptually, a resource object is composed of:

a. an integer counter (initially positive, default 1),
b. a queue of waiting tasks (initially empty).

A resource object always satisfies the following invariants:

- counter >= 0 mutually implies queue empty
- counter <= 0 mutually implies length of queue = abs(counter)
- counter = (initial value minus number of successful GET operations plus number of RELEASE operations).

Once created (CREATE) a resource may be obtained (GET) and then released (RELEASE); it may be observed (COUNT, VALUE) and deleted (DESTROY). A resource may be simultaneously owned by a maximum of CAPACITY tasks. The GET procedures can either cause unconditional waiting or waiting with a time-out.

Buffers

Issue. Real-time applications need some kind of communication object in order to efficiently communicate asynchronously between tasks.

Proposal. The interface is a generic package defining the private BUFFER type.

```
with QUEUING_DISCIPLINE;
use QUEUING_DISCIPLINE;
generic
   type MESSAGE is private;
   DEFAULT_MESSAGE : in MESSAGE;
   RECEIVE_QUEUING_DISCIPLINE : DISCIPLINE := FIFO_QUEUING;
   SEND_QUEUING_DISCIPLINE : DISCIPLINE := FIFO_QUEUING;
package BUFFERS is

   type BUFFER is private;

   NULL_ACCESSOR: constant BUFFER;
   IMMEDIATELY: constant DURATION := 0.0;
```

```
    NON_EXISTENT_BUFFER: exception;
    INVALID_BUFFER_NAME: exception;
    NON_EXISTENT_MESSAGE: exception;
    BUFFER_DESTROYED: exception;

    MAX_CAPACITY : constant POSITIVE := <implementation defined>;
    MAX_WAITING_TASKS : constant POSITIVE := <implementation defined>;

    type CAPACITY_RANGE is range 1..MAX_CAPACITY;
    type MESSAGE_COUNT_RANGE is range 0..MAX_CAPACITY;
    type COUNTER_RANGE is range -MAX_WAITING_TASKS .. MAX_CAPACITY;
    type WAITING_RANGE is range 0..MAX_WAITING_TASKS;

    function CREATE(CAPACITY: in CAPACITY_RANGE := 1;
                    NAME: in STRING := "" ) return BUFFER;
    function CAPACITY (B: in BUFFER) return CAPACITY_RANGE;

    procedure RECEIVE( R: in BUFFER; M: out MESSAGE);
    procedure RECEIVE(B: in BUFFER;
                    M: out MESSAGE;
                    PASSED: out BOOLEAN;
                    TIME_OUT: in DURATION := IMMEDIATELY);

    procedure SEND( B: in BUFFER; M: in MESSAGE);
    procedure SEND(B: in BUFFER;
                    M: in MESSAGE;
                    PASSED: out BOOLEAN;
                    TIME_OUT: in DURATION := IMMEDIATELY);

    procedure DESTROY( B: in out BUFFER);

    function RECEIVE_COUNT( B: in BUFFER) return WAITING_RANGE;
    function SEND_COUNT( B: in BUFFER) return WAITING_RANGE;

    function MESSAGE_COUNT( B: in BUFFER) return MESSAGE_COUNT_RANGE;
    function MESSAGE_VALUE( B: in BUFFER; I: in CAPACITY_RANGE :=1)
            return MESSAGE;
private
    type BUFFER is <implementation defined>;
    NULL_ACCESSOR: constant BUFFER := <implementation defined>;
end BUFFERS;
```

Conceptually, a buffer object is composed of:

a. a bounded FIFO queue of messages (initially empty),
b. a counting semaphore to manage the tasks waiting to receive a message (the initial value of the semaphore is 0, meaning that it is free),
c. a counting semaphore to manage the tasks waiting to send a message (the initial value of the semaphore is CAPACITY, which is the maximum number of messages in the BUFFER).

A buffer object always satisfies the following invariants:

a. queue of messages is not empty mutually implies "receive semaphore" is free
b. queue of messages is not full mutually implies "send semaphore " is free
c. queue of messages is empty mutually implies "receive semaphore" is busy
d. queue of messages is full mutually implies "send semaphore " is busy
e. length of message queue = (number of successful SEND operations minus number of successful RECEIVE operations).

Once created (CREATE) a buffer may be used by tasks to send (SEND) typed messages. Such messages may be consumed (RECEIVE). CAPACITY messages may be kept in the buffer. A buffer may be observed (SEND_COUNT, RECEIVE_COUNT, MESSAGE_COUNT, MESSAGE_VALUE) and deleted (DESTROY). Both SEND and RECEIVE procedures can cause conditional and unconditional waiting.

The formal generic parameter MESSAGE type conveys the description of the data copied during the communication. The use of access types within the data is as unsafe as handling access types in subprogram or entry parameters.

The formal generic parameters RECEIVE_QUEUING_DISCIPLINE and SEND_QUEUING_DISCIPLINE convey the disciplines used to manage the receiving and sending queues associated with each buffer object.

Events

Issue. Real-time applications need some kind of synchronization object in order to efficiently notify any waiting tasks upon the occurrence of a latched condition.

Proposal. The interface is a package defining the private EVENT type.

```
package EVENTS is

    type EVENT is private;
    type EVENT_STATE is (UP, DOWN);

    NULL_ACCESSOR: constant EVENT;
    IMMEDIATELY: constant DURATION := 0.0;

    NON_EXISTENT_EVENT: exception;
    INVALID_EVENT_NAME: exception;
    EVENT_DESTROYED: exception;

    MAX_WAITING_TASKS : constant := <implementation defined>;
    type WAITING_RANGE is range 0..MAX_WAITING_TASKS;

    function CREATE(INITIAL: in EVENT_STATE := DOWN;
                    NAME: in STRING := "") return EVENT;

    procedure WAIT (E: in EVENT);
    procedure WAIT(E: in EVENT;
                PASSED: out BOOLEAN;
                TIME_OUT: in DURATION := IMMEDIATELY);

    procedure SET (E: in EVENT);
    procedure RESET (E: in EVENT);
    procedure TOGGLE (E: in EVENT);

    procedure DESTROY (E: in out EVENT);
    function COUNT (E: in EVENT) return WAITING_RANGE;

    function STATE (E: in EVENT) return EVENT_STATE;
private
    type EVENT is <implementation defined>;
    NULL_ACCESSOR: constant EVENT := <implementation defined>;
end EVENTS;
```

Conceptually, an event is composed of a bi-valued state variable (the states are often called up and down), and a set of waiting tasks (initially empty).

An event object always satisfies the following invariants:

a. event = UP implies no waiting task
b. event = DOWN implies existence of at least one waiting task.

Once created (CREATE) an event may be set (SET) to the state "condition has occurred" or reset (RESET). Tasks may wait for this occurrence (WAIT). It may be observed (COUNT, STATE) and deleted (DESTROY).

Blackboards

Issue. Real-time applications need some kind of communication object in order to efficiently make messages visible between tasks.

Proposal. The interface is a generic package defining the private BLACKBOARD type.

```
generic
   type MESSAGE is private;
   DEFAULT_MESSAGE : in MESSAGE;
package BLACKBOARDS is

   type BLACKBOARD is private;
   type BLACKBOARD_STATE is (VALID, INVALID);

   NULL_ACCESSOR: constant BLACKBOARD;
   IMMEDIATELY: constant DURATION := 0.0;

   NON_EXISTENT_BLACKBOARD: exception;
   INVALID_BLACKBOARD_NAME: exception;
   BLACKBOARD_DESTROYED: exception;

   MAX_WAITING_TASKS : constant POSITIVE := <implementation defined>;
   type WAITING_RANGE is range 0..MAX_WAITING_TASKS;

   function CREATE (NAME: in STRING :="") return BLACKBOARD;
   function CREATE(INITIAL: in MESSAGE;
                   NAME: in STRING := "") return BLACKBOARD;

   procedure READ(B: in BLACKBOARD; M: out MESSAGE);
   procedure READ(B: in BLACKBOARD;
                  M: out MESSAGE;
                  PASSED: out BOOLEAN;
                  TIME_OUT: in DURATION := IMMEDIATELY);

   procedure DISPLAY(B: in BLACKBOARD; M: in MESSAGE);
   procedure CLEAR (B: in BLACKBOARD);
   procedure DESTROY (B: in out BLACKBOARD);
   function COUNT (B: in BLACKBOARD) return WAITING_RANGE;
   function STATE (B: in BLACKBOARD) return BLACKBOARD_STATE;
private
   type BLACKBOARD is <implementation defined>;
   NULL_ACCESSOR: constant BLACKBOARD:= <implementation defined>;
end BLACKBOARDS;
```

Conceptually, a blackboard object is composed of:

a. a variable of type MESSAGE (to display the message),
b. a validity indicator for the message,
c. a set of waiting tasks (initially empty).

A blackboard object always satisfies the following invariants:

a. blackboard valid implies no waiting task
b. set of waiting tasks non empty implies blackboard invalid.

Once created (CREATE) a blackboard may be written on (DISPLAY). The written typed information may be read (READ) by tasks until cleared (CLEAR). A blackboard may be observed (COUNT, STATE) and deleted (DESTROY). The READ procedures cause conditional and unconditional waiting.

The formal generic parameter MESSAGE type conveys the description of the data copied during the communication. The use of access types within such data is as unsafe as handling access types in subprogram or entry parameters.

Pulses

Issue. Real-time applications need some kind of synchronization object in order to efficiently notify any waiting tasks upon the occurrence of a pulsed condition.

Proposal. The interface is a package defining the private PULSE type.

```
package PULSES is

    type PULSE is private;

    NULL_ACCESSOR: constant PULSE;
    IMMEDIATELY : constant duration := 0.0;

    NON_EXISTENT_PULSE: exception;
    INVALID_PULSE_NAME: exception;
    PULSE_DESTROYED: exception;

    MAX_WAITING_TASKS : constant POSITIVE := <implementation defined>;
    type WAITING_RANGE is range 0..MAX_WAITING_TASKS;

    function CREATE (NAME: in STRING := "") return PULSE;

    procedure WAIT (P: in PULSE);
    procedure WAIT (P: in PULSE;
                    PASSED: out BOOLEAN;
                    TIME_OUT: in DURATION := IMMEDIATELY);

    procedure SET (P: in PULSE);

    procedure DESTROY (P: in out PULSE);

    function COUNT (P: in PULSE) return WAITING_RANGE;
private
    type PULSE is <implementation defined>;
    NULL_ACCESSOR: constant PULSE := <implementation defined>;
end PULSES;
```

Conceptually, a pulse object is composed of a set of waiting tasks (initially empty).

Once created (CREATE) a pulse may be set (SET) to notify such an occurrence to the tasks waiting for it (WAIT). This occurrence is not latched. A pulse may be observed (COUNT) and deleted (DESTROY). The WAIT procedures cause conditional and unconditional waiting.

Broadcasts

Issue. Real-time applications need some kind of communication object in order to efficiently broadcast messages to multiple tasks.

Proposal. The interface is a generic package defining the private BROADCAST type.

```
generic
   type MESSAGE is private;
   DEFAULT_MESSAGE : in MESSAGE;
package BROADCASTS is

   type BROADCAST is private;

   NULL_ACCESSOR: constant BROADCAST;

   NON_EXISTENT_BROADCAST: exception;
   INVALID_BROADCAST_NAME: exception;
   BROADCAST_DESTROYED: exception;

   MAX_WAITING_TASKS : constant POSITIVE := <implementation defined>;
   type WAITING_RANGE is range 0..MAX_WAITING_TASKS;

   function CREATE (NAME: in STRING := "") return BROADCAST;

   procedure RECEIVE(B: in BROADCAST; M: out MESSAGE);
   procedure RECEIVE(B: in BROADCAST;
                     M: out MESSAGE;
                     PASSED: out BOOLEAN;
                     TIME_OUT: in DURATION );

   procedure SEND(B: in BROADCAST; M: in MESSAGE);

   procedure DESTROY (B: in out BROADCAST);
   function COUNT (B: in BROADCAST) return WAITING_RANGE;
private
   type BROADCAST is <implementation defined>;
   NULL_ACCESSOR: constant BROADCAST := <implementation defined>;
end BROADCASTS;
```

Conceptually, a broadcast object is composed of a set of tasks waiting for a message(initially empty).

Once created (CREATE) a broadcast may be used to send (SEND) a typed message to all the tasks waiting for it (RECEIVE). This message is consumed by a RECEIVE operation. A broadcast may be observed (COUNT) and deleted (DESTROY). The RECEIVE procedures cause conditional and unconditional waiting.

The formal generic parameter MESSAGE type conveys the description of the data copied during the communication. The use of access types within such data is as unsafe as handling access types in subprogram or entry parameters.

Barriers

Issue. Real-time applications need some kind of synchronization object in order to efficiently control the simultaneous resumption of some fixed number of waiting tasks.

Proposal. The interface is a package defining the private BARRIER type.

```
package BARRIERS is
   type BARRIER is private;

   NULL_ACCESSOR: constant BARRIER;

   NON_EXISTENT_BARRIER : exception;
   INVALID_BARRIER_NAME : exception;
   BARRIER_DESTROYED : exception;

   MAX_CAPACITY : constant POSITIVE := <implementation defined>;
   type CAPACITY_RANGE is range 1..MAX_CAPACITY;

   type WAITING_RANGE is range 0..MAX_CAPACITY;

   function CREATE(CAPACITY: in CAPACITY_RANGE;
                   NAME: in STRING := "") return BARRIER;

   function CAPACITY (B: in BARRIER) return CAPACITY_RANGE;

   procedure WAIT (B: in BARRIER);

   procedure DESTROY (B: in out BARRIER);
   function COUNT (B: in BARRIER) return WAITING_RANGE;
   function VALUE (B: in BARRIER) return CAPACITY_RANGE;
private
   type BARRIER is <implementation defined>;
   NULL_ACCESSOR: constant BARRIER := <implementation defined>;
end BARRIERS;
```

Conceptually, a barrier object is composed of:

a. a non negative counter (initially equal to the capacity of the barrier)
b. a pulse to manage the tasks waiting at the barrier.

A Barrier object always satisfies the invariants number of waiting tasks = (capacity - counter).

Once created (CREATE) a barrier may be waited at (WAIT) until CAPACITY tasks are waiting. When this condition occurs the CAPACITY waiting tasks are resumed simultaneously. A barrier may be observed (COUNT, VALUE, CAPACITY) and deleted (DESTROY).

Mutually Exclusive Access to Shared Data

Issue. In many applications the overhead of protecting shared data using a task is too great; furthermore it is not possible to use pragma SHARED for all data types. For portability, there should be a standard mechanism for mutually exclusive access to shared data.

Proposal. A generic package is proposed which when instantiated will allow mutually exclusive access to a shared data item with an appropriate queuing discipline.

```
with QUEUING_DISCIPLINE;
generic
   type ITEM is private;
   INITIAL_VALUE : ITEM;
   QUEUING : QUEUING_DISCIPLINE.DISCIPLINE;
package SHARED_DATA_TEMPLATE is
      type SHARED_DATA is limited private;
```

```
   procedure WRITE(TO_OBJECT: in out SHARED_DATA; NEW_VALUE: in ITEM );
   function VALUE_OF(OBJECT: in SHARED_DATA ) return ITEM;
private
   type SHARED_DATA is <implementation-defined>;
end SHARED_DATA_TEMPLATE;
```

After instantiating the generic with the required queuing discipline, a shared data object is created by declaring an object of type SHARED_DATA. The object will be automatically initialized to INITIAL_VALUE. The object can be given a new value by using the WRITE procedure. It can be read by using the VALUE_OF function. VALUE_OF and WRITE operations are mutually exclusive, successive read operations may occur in parallel but successive write operations are mutually exclusive. When tasks are blocked they are queued according to the selected discipline.

Shared Locks

Issue. Some applications cannot tolerate the overhead of Ada tasking and rendezvous for simple resource control, even when streamlined tasking paradigms such as "trivial entries" are provided. Some applications require that certain tasks ("readers") be granted concurrent shared access to a resource, whereas other tasks ("writers") be granted exclusive access to the resource. Hardware and/or operating systems usually provide instructions (such as "compare and swap", "test and set", or "fetch and add") that can be used to build fast conditional locking mechanisms with appropriate queuing disciplines and levels of resource sharing. A common Ada interface to such capabilities should be provided to enhance portability.

Proposal. A generic package is proposed to provide combinations of the desired resource access (exclusive only versus shared and exclusive) plus the queuing discipline (if any) to be used when the lock is unavailable:

```
with QUEUING_DISCIPLINE;
generic
   QUEUING : in QUEUING_DISCIPLINE.DISCIPLINE;
   -- type of queuing to be used when the lock is unavailable
   ALLOW_SHARED_ACCESS : in BOOLEAN;
   -- true -> shared lock, false -> exclusive lock
package GENERIC_LOCK is

   type LOCK_STATUS_TYPE is ( NOT_LOCKED, SHARED, EXCLUSIVE );
   subtype LOCK_ACCESS_SUBTYPE is
      LOCK_STATUS_TYPE range SHARED .. EXCLUSIVE;
   type LOCK_TYPE is limited private;

   LOCK_ALREADY_OWNED_ERROR : exception;
      -- from LOCK or ATTEMPT_LOCK
   LOCK_NOT_OWNED_ERROR : exception;
      -- from UNLOCK
   LOCK_NOT_SHARABLE_ERROR : exception;
      -- from LOCK or ATTEMPT_LOCK
   LOCK_NOT_INITIALIZED_ERROR : exception;
      -- from any subprogram except INITIALIZE_LOCK

   procedure INITIALIZE_LOCK( LOCK : in out LOCK_TYPE );
   procedure CREATE( LOCK : in out LOCK_TYPE )
      renames INITIALIZE_LOCK;

   procedure FINALIZE_LOCK( LOCK : in out LOCK_TYPE );
   procedure DESTROY( LOCK : in out LOCK_TYPE )
      renames FINALIZE_LOCK;
```

```
    procedure LOCK(LOCK : in out LOCK_TYPE;
                   FOR_USE : in LOCK_ACCESS_SUBTYPE := EXCLUSIVE );
    procedure ATTEMPT_LOCK
                   (LOCK : in out LOCK_TYPE;
                    FOR_USE : in LOCK_ACCESS_SUBTYPE := EXCLUSIVE;
                    OBTAINED : out BOOLEAN );

    procedure UNLOCK( LOCK : in out LOCK_TYPE );
    procedure ATTEMPT_UNLOCK( LOCK : in out LOCK_TYPE );
    procedure ATTEMPT_UNLOCK(  LOCK : in out LOCK_TYPE;
                               RELEASED : out BOOLEAN );

    procedure BREAK_LOCK( LOCK : in out LOCK_TYPE );

    function GLOBAL_LOCK_STATUS( LOCK : in LOCK_TYPE )
       return LOCK_STATUS_TYPE;
    function LOCAL_LOCK_STATUS( LOCK : in LOCK_TYPE )
       return LOCK_STATUS_TYPE;
private
    type LOCK_TYPE is <implementation defined>;
end GENERIC_LOCK;
```

Shared locks are created (INTIALIZE_LOCK and CREATE). Then they may be locked (LOCK and ATTEMPT_LOCK), causing the caller to unconditionally and conditionally wait until the shared lock is unlocked. The caller may request exclusive or shared access (if permitted by the instantiation of the GENERIC_LOCK package). The caller may be queued (according to the queuing discipline of the instantiation) if the request can not be made. There will be less queuing when all callers request shared access. A shared lock can be unlocked by either the current owner (UNLOCK) or some other caller ATTEMPT_UNLOCK). If this situation absolutely calls for breaking the current hold on the shared locked, the caller may break the lock (BREAK_LOCK) at great risk. Any caller can get the status of locks (GLOBAL_LOCK_STATUS and LOCAL_LOCK_STATUS). Finally all shared locks should be destroyed (FINALIZE_LOCK and DESTROY_LOCK) when they are no longer needed.

Signals

Issue. Real-time applications need a means to asynchronously signal an entry point or procedure upon the occurrence of a specific condition. Such a notification may be accompanied by the communication of a message associated with the signal. Asynchronous activations can be implemented in Ada, but at the cost of agent tasks.

Proposal. The interface consists of two generic packages :

```
generic
     type PARAMETER is private;
     with procedure TO_BE_CALLED( PARAM : in PARAMETER );
package SIGNAL_WITH_PARAMETER is
     procedure NON_WAITING( PARAM : in PARAMETER );
end SIGNAL_WITH_PARAMETER;

generic
   with procedure TO_BE_CALLED;
package SIGNAL is
   procedure NON_WAITING;
end SIGNAL;
```

The Signals Entry behaves as if an agent task were used to transfer the signal and associated message to the target procedure or task entry, even though the implementation may not actually use an Ada task. The semantics of the agent task are that, upon creation, it has the priority of the invoking (initiating) thread of control, if dynamic priorities are available to the implementor of the SIGNALS capability; otherwise the agent task has the highest software priority in the system. Using the priority of the signaling thread of control is the preferred implementation. The existing Ada rules for priorities between tasks within rendezvous apply to the interactions between the agent task and the invoking thread. On the receiving end, the asynchronous signal has the same semantics as a normal call (to either a procedure or a task entry). Similarly, the effect of all other CIFO Entries, such as Priority Inheritance Discipline, are as if an Ada task were being used to transmit the signal.

The generic package SIGNAL is a simplification of SIGNAL_WITH_PARAMETER which corresponds to the case where no data is sent with the signal.

A NON_WAITING caller never waits. If the callee has disappeared or is not callable at NON-WAITING calling time, then the call is lost. The asynchronous property does not belong to the callee, it belongs to the caller.

Asynchronous Transfer Of Control

Issue. At the Second International Workshop on Real-Time Ada Issues, three requirements for Asynchronous Transfer of Control were identified. These requirements are restated here:

1) Fault Recovery - requires either stopping a task or altering its flow of control due to an occurrence of a fault.
2) Mode Changes - may require stopping an application or altering its flow of control. For example, aborting a bombing run to change to a defensive mode.
3) Partial Computations - A task may process an algorithm which gives a first approximation of a result (partial result) and then refines this result (giving progressively better refinements of the result as it is allowed more time to compute).

At the Third International Workshop on Real-Time Ada Issues, the Asynchronous Transfer of Control Working Group endorsed Tucker Taft's Ada Revision Request (00083) for implementing asynchronous transfers via a modified form of the select statement. The Joint Integrated Avionics Working Group - Common Ada Run Time Working Group (JIAWG/CART) subsequently endorsed this request as also fulfilling their requirements for asynchronous transfers.

The Taft proposal is reproduced here:

```
select
      select_alternative
{ or
      select_alternative }
and
      sequence_of_statements
end select;
```

The semantics of the above construct are as follows. Normal processing is performed on select alternatives to determine which ones are open. Selection of one such open alternative takes place immediately if a rendezvous is possible. If no rendezvous is possible but a delay alternative of less than or equal to zero seconds is open, that alternative is executed. Otherwise, the sequence_of_statements following the "and" begins execution. If the sequence_of_statements completes execution, then the select statement as a whole is completed. If prior to completion of the sequence_of_statements a delay alternative expires or a call is made to an open accept alternative, the sequence_of_statements is abandoned and control is transferred asynchronously to the appropriate open select alternative.

The following example illustrates the usage of the modified select:

```
task TAFT_EXAMPLE is
   entry BREAK(...);
end TAFT_EXAMPLE;

task body TAFT_EXAMPLE is
begin
   loop
      select
         accept BREAK(...) do
            HANDLE_BREAK;
         end BREAK;
         RECOVER_AFTER_BREAK;
      or
         delay TIMEOUT;
         RECOVER_AFTER_TIMEOUT;
      and
         DO_WORK_ALLOWING_BREAK;
      end select;
   end loop;
end TAFT_EXAMPLE;
```

Proposal. This CIFO Entry provides a generic package to approximate the semantics of Taft's modified select statement within the confines of the 1983 language standard. This package can be thought of as creating an asynchronous agent to execute the sequence of statements following the AND in the Taft proposal, and exports a facility to asynchronously abandon that execution. The generic specification is as follows:

```
generic
   with procedure AGENT_ACTIONS;
   -- AGENT_ACTIONS encapsulates the sequence
   -- of statements following the AND in the
   -- modified select.
   with procedure AGENT_DONE;
   -- AGENT_DONE is intended to be an entry
   -- to be called to signal completion of
   -- AGENT_ACTIONS.
package ASYNCH_AGENT is
   procedure DESTROY_AGENT;
   -- DESTROY_AGENT causes the asynchronous
   -- abandonment of AGENT_ACTIONS.
end ASYNCH_AGENT;
```

The semantics of the body for ASYNCH_AGENT are described by the following: (Note that the following is for illustrative purposes only. The actual implementation may be able to utilize a simplified method of concurrence in implementing the body of the package.)

```
package body ASYNCH_AGENT is
      task AGENT;
      task body AGENT is
      begin
            AGENT_ACTIONS;
            AGENT_DONE;
      end AGENT;

      procedure DESTROY_AGENT is
      begin
            abort AGENT;
      end DESTROY_AGENT;
end ASYNCH_AGENT;
```

The following example illustrates the intended use of the generic package:

```
task TAFT_EXAMPLE_83 is
    entry BREAK(...);
    entry ASYNCH_DONE; -- new entry
end TAFT_EXAMPLE_83;

task body TAFT_EXAMPLE_83 is
begin
    loop
        declare
            procedure DO_WORK_ALLOWING_BREAK is
                ...
            end DO_WORK_ALLOWING_BREAK;
            package ASYNCH is
                new ASYNCH_AGENT (DO_WORK_ALLOWING_BREAK, ASYNCH_DONE);
        begin
            select
                accept BREAK(...) do
                    ASYNCH.DESTROY_AGENT;
                    HANDLE_BREAK;
                end BREAK;
                RECOVER_AFTER_BREAK;
            or
                delay TIMEOUT;
                ASYNCH.DESTROY_AGENT;
                RECOVER_AFTER_TIMEOUT;
            or
                accept ASYNCH_DONE; -- new entry
            end select;
        end;
    end loop;
end TAFT_EXAMPLE_83;
```

A.3 Interrupt Support.

Interrupt Management

Issue. The LRM (13.5.1) does not define the manner of managing interrupts on the target, since they are highly implementation dependent. Typical architectures incorporate either a level oriented mechanism, in which interrupts are specified by number, or a named mechanism, in which interrupts are individually named. A common format for controlling and interrogating either individually-named or level-oriented interrupts is thus desirable. Clearly, this sort of utility is very machine dependent, and will no doubt be bound differently for each machine. This proposal is concerned with the management of very low-level hardware, whereas preemption is concerned with software scheduling and dispatching (see Time Critical Sections CIFO entry).

Proposal. This Entry proposes a package of services to control the occurrences and masking of interrupts.

```
package INTERRUPT_MANAGEMENT is
    type INTERRUPT_ID is <implementation-defined discrete type>;
    type INTERRUPT_LIST is array( INTERRUPT_ID ) of BOOLEAN;

    ENABLE_FAILURE : exception;
```

```
procedure ENABLE( INTERRUPT : in INTERRUPT_ID );
procedure DISABLE( INTERRUPT : in INTERRUPT_ID );
function ENABLED return INTERRUPT_LIST;

procedure MASK( INTERRUPTS : in INTERRUPT_LIST );
procedure UNMASK( INTERRUPTS : in INTERRUPT_LIST );
function MASKED return INTERRUPT_LIST;
end INTERRUPT_MANAGEMENT;
```

Procedure ENABLE will make it possible for the specified interrupt to occur (in contrast to allowing the interrupt arbitration system to pass it on once it actually has occurred, which is accomplished by MASK). The procedure DISABLE will disable the interrupt specified from occurring. Calls to ENABLE which fail will raise ENABLE_FAILURE. Calls to DISABLE which fail have no effects. However, procedures ENABLE and DISABLE have an effect that is implementation-dependent with respect to their effect on any interrupts other that those specified in the call. For example, the hardware may be such that a call to DISABLE will disable the specified interrupt and all "lower-level" interrupts as well. The implementation is expected to document this kind of effect.

Procedure MASK takes a list of interrupts, where those specified as "true" will not be accepted if they occur and those that are set to "false" will not be affected in any way. Thus, procedure ENABLE is used to control whether those interrupts are possible, in a hardware/device context, and procedure MASK controls whether an interrupt is recognized once it does occur. Calls to MASK and UNMASK interrupts which are not enabled have no effects. Procedure UNMASK operates in opposite manner from MASK. Function MASKED returns an array of type INTERRUPT_LIST.

Trivial Entries

Issue. An important special case of Ada rendezvous is the utilization of a rendezvous with an empty accept body for the sole purpose of optimizing the performance of task synchronization.

Proposal. The pragma

```
pragma TRIVIAL_ENTRY( NAME : <entry_simple_name> );
```

may appear within a task specification after an entry declaration. Its argument must be the simple name of an entry. This pragma conveys to the implementation the information that the entry at hand has only "trivial" accept statements. A trivial accept statement is one that does not have a sequence of statements, i.e. a trivial accept statement is of the form:

```
accept <entry_simple_name>;
```

If the information conveyed by the pragma is not correct, the Ada program is erroneous. In this case, the pragma should be ignored and a warning message issued by the compiler.

Fast Interrupt Pragmas

Issue. Transfer of control to an accept statement for an interrupt entry is slower than transfer of control to a traditional interrupt routine (whose address has been loaded into a hardware interrupt vector). This is because in the case of the Ada interrupt rendezvous, various tasking data structures in the runtime environment have to be read and updated. The difference in speed is likely to prohibit the use of Ada for many real-time applications.

Proposal. This proposal consists of two pragmas, INTERRUPT_TASK and MEDIUM_FAST_INTERRUPT_ENTRY, and an enumeration type INTERRUPT_TASK_KIND. The enumeration type declaration appears in package SYSTEM and is defined as follows:

```
type INTERRUPT_TASK_KIND is ( SIMPLE, SIGNALLING );
```

A given implementation may support additional enumeration values.
The first pragma

```
pragma INTERRUPT_TASK( KIND : INTERRUPT_TASK_KIND )
```

is only allowed within a task specification for a single task. It specifies that this task contains only the actual statements to be directly executed when the interrupt occurs within a single accept statement for that entry. This is commonly called an interrupt service routine. There are restrictions on the format and content of the task to ensure predictable behavior, to ensure correct interrupt service manners, and to prevent it from being called from another task. The difference between a fast interrupt task that is SIMPLE or SIGNALLING is that a SIGNALLING task is permitted to make a conditional entry call to a TRIVIAL entry of another task.
The second pragma

```
pragma MEDIUM_FAST_INTERRUPT_ENTRY( NAME : <entry_simple_name> );
```

may appear within a task specification after an entry declaration. Its argument must be the simple name of an entry, and that entry must be an interrupt entry. This pragma permits looser set of restrictions on the associated at the cost of slower interrupt response. The task with a medium fast interrupt entry is permitted to have statements outside of the accept statement for that entry and it may reference non-local values. The result is the time needed to transfer control to the accept statement in a fast interrupt task or in a signalling interrupt task is of the same order of magnitude as the time required by the state saving portion of a traditional interrupt routine. The exact time is implementation-dependent. Meanwhile the time needed to transfer control to the accept statement for a medium fast interrupt entry lies between the time required in the case of a fast interrupt task, and the time needed for an ordinary interrupt entry. The exact time is implementation-dependent.

A.4 Miscellaneous Services.

Task Identifiers

Issue. Several RTE extensions described in this catalogue require a means of specifying tasks as parameters to RTE procedures, where the Ada typing rules would not permit using the name of the task. In addition, in the writing of general schedulers and resource managers there is need for a means of storing information about tasks in tables, and for a way of associating a storable identifier with each task, beyond the basic capabilities provided by the language.

Proposal. An implementation-defined package:

```
package TASK_IDS is
   type TASK_ID is private;

   TASK_IDS_CHECKED : constant BOOLEAN := <implementation-defined>;

   TASK_ID_ERROR, PASSIVE_TASK_ERROR : exception;
```

```
   function NULL_TASK return TASK_ID;
   function SELF return TASK_ID;
   function MASTER_TASK return TASK_ID;
   function CALLER return TASK_ID;
   function CALLABLE( T : TASK_ID ) return BOOLEAN;
   function TERMINATED( T : TASK_ID ) return BOOLEAN;
private
   type TASK_ID is <implementation-defined>;
end TASK_IDS;
```

This package provides the type TASK_ID and several functions for obtaining the identifier of a particular task and determining its status. Task IDs are assumed to be unique across an Ada program's life time. If an operation is performed on a task which is no longer in existence then the exception TASK_ID_ERROR will be raised.

The function SELF returns the task ID of whatever task calls it. If the main program calls SELF then the task ID of the environment task is returned. The function MASTER_TASK returns the task ID of the task on which the task calling the function is directly dependent (see LRM 9.4 for a detail definition of dependent tasks and their masters). The function CALLER, if called from within an accept, returns the task ID of the partner task. The other functions (NULL_TASK, CALLABLE, and TERMINATED) are clearly defined by their names.

Queuing Disciplines

Issue. Several RTE extensions described in this catalogue provide a means of blocking and scheduling a task. In general there are several queuing disciplines that can be used with these Entries.

Proposal. This Entry defines the type which will be used to indicate which discipline is required when instantiating other CIFO Entries.

```
package QUEUING_DISCIPLINE is
   type DISCIPLINE is ( ARBITRARY_QUEUING, FIFO_QUEUING,
                   PRIORITY_QUEUING, SPINNING );

   UNSUPPORTED_DISCIPLINE : exception;
end QUEUING_DISCIPLINE;
```

If ARBITRARY_QUEUING is selected, the queuing discipline is implementation-defined. If FIFO_QUEUING is selected then queuing is on a first-in, first-out basis. If PRIORITY_QUEUING is selected queuing is determined by the priority of the tasks involved. If SPINNING is selected then there is no queuing. The exact spinning policy depends on the implementation, but an example might be for a multiprocessor system a task would continually attempt to get the service until the service was available, only releasing the processor if preempted. With priority queuing, it may happen that a queue contains more than one task at the same priority. In this case, the "PRIORITY" discipline uses FIFO ordering.

Pre-elaboration of Program Units

Issue. Real-time applications frequently require that programs (and tasks) be able to start up more quickly than if all the work of elaboration is done at execution time. A well-defined class of constructs, defined similarly to static expressions but larger in scope, is needed such that a programmer can rely on the elaboration of these constructs not taking any execution time. Constructs whose elaboration does not take any execution time is called "pre-elaborated". Runtime elaboration of constant data structures and a priori known tasks is not consistent with many embedded systems' power-up and restart requirements.

Proposal. This Entry proposes a pragma that appears in a declarative part.

```
pragma PRE_ELABORATE( [ <identifier_list> ] );
```

It will request the compilation system (i.e., compiler/linker) to pre-elaborate the indicated list of data structures and program units. If the optional identifier list is omitted, all possible entities will be pre-elaborated, in the program unit where the pragma appears, and a list of those entities that cannot be pre-elaborated will be produced by the compilation system. Pre-elaborated objects should be ROM-able. The complete list of pre-elaboratable constructs is extensive and can be found in the CIFO.

An implementation supporting this feature shall include the following constant declaration in package SYSTEM:

```
SUPPORTS_PREELABORATION : constant BOOLEAN := TRUE;
```

Access Values That Designate Static Objects

Issue. In many embedded systems, it is necessary to manipulate references to static objects. An object may need to be static because it is located in read-only memory, or it is accessed by an I/O processor directly (DMA), or because it is a pre-elaborated constant, or for other reasons. It may be necessary to refer to such an object indirectly. For example, a reference to the object may appear as an actual parameter of a procedure or as the value of a function. Also, groups of static objects are sometimes logically viewed as arrays, while they do not have all the physical properties of arrays, such as contiguity in memory. In these cases, the logical view can be implemented as an array of references.

Proposal. This proposal consists of a generic function, a pragma, and a Boolean constant as defined in the following:

```
generic
    type OBJECT is limited private;
    type ACCESS_TYPE is access OBJECT;
function MAKE_ACCESS_VALUE( STATIC : OBJECT ) return ACCESS_TYPE;
```

Assume a type OT and a corresponding access type AOT, and assume the generic instantiation:

```
function ACCESS_TO is new MAKE_ACCESS_VALUE( OT, AOT );
```

If OBJ is of type OT, the value ACCESS_TO(OBJ) will be an access value that designates OBJ in the same way in which the access value returned by an allocator designates the corresponding dynamically allocated object.

Because this feature may require special compiler support, an implementation shall also include an implementation-defined pragma:

```
pragma MAY_MAKE_ACCESS_VALUE( <type_mark> );
```

This pragma is to be specified for every type or subtype for which a programmer intends to instantiate MAKE_ACCESS_VALUE. This pragma must appear in the same declarative part as the named type, and must appear before any forcing occurrence (see LRM 13.1) of the named type.

The implementation shall also supply a Boolean constant in package SYSTEM named:

```
MAKE_ACCESS_SUPPORTED : constant BOOLEAN := <Boolean value>;
```

which indicates whether or not the feature is supported.

Passive Task Pragma

Issue. Many tasks can be implemented as either active or passive entities. Active tasks require separate threads of control that can be independently scheduled by the run-time system. Passive tasks are those that do not require threads of control. For passive tasks, entry calls can be transformed into procedure calls, avoiding the cost of task switching. The memory required for the implementation of passive tasks is negligible, roughly equivalent to simple objects such as semaphores. The application must have control over which tasks are passive and which are active.

Numerous Ada abstractions are represented using intermediate tasks such as server tasks or agent tasks which are inherently passive. If the implementation cannot detect and optimize such tasks, their cost can be prohibitive for many real-time applications.

Proposal. A new pragma is proposed:

```
pragma THREAD_OF_CONTROL( DESIRED : BOOLEAN );
```

which is allowed within a task specification both for a single task and a task type and whether the immediately enclosing task is to be implemented as an active or passive task.

At a minimum, an implementation that supports passive tasks should allow passive tasks of either of the following two forms:

1) Simple accept statements

```
task body T is
   <restricted_declarative_part>
begin
   loop -- optional loop
      accept E1(...) do
         ...                          -- optional accept body
      end E1;
      .
      .
      accept En(...) do
         ...                          -- optional accept body
      end;
   end loop;
end T;
```

2) Selective wait statement

```
task body T is
   <restricted_declarative_part>
begin
   loop                           -- optional loop
      select
         when <condition> =>      -- optional guard
            accept E1(...) do
               ...                -- optional accept body
            end E1;
```

```
      or
         .
         .
      or when <condition> =>          -- optional guard
            accept En(...) do
               ...                    -- optional accept body
            end En;
      or when <condition> =>
            terminate;                -- optional
      end select;
   end loop;
end T;
```

`<restricted_declarative_part>` consists of any declaration except declarations of dependent tasks, inner packages, objects of dynamic size or access types. Additionally, the default initialization for any declaration is restricted from calling user-defined functions.

In both forms the following restrictions apply :

1) In the selective wait, no delay alternative or else part is allowed.
2) Nested accept statements are not allowed.
3) Entry families are not supported.
4) In the task body there is one and only one accept statement for each entry declared in the task specification.
5) The specification of storage size for a task activation is not allowed for passive task and is ignored by the implementation if present.
6) Passive tasks may not have dependent tasks.
7) No exception handler is allowed for the task body.
8) The guard expressions (<condition>) must not contain calls to user-defined functions.
9) The only statement allowed outside of select and accept bodies is an unconditional loop.

An implementation is free to provide additional forms of passive tasks, or to eliminate some of the above restrictions. An implementation must clearly define the circumstances under which a task is eligible for implementation as a passive entity.

Unchecked Subprogram Invocation

Issue. Ada provides the capability to take the address of any program unit (LRM 13.5, 13.7.2) but the language does not guarantee that all implementations provide the corresponding capability to invoke that unit by its address.

Proposal. An implementation-defined pragma shall be supported, of the following form:

```
pragma INVOKE_BY_ADDRESS( <subprogram_name> );
```

An Ada language implementation supporting this feature shall permit the use of a subprogram address clause as a means for calling a subprogram via an address that is determined at run time. Support for this feature shall be indicated by inclusion of the following constant declaration in package SYSTEM:

```
SUPPORTS_INVOCATION_BY_ADDRESS : constant BOOLEAN := TRUE;
```

Implementations supporting this feature shall recognize a pragma INVOKE_BY_ADDRESS, whose semantics are defined below. This pragma takes a subprogram name as its only argument.

The code sketch below illustrates how this feature could be used to call subprogram SOME_PROCEDURE with arguments Z and W.

```
CALL_TABLE : array ( 1 .. N ) of SYSTEM.ADDRESS;
...
CALL_TABLE(I) := SOME_PROCEDURE'ADDRESS;
...
declare
   procedure P( X : in INTEGER; Y : out INTEGER );
   pragma INTERFACE(SOME_LANGUAGE,P);
   pragma INVOKE_BY_ADDRESS(P);
   for P use at CALL_TABLE(I);
begin
   ...
   P( Z, W );
   ...
end;
```

Data Synchronization Pragma

Issue. The use of CIFO entries for Ada task synchronization will lead to errors if the user assumes that these entries are synchronization points. Some CIFO users, unaware of the risk involved, will naturally want to use these entries to implement protocols for sharing data among Ada tasks. If the Ada compiler being used has optimizations suppressed or does not perform a high degree of optimization, this approach to data sharing may work, accidentally. Unfortunately, with an Ada compiler that does perform a high degree of optimization, this approach to data sharing has a high probability of failure. As highly optimizing compilers become more common, this problem will occur more often.

The problem arises because an Ada compiler will not recognize the invocation of CIFO entries as a synchronization point as it would a task entry call. To solve the problem, the synchronization points and the data shared must be identified for the compiler. If this is done, the CIFO task synchronization entries can be used to implement data sharing. The pragma SHARED is limited to scalars and access types, a small subset of the variables types that need to be shared. The proposed pragma SHARED_DATA eliminates these restrictions.

Proposal. The proposed pragma designates a variable that is permitted to be a scalar, access type, or an aggregate type as shared and requires every read or update of the variable or its components within the scope of its declaration to be treated as a synchronization point by the compiler.

```
pragma SHARED_DATA ( <variable_name> );
```

The effect of pragma SHARED_DATA is to force the compiler to allocate storage for the shared variable, to read a value from storage when the variable or any of its components is referenced, and to write a value to storage when the variable or any of its components is updated. With shared cached memory, the cache entry should be written to memory or flushed as appropriate. The effect of pragma SHARED_DATA is to maintain data coherency.

Dynamic Storage Management

Issue. The freedom which the Ada standard leaves to the language implementor with regard to dynamic storage management makes it difficult for application programmers to program time and memory-constrained applications. Two particular manifestations of this problem are: (1) Ada Runtime Environment routines for storage management may use up significant amounts of processor time at times not predictable by the application programmer; (2) dynamic storage may be exhausted without any warning to the application program, and the STORAGE_ERROR exception may be raised too late or in a section of the program where recovery is not possible.

This proposal is intended to provide low-cost implementations of dynamic storage management for those resource-constrained applications that require dynamic storage allocation and recovery, but where the more general schemes would be too time-consuming.

Proposal. Two packages are proposed: (1) POOLS to define storage pools, and (2) GIVE_AND_TAKE to assign designated user data types to be allocated from these pools:

```
package POOLS is
   type POOL_ID is private;
   type BLOCK_POINTER is <implementation defined>;

   NULL_BLOCK_POINTER : constant BLOCK_POINTER := <implementation
defined>;

   type NUMBER_OF_FREE_BLOCKS is range 0 .. <implementation defined>;
   subtype NUMBER_OF_BLOCKS is
      NUMBER_OF_FREE_BLOCKS range 1 .. <implementation defined>;
   type NUMBER_OF_STORAGE_UNITS_PER_BLOCK is range <implementation
defined>;

   POOL_STORAGE_ERROR         : exception;
   POOL_BLOCKS_STILL_IN_USE   : exception;
   POOL_ID_INVALID             : exception;
   POOL_BLOCK_UNAVAILABLE     : exception;
   POOL_BLOCK_SIZE_TOO_SMALL  : exception;

   function NEW_POOL(  POOL_SIZE : NUMBER_OF_BLOCKS;
                   BLOCK_SIZE : NUMBER_OF_STORAGE_UNITS_PER_BLOCK )
      return POOL_ID;
   function CREATE_POOL( POOL_SIZE : NUMBER_OF_BLOCKS;
                   BLOCK_SIZE : NUMBER_OF_STORAGE_UNITS_PER_BLOCK )
      return POOL_ID renames NEW_POOL;

   procedure RELEASE_POOL( POOL : in POOL_ID );
   procedure CONDITIONAL_DESTROY_POOL( POOL : in POOL_ID )
      renames RELEASE_POOL;
   procedure UNCONDITIONAL_RELEASE_POOL( POOL : in POOL_ID );
     procedure UNCONDITIONAL_DESTROY_POOL( POOL : in POOL_ID )
      renames UNCONDITIONAL_RELEASE_POOL;

   procedure EXTEND_POOL( POOL : in POOL_ID;
                       EXTENSION_SIZE : in NUMBER_OF_BLOCKS );

   function GET_BLOCK( POOL : POOL_ID ) return BLOCK_POINTER;

   procedure FREE_BLOCK( POOL : POOL_ID; BLOCK : in out BLOCK_POINTER );

   function POOL_SIZE( POOL : POOL_ID ) return NUMBER_OF_BLOCKS;
   function BLOCK_SIZE( POOL : POOL_ID ) return
      NUMBER_OF_STORAGE_UNITS_PER_BLOCK;
   function FREE_STORAGE_BLOCKS( POOL : POOL_ID )
      return NUMBER_OF_FREE_BLOCKS;
private
   type POOL_ID is <implementation defined>;
end POOLS;
```

```
with POOLS;
generic
   POOL : POOLS.POOL_ID;
   type DESIGNATED_SUBTYPE is limited private;
package GIVE_AND_TAKE is
   -- *** WARNING: This access type may NOT be used with "new",
   -- *** "UNCHECKED_DEALLOCATION", or "pragma CONTROLLED".
   type POINTER is access DESIGNATED_SUBTYPE;

   function NEW_BLOCK return POINTER;
   procedure RELEASE_BLOCK( BLOCK : in out POINTER );
end GIVE_AND_TAKE;
```

The semantics of these packages are fairly straightforward and clearly indicated by the subprogram names. The real significance of this Entry lies in the implementation, which must guarantee that:

1. all subprograms in these packages execute safely in a multitasking environment
   [NOTE: This requirement may necessitate the use of storage synchronization mechanisms (e.g. locks) that in turn may result in tasks being blocked. The implementation must document any calls which are blocking.]
2. the execution time of allocation of a block from a storage pool is bounded by a (small) constant
3. the execution time of returning of a block to a storage pool is bounded by a (small) constant

The actual execution times are implementation defined and must be documented for each implementation.

Disclaimer. CIFO is the result of concerted effort by well-qualified team of volunteer application builders and Ada vendors. However, it has not had the amount of rigorous outside review that is given to formal standard, nor has it been through a balloting process as rigorous as that of a formal standard. Furthermore, ARTEWG has endeavored to expedite the release of this version, so that it can be relevant before culmination of the Ada9X effort. ARTEWG is convinced that this version is a significant improvement over previous versions of CIFO. However, **users and vendors are warned that semantic ambiguities may remain.**

Towards Ada 9X
A. Burns, Ed.
IOS Press, 1992

Some Proposed Ada 9X Mappings

Bill Taylor

Transition Technology, 96 Glanrhyd, Cwmbran, Gwent NP44 6TZ, UK

Abstract: The revision of the current Ada language standard has reached the stage where proposed mappings to satisfy the requirements are stabilising. This paper shows by example how designs expressed in Ada-83 can be re-expressed in Ada-9X using three proposed major new features: Object Oriented Programming, Hierarchical Libraries and Protected Records.

1. Introduction

The latest draft Ada 9X Mapping Specification [2] for the revision of the current Ada standard [1] was published in August 1991. This paper gives a brief introduction to the capabilities offered by three major new features, by comparing an implementation in Ada-9X with one in Ada-83. The selected features are:

- *Type Extension*, to allow an Object-Oriented style of programming, with the benefits of re-use and reduced recompilation;

- *Hierarchical Libraries*, with the prime benefit of reduced recompilation;

- *Protected Records*, which offer a portable alternative to rendezvous to achieve data synchronisation.

2. Windowing System - Ada-83

To illustrate the capabilities offered by the proposed Object Oriented Programming features in Ada 9X, a very simple windowing system will be used. Three kinds of window are supported: *Simple* windows which are displayed as a box, *Labeled* windows which have an additional label, and *Composite* windows which are labeled and consist of a set of windows each of which can be of any kind.

The specification and body of this package are shown in Figures 1 and 2. The following points should be noted:

- The different kinds of window are represented by an enumeration type (1).

- The type Window is a variant record so that a composite window, comprising a set of heterogeneous windows, can be implemented as a list (2).

- The structure of the type Window is defined using a variant part (3).

- The implementation of Display involves a case statement (4).

```
package Window_System is
    type Coordinate is private;
    type Text is new String (1 .. 32);
    type Window_Kind is (Simple, Labeled, Composite);   -- (1)
    type Window (Kind : Window_Kind);
    type Window_Ptr is access Window;
    type Window (Kind : Window_Kind) is                 -- (2)
        record
            Position : Coordinate;
            Next : Window_Ptr;
            Encloser : Window_Ptr;
            case Kind is                                -- (3)
                when Simple =>
                    null;
                when others =>
                    Label : Text;
                    case Kind is
                        when Simple | Labeled =>
                            null;
                        when others =>
                            First : Window_Ptr;
                    end case;
            end case;
        end record;

    procedure Display (W : Window);
private
    type Coordinate is
        record
            Low_X, Low_Y, High_X, High_Y : Integer;
        end record;
end Window_System;
```

Figure 1 - Package Specification Window_System

Consider, how the Window_System software could be adapted to add a new kind of window, such as Coloured_Window, which is a special kind of Labeled_Window. The necessary steps are:

1. Add an extra enumeral to the enumeration type Kind.

2. Change the definition of Window to allow for the extra variant.

3. Change the body of Window_System to allow for the extra case.

4. Recompile all existing clients of Window_System.

5. Re-test all existing users of Window_System

3. Windowing System - Ada-9X

3.1 A Simple Window

In the Ada 9X equivalent, the enumeration type (Kind) is unnecessary. Instead, each of the different window kinds has its own package. The first package defines

```
package body Window_System is
    procedure Draw_Box (Position : Coordinate) is separate;
    procedure Draw_Label (Label_Text : Text;
                          Position : Coordinate) is separate;
    procedure Display (W : Window) is
    begin
        case W.Kind is                                    -- (4)
            when Simple =>
                Draw_Box (W.Position);
            when Labeled =>
                Draw_Box (W.Position);
                Draw_Label (Label_Text => W.Label,
                            Position => W.Position);
            when Composite =>
                Draw_Box (W.Position);
                Draw_Label (Label_Text => W.Label,
                            Position => W.Position);
                declare
                    Ptr : Window_Ptr := W.First;
                begin
                    while Ptr /= null loop
                        Display (Ptr.all);
                    end loop;
                end;
        end case;
    end Display;
end Window_System;
```

Figure 2 - Package Body Window_System

```
package Windows is
    type Coordinate is private;
    type Window;
    type Window_Ptr is access Window'Class;              -- (5)
    type Window is
        tagged record                                    -- (6)
            Position : Coordinate;
            Next : Window_Ptr;
            Encloser : Window_Ptr;
        end record;

    procedure Display (W : Window);
private
    type Coordinate is
        record
            Low_X, Low_Y, High_X, High_Y : Integer;
        end record;
end Windows;
```

Figure 3 - Package Specification Windows

```
package body Windows is
    procedure Draw_Box (Position : Coordinate) is separate;
    procedure Display (W : Window) is
    begin
        Draw_Box (W.Position);
    end Display;
end Windows;
```

Figure 4 - Package Body Windows

3.2 A Labeled Window

A labeled window is defined by extending from the simple window and adding a Label component. See Figures 5 and 6.

```
with Windows; use Windows;
package Labeled_Windows is
    type Labeled_Window (Label_Length : Natural)
        is new Windows.Window
        with record
            Label : String (1 .. Label_Length);
        end record;

    procedure Display (Lw : Labeled_Window);   -- displays border
                                               -- and label (7)
end Labeled_Windows;
```

Figure 5 - Package Specification Labeled_Windows

```
package body Labeled_Windows is
    procedure Draw_Label (Label_Text : Text;
                          Position : Coordinate) is separate;
    procedure Display (Lw : Labeled_Window) is
    begin
        Display (Window (Lw));                        -- (8)
        Draw_Label (Label_Text => Lw.Label,
                    Position => Lw.Position);
    end Display;
end Labeled_Windows;
```

Figure 6 - Package Body Labeled_Windows

Note that:

- If a declaration for Display (7) had not been provided then the Display provided by Window would have been inherited (as in Ada-83 rules for derived types) but any Labeled_Window would be displayed as if it were a simple window.

- By converting the parameter Lw to a Window (8), the Display operation for type Window is called.

3.3 A Composite Window

Similarly, a composite window is defined by extending from the labeled window and adding a First component to point to the first sub-window. See Figures 7 and 8.

```ada
with Labeled_Windows; use Labeled_Window;
package Composite_Windows is
    type Composite_Window is new Labeled_Window
        with record
            First : Window_Ptr;
        end record;

    procedure Display (Cw : Composite_Window);
    -- displays border, label and contents
end Composite_Windows;
```

Figure 7 - Package Specification Composite_Windows

```ada
package body Composite_Windows is
    procedure Display (Cw : Composite_Window) is
        Ptr : Window_Ptr := Cw.First;
    begin
        Display (Labeled_Window (Cw));
        -- display border and label

        while Ptr /= null loop
            Display (Ptr.all);   -- dispatch to proper display (9)
            Ptr := Ptr.Next;
        end loop;
    end Display;
end Composite_Windows;
```

Figure 8 - Package Body Composite_Windows

Note how the call to Display (9) dispatches on the tag of *Ptr.all*. If the type of Ptr.all is Window then Windows.Dispatch will be executed. If the type of Ptr.all is Labeled_Window then Labeled_Windows.Dispatch will be executed. If the type of Ptr.all is Composite_Window then Composite_Windows.Dispatch will be executed.

3.4 A Coloured Window

Now consider, how the above Ada 9X implementation could be adapted to add a new kind of window, such as Coloured_Window, which is a special kind of Labeled_Window. The necessary steps are:

1. Define a new package (Coloured_Windows) with a new type (Coloured_Window) extended from Labeled_Window and with a redefined Display operation, as in Figure 9.

2. Provide a body for Coloured_Windows, as in Figure 9.

3. Compile and test Coloured_Windows.

Note that there is no need to change any existing software (and hence no need to test any existing clients). Because Coloured_Window belongs to Window'Class a composite window can enclose coloured windows and the package Composite_Windows does not have to be changed to achieve this. In particular, Composite_Windows.Display will execute correctly without being changed, even though it was written without any knowledge of the existence of coloured windows.

```ada
with Labeled_Windows; use Labeled_Window;
package Coloured_Windows is
    type Coloured_Window is new Labeled_Window
        with record
            Colour : Colour_Type;
        end record;

    procedure Display (Cw : Coloured_Window);
    -- displays border, label and contents
end Coloured_Windows;

-------------------------------------------------------------------

package body Coloured_Windows is
    procedure Display (Cw : Coloured_Window) is
        Ptr : Window_Ptr := Cw.First;
    begin
        Display (Labeled_Window (Cw)); -- display border and label

        while Ptr /= null loop
            Display (Ptr.all); -- dispatch to proper display (9)
            Ptr := Ptr.Next;
        end loop;
    end Display;
end Coloured_Windows;
```

Figure 9 - Package Specification and Body Coloured_Windows

4. Hierarchical Libraries

There are two major limitations in the structuring of a large "package" in Ada:

- A large package specification cannot be decomposed if the private part needs to be shared by the constituent packages. One specification implies that any change will obsolete all clients.

- A large package body cannot be decomposed if the private part needs to be shared by the supporting packages. The use of subunits is an option but any change to a subunit specification will obsolete all the subunits.

The solution is to introduce the concept of a library package being a *parent package*, having any number of *child packages*. Posix is an example of a package with an enormous specification in Ada-83. In Ada 9X, however, the Posix package would be relatively small, only defining a set of shared private types (see Figure 10). A child package (such as Posix.File_Manager in Figure 10) has visibility of the private part of its parent. A client can *with* (and access) a child package in the same way as an Ada-83 package, but using dot notation, as in the use of Posix.File_Manager in Figure 11.

An additional capability is to designate a child package as being *private*, as in Figure 12, with the property that it is only visible to its parent (library) package or any child packages of its parent. A child package can have further child packages.

```
    package Posix is
        type Descriptor is private;
    private
        type Descriptor is new Natural;
    end Posix;


    ------------------------------------------------------------------


    package Posix.Exceptions is
        File_Descriptor_Error : exception;
        File_Name_Error : exception;
        Permission_Error : exception;
    end Posix.Exceptions;


    ------------------------------------------------------------------


    with Posix.Exceptions;
    package Posix.File_Manager is
        type Mode is (Read_Only, Write_Only, Read_Write);
        function Open (Name : String;
                       Of_Mode : Mode) return File_Descriptor;
        procedure Close (File : in out File_Descriptor);
    end Posix.File_Manager;
```

Figure 10 - Package Specifications for Posix

5. Buffer Task - Ada-83

One of the Requirements for Ada 9X was to "ensure that common programming paradigms can be implemented with predictably efficient performance". One

```
with Posix;
with Posix.File_Manager;
with Posix.Exceptions;
procedure Posix_User is
    File : Posix.File_Descriptor;
begin
    File := Posix.File_Manager.Open
                (Name => "File_Name",
                 Mode => Posix.File_Manager.Read_Only);
        -- etc
    Posix.File_Manager.Close (File);
exception
    when Posix.Exceptions.File_Name_Error =>
        null;            -- do whatever is necessary
end Posix_User;
```

Figure 11 - Package Specification Posix_User

```
private
package Posix.Descriptor_Manager is
    function Allocate return Posix.File_Descriptor;
    procedure Deallocate (D : in out Posix.File_Descriptor);
end Posix.Descriptor_Manager;
```

Figure 12 - Package Specification Posix.Descriptor_Manager

```
task type Buffer is
    entry Put (D : in Data);
    entry Get (D : out Data);
end Buffer;
```

Figure 13 - Task Type Buffer

common paradigm is controlled access to shared data, for example a cyclic buffer. In Ada-83 there are three approaches, each with its own drawback:

- Use a buffer task and perform a rendezvous to Put and Get data, as illustrated in Figures 13 and 14, which is a heavyweight solution and incurs a significant performance penalty;

- Rely on a *passive task* optimisation, which is compromises portablility;

- use extra-lingual techniques (such as CIFO or a proprietary equivalent), which are totally non-portable.

```
task body Buffer is
    Length : constant := 32;
    Count : Natural := 0;
    Inptr, Outptr : Positive := 1;
    Store : array (1 .. Length) of Data;
begin
    loop
        select
            when Count < Length =>
                accept Put (D : in Data) do
                    Store (Inptr) := D;
                    Inptr := (Inptr mod Length) + 1;
                    Count := Count + 1;
                end Put;
            or
            when Count > 0 =>
                accept Get (D : out Data) do
                    D := Store (Outptr);
                    Outptr := (Outptr mod Length) + 1;
                    Count := Count - 1;
                end Get;
        end select;
    end loop;
end Buffer;
```

Figure 14 - Task Body Buffer

```
protected type Buffer is
    entry Put (D : in Data);
    entry Get (D : out Data);
private record
    Length : constant := 32;
    Count : Natural := 0;
    Inptr, Outptr : Positive := 1;
    Store : array (1 .. Length) of Data;
end Buffer;

------------------------------------------------------------------

protected body Buffer is
    entry Put (D : in Data)
        when Count < Length is              -- (10)
    begin
        Store (Inptr) := D;
        Inptr := (Inptr mod Length) + 1;
        Count := Count + 1;
    end Put;

    entry Get (D : out Data)
        when Count > 0 is
    begin
        D := Store (Outptr);
        Outptr := (Outptr mod Length) + 1;
        Count := Count - 1;
    end Get;
end Buffer;
```

Figure 15 - Protected Type Buffer and body

6. Buffer Protected Record - Ada-9X

The objective in Ada 9X is to get a portable, efficient solution to this problem. It is based on the concept of a *Protected Record*. Associated with a Protected Record are a set of protected operations (functions, procedures and entries). Functions offer read_only access to the protected data (Length, Count, Inptr, Outptr and Store) and can be executed in parallel. Procedures offer exclusive read/write access but cannot suspend the caller. Entries also offer exclusive read/write access but will suspend the caller until the *barrier condition* is True (see (10) in Figure 15). Objects named in the barrier condition are restricted to protected data and global data, in particular, formal parameters cannot be accessed. This ensures that all waiting callers are waiting on the same condition.

7. Mutual Exclusion - Ada-83

Another example of controlled access to shared variables is the simple case of an object to allocate the next number in a sequence, such as Posix.File_Descriptor (which is simply an Integer). The Ada-83 solution is shown in Figures 16 and 17.

```ada
task Counter is
    entry Get_Next (New_Value : out Positive);
    entry Get_Last (Last_Value : out Positive);
end Counter;
```

Figure 16 - Task Counter

```ada
task body Counter is
    Value : Natural := 0;
begin
    loop
        select
            accept Get_Next (New_Value : out Positive) do
                Value := Value + 1;
                New_Value := Value;
            end Get_Next;
        or
            accept Get_Last (Last_Value : out Positive) do
                Last_Value := Value;
            end Get_Last;
        end select;
    end loop;
end Buffer;
```

Figure 17 - Task Body Counter

8. Mutual Exclusion - Ada-9X

In Ada 9X, the counter is implemented as a protected record. Because there are no barrier conditions for the protected operations - there were no guards in the Ada 83 solution - they can be implemented as subprograms. See Figures 18 and 19. Note that Get_Next cannot be a function because it changes the (protected) state of the object.

```
protected Counter is
    procedure Get_Next (New_Value : out Positive);
    function Get_Last return Positive;
private record
    Value : Natural := 0;
end Counter;
```

Figure 18 - Protected Counter

```
protected body Counter is
    procedure Get_Next (New_Value : out Positive) is
    begin
        Value := Value + 1;
        New_Value := Value;
    end Get_Next;

    function Get_Last return Positive is
    begin
        return Value;
    end Get_Last;
end Counter;
```

Figure 19 - Protected Body Counter

REFERENCES

[1]   ANSI/MIL-STD-1815A-1983, Ada Reference Manual, 1983.

[2]   Ada 9X Mapping Document, Volumes I and II, Intermetrics Inc., August 1991.

Asynchronous Transfer of Control in Ada 9X[1]

By Offer Pazy[2]

Abstract

The need for an Asynchronous Transfer of Control (*ATC*) mechanism in Ada has been discussed by real-time experts in the last several years [8, 9, 10]. There is consensus today that the lack of such a mechanism in Ada 83 [15] significantly affects the ability to construct reliable systems in the fault-tolerance and real-time domains. This need was recognized by the Ada 9X project and a specific requirement was formulated to address that deficiency [5]. This paper will describe the proposed change to the language as currently formulated by the Mapping Revision Team (*MRT*).

1. Introduction

1.1. Background: The Need

The synchronous nature of Ada 83 has been identified by many as a potential deficiency for the programming of certain paradigms in real-time and fault-tolerant systems. Since there is no way to alter the flow of execution of an Ada task asynchronously, there is also no convenient way to inform it about unexpected events and to direct it to respond to them accordingly. This deficiency was identified by several Ada Revision Requests (*ARR*'s) [6] (ARR numbers 83, 106, 196, 384, 651, 656, 768) and by the various International Workshops on Real-Time Ada Issues [8, 9, 10]. As a result, the requirements document for the Ada 9X revision [5] explicitly calls for providing such a capability. Requirement R5.3-A(1) says "Ada 9X shall allow the execution of a sequence of statements to be abandoned in order to execute a different sequence within the same task." We will not repeat here the entire body of experience that has lead to the formulation of this requirement, but rather we will briefly enumerate the primary examples: detection and response to time overruns, mode-changes, partial computations, and responding quickly to external events, in particular, faults. In the latter case, it is crucial that the thread of control (the Ada task) will stop its normal execution immediately and either be prevented from doing anything else or start its recovery sequence.

All of these requirements are addressed by the proposed change.

---

[1]This paper has been produced under the sponsorship of the Ada 9X Project Office under contract F08635-90-C-0066.

[2]Author's current addresses: Paper -- Intermetrics Inc., 733 Concord Ave, Cambridge MA 02138-1002, Email -- <offer@inmet.inmet.com>

1.2. Organization

We start with a brief discussion of the alternative approaches that have been proposed to solve this problem. These approaches are well-documented in the literature. The main two approaches are the *asynchronous exceptions* [14, 1, 11, 16, 18] and the *dedicated task* approach. The limitations and problems with the above approaches will be discussed. Then, a description of the proposed change is given, followed by a rationale for the specific semantics, and a discussion of the various alternatives that were considered by the MRT. An analysis of implementation issues with regard to real-time systems concludes that part.

We close with a number of examples which emphasize on the composability of the proposed feature, and the ability to construct high-level abstractions such as mode-changes, detection of missed deadlines and more. Specific, more subtle ramifications of the proposed semantics will be discussed with these examples to evaluate the user-friendliness and the expressive power of the new language constructs. A summary of the approach will conclude the paper.

Throughout this paper we will use the terms *selects with an abortable final part* and *select-in* interchangeably.

2. Other approaches

Several approaches have been suggested during the last decade to address the ATC problem in Ada. Some of these solutions are compatible with Ada 83 and some require changes to the standard and were suggested mainly as ideas for the forthcoming project to revise the language. While these approaches have been discussed frequently in the literature, we mention them here as a context in which to discuss the proposed change, and attempt to show which of the problems and deficiencies of these approaches are solved by the proposed change.

2.1. Creating and Aborting a Task

One solution that has been suggested is to encapsulate the abortable computation or logic in a separate task; the triggering event (delay expiration, fault, or an external event) will simply abort that task. The next time that the same computation needs to start a new task will be created.

Several problems exist with this approach. From a user perspective, it is not always convenient to separate the abortable code from the main computation. Furthermore, the solution does not scale easily to encapsulate larger processing that may need to be aborted, such as mode changes, when a set of tasks need to either be stopped or change what they are doing. Also, when a task aborts, not just its thread of control is affected; a task in Ada represents more than just that. It has context, data (which may be the result of extensive computation), and potential entries with callers queued on them. Killing this task is often more radical than what is needed. A replacement task, which will be created later *instead* of the aborted one, is not considered in Ada as the same entity but as a new one. All pending callers on entries of the aborted task will get TASKING_ERROR, and will have to have the logic to understand how to react (as opposed to a *simple* task failure). A manager task will have to notify all the interested tasks of the identity of the new server, and in turn they will have to re-issue the calls. Programming such a solution for a large-scale application, while guaranteeing freedom from races, is considered very complicated and error-prone [4, p. 403] (and will also require a powerful broadcast mechanism or an ATC by itself). Also, there is the issue of performance and efficiency of implementations both in terms of time and space. Task creation and abortion are still considered two of the heavier operations in Ada tasking, and it has not been proven yet that tasks in Ada can be created and aborted as fast as light-weight threads in other languages or operating systems [13]. Finally, the danger of memory leaks after the abortion is a very serious one. Even a clever implementation cannot always reclaim all storage occupied by the aborted tasks since the information about this storage may be present only at the user level.

2.2. Asynchronous Exception

Another approach, which is commonly known as the *Asynchronous Exception* (AE), was originally suggested as the FAILURE exception in preliminary Ada [12]. It was later decided to drop this feature because of its implementation consequences [4 p. 286, 2, 17]and the belief that it was too similar to the **abort** to be justified as a separate feature. Since then, many have suggested reinstating this capability in one form or another. While some variations exist among the various proposals, the fundamental capability is for one task to asynchronously raise an exception in another.

The main problems that have been identified with asynchronous exceptions are as follows: There is no clear way to define the regions in which the affected task is willing to *accept* the AE, and the regions where it wants to be protected from interruption. The desired semantics regarding what happens when AE's are blocked or when more than one AE is sent to a task are not clear. It is not clear what are the desired relationships between asynchronous and synchronous exceptions (e.g., what should happen when **new** is about to raise STORAGE_ERROR and at the same time an AE is sent to that task. It is usually application-dependent which exception should override the other). There was no easy way to send an AE to a set of tasks, a requirement that is often associated with mode-changes and fault-tolerant systems. In addition, with AE, there is always the danger of the exception being lost by **when others** (unless a special rule is defined), or by a more deeply nested procedure. The latter problem is particularly complicated for the design of systems with multiple modes. There, a request for a mode-change should affect the most global "controller" as soon as possible and be handled there, and not by various local routines "on the way". Finally, such exceptions may be undesirably propagated through a rendezvous when the caller is not expecting such a situation and is not ready to handle it.

To summarize, the way to address and resolve the above problems, and the inherent race-conditions which were present in any attempt to define AE's, were not evident. It seems that there is very little in common between regular, synchronous, exceptions and asynchronous ones, and any attempt to unify them could result in a more cumbersome and error-prone facility.

3. The Proposed Change

This section highlights the main characteristics and features of the proposed asynchronous transfer of control mechanism for Ada 9X. The detailed description appear in the Mapping Specification document [7, 9.9.2, 9.9.3, 9.12]; we will concentrate here on the important aspects of the change, the rationale for certain decisions, and some of the alternatives that were considered by the MRT.

The support for ATC in Ada 9X is through the **select** construct with an abortable final part. A portion of the new syntax is presented below:

```
select
  event_alternative
  sequence_of_statements
or
  event_alternative
  sequence_of_statements
or
  ...
in
  handled_sequence_of_statements
end select;
```

Like any other selective entry call, several alternatives may appear before the **in** keyword. Each alternative represents an interrupting event and may be either an entry call or a delay statement. When an event alternative is selected (it is guaranteed that only one such event will take effect), it will interrupt the sequence of statements in the abortable final part (after the **in** keyword). This sequence of statements will then begin finalizing itself (if finalization routines or an exit handler are defined) and transfer control to the sequence of statements of the interrupting alternative. As part of aborting that sequence, dependent tasks will be aborted. If the final part completes its execution before any interrupting event has occurred, all pending entry calls or delays are cancelled. While in the final part, no limitations exist on the kind of constructs that can be used, including the nesting of another select with an abortable final part. However, issuing another entry call on a protected record entry, may yield unpredictable results, since the queuing policy in effect for the program, will determine which call will be accepted first, and hence which scope will be aborted.

It is important to remember that the default state of a task is insensitive to ATC's (except to **abort** statements which are directed at entire tasks). Only when the task expresses explicitly its desire to handle ATC's, will they take effect.

In order to protect user data structures and ensure the consistency of the program's data base, abort is deferred in certain regions of code. These regions include rendezvous, operations on protected records, when finalizing objects, and when executing an *exit_handler* which contains a *when abort* choice.

Abort is deferred in an *exit_handler* with an *abort* choice, since the presence of such a choice means that the corresponding code relies on certain finalization operations in the case of an abort. If the abort occurs before the normal processing completes, the handler will execute. However, if the processing has just completed and the exit handler is executing (for another choice), aborting the code then will be contrary to the user expectations. In addition, while performing critical finalization operations in the abort handler, an abort from an outer scope should be deferred in order to let the finalization complete normally.

If several select constructs, with abortable final parts are nested within each other, each one of them can be aborted depending on the specific interrupting event. When a final part is aborted, all nested selects will be aborted as well. While the precedence of which scope to abort is from the outermost scope (to prevent *local* handling of global events), the finalization of all aborted scopes will proceed from the innermost scope outward. This is done to ensure that all scopes are properly finalized and data structures maintain their consistency under all circumstances. When a certain scope is aborted, all outer scopes (of selects with an abortable final part) are not affected and remain *sensitive* to their corresponding events.

The finalization rules ensure data integrity and proceed from innermost scope to the outside. This process can be perceived as cleaning up the aborted execution. However, the finalization sequence does not always know the exact reason for the abort (if more than one interrupting event exists or multiple *select-in*'s are nested), and therefore cannot perform the clean-up which is particular to the specific interrupting event. If such a cleanup is necessary, it can be accomplished by the sequence of statements after the interrupting event (which is unique to the interrupting reason). This sequence of statements can also be used to prepare for future processing (such as in mode-change). Note that if no alternative is selected before the abortable final part has completed, none of the sequence of statements following the events will execute. Finally, the user has full control over the speed and latencies incurred with an ATC. Elaborated finalization code is not always necessary or desired; in fact, finalization can be very short or even empty, thus achieving a very fast transfer of control.

Using the select construct, the user has the capability to construct the abortable regions based on the system's design; to assign preferences, to limit the regions in which ATC's can take effect, the amount of latency in responding to ATC's, and the degree of finalization and recovery after each ATC. By using entry calls, the triggering event occurs asynchronously with the abortion sequence, thus it is suitable for interrupt handlers. The ability to specify delays (including user-defined timers, see [7, G.1.6]together with entry calls, and the capabilities mentioned above allow for the composition of high-level interruptible abstractions, or for the construction of common primitives which can work safely in the presence of ATC's.

In summary, by supporting asynchronous transfer of control as part of a selective entry call, several useful properties are provided:

1. The statements which are abortable are clearly bracketed in the abortable final part.

2. The asynchronous transfer of control is directly tied to the acceptance of an entry call or the expiration of a delay. This allows the transfer to occur without requiring another task to explicitly signal each task being interrupted, in contrast to what is possible with abort.

3. Any one of a set of events, represented by the select alternatives, can be used to trigger the asynchronous transfer. Which event occurred can be determined, because the sequence of statements of the corresponding alternative is executed.

4. The asynchronous transfer cannot be mistakenly redirected by a local handler, as might happen with a mechanism based on asynchronous exceptions.

The MRT has considered another alternative to the *select-in* construct. This solution would have allowed *accept* alternatives as the interrupting events. This idea was rejected due to complexities in the semantic model and implementation difficulties. Some of the main problems were:

Providing such a capability would open up the possibility of more than one entry being open for a task concurrently, each represents a separate activity. In addition to the semantic problems, such as the order and the preference of acceptance and the possibility for a self deadlock, it was believed to be troublesome for implementations.

It was not clear when the aborting process should begin after the interrupting event was accepted. Since the accept body may be non-trivial (i.e., has a *do-end*) and since semantically it is executed by the same task, there were severe trade-offs between ease of implementation and immediacy of the abort. We did not want to create a situation in which a task would need two threads of control to accomplish that part.

Usually, the task which signals the interrupting event (in whatever form) needs to do it asynchronously. It is common to have interrupt handlers do this, and these cannot block until the acceptance of the abort request. But abort requests usually require acknowledgement as to the success of the delivery of the request. With the available timed, conditional, and unconditional entry calls, there was no way to program such an abort request, while avoiding blocking and receiving the acknowledgement. This is particularly true when the affected task is in a loop which contains various states such as: *just-before-being-interruptible, interruptible, aborted-by-another-task* and *just-finished-the-abortable-region.* It is usually undesirable to leave the abort request pending for the next cycle if the affected task has already finished its processing before the abort request was sent.

Finally, using protected records, the bandwidth between the aborting and aborted tasks can be arbitrarily large, as specified by the application, using **in** and **out** parameters to the corresponding entry calls and procedures. With AE's, the bandwidth was severely limited to distinct exception names or to only one reason in the case of the FAILURE exception.

4. Examples

A key goal of the design of the proposed changes was to provide a user with building blocks to enable him to construct his own high-level abstractions. It was felt that there is no way that a language could have built into it all of the various primitives and abstractions necessary for real-time applications. Instead, by providing a small set of low-level and efficient mechanisms, a set that can be used to compose other primitives, it is believed that the language can remain relatively small, but still powerful. In any review of the proposed changes, it is important to evaluate the proposals along these lines.

The low-level nature of the constructs suggests that very efficient implementations can be developed, thus using them to build higher-level constructs that should not incur undue overhead. Furthermore, the close interaction with the proposed Ada 9X priority model and proposed scheduling policies (see [7, G.1.3, G.1.4], allow these building blocks to coexist with others, and to consistently follow application specific policies. Finally, the freedom from races as is guaranteed by the *CLAIM* mechanism (see 5.2) and the rules of protected records provide for a safe and robust usage of these features.

Below, we present some simple examples to demonstrate various ways to use the proposed features.

4.1. Partial Computations

```
task body T is
begin
    Result_Pr.Update (Initial_Approximation);
    select
        delay until End_Of_Quota;
    in
        while Error > Epsilon loop
            Improve_Result (Var);
            Result_Pr.Update(Var);
        end loop;
    end select;
end T;
```

After establishing an initial approximation of the calculation, the task enters a loop for improving the result, while at the same time being "sensitive" to the delay expiration (in this case, the delay is a user-defined one which measures CPU usage time). When the delay expires, the loop is abandoned and the last good result is remembered. The use of a protected procedure (*Update*) to maintain the global location of the result, ensures that actual updates will be performed atomically.

4.2. Detection of Missed Deadlines

```
task body T is
begin
   loop
      delay until Next_Cycle;
      select
         Manager.Wait_For_Overrun;
         Process_Overrun;
      in
         Do_Something;
      end select;
      Update_Next_Cycle;
   end loop;
end T;
```

The task suspends until the time for its next cycle arrives. It then calls the manager to request a notification when an overrun occurs, and starts its work. If the work is completed before an overrun occurs, the entry call is cancelled and a new cycle starts. Otherwise, the normal processing is aborted and *Process_Overrun* is called. (Depending on the specifics of the problem, *Process_Overrun* may raise an exception so that a new cycle will not start).

4.3. Mode Changes

Example of a program-wide mode change:

```
type System_Mode is
   (Normal, Mode2, Mode3, ...);

protected Mode_Manager is

   procedure Set_Mode(M : System_Mode);

   function Get_Mode return System_Mode;

   entry Wait_For_Mode_Change(System_Mode)
      (New_Mode : out System_Mode);
      -- The family index is the Mode of the caller
      -- Entry returns when system mode does not
      -- equal mode of caller, with New_Mode
      -- indicating the new system mode.

private record
   Current_Mode : System_Mode := Normal;
end Mode_Manager;


protected body Mode_Manger is
```

```
procedure Set_Mode(M : System_Mode) is
begin
    -- Record new mode
    Current_Mode := M;
end Set_Mode;

function Get_Mode return System_Mode is
begin
    return Current_Mode;
end Get_Mode;

entry Wait_For_Mode_Change
    (for Old_Mode in System_Mode)
    (New_Mode : out System_Mode)
       when Old_Mode /= Current_Mode is
begin
    New_Mode := Current_Mode;
end Wait_For_Mode_Change;

end Mode_Manager;
```

-- Here is a typical task which reacts to mode changes:

```
task body Typical_Task is

    My_Mode : System_Mode := Normal;
    New_Mode : System_Mode;

begin
    loop
        select
            Mode_Manager.Wait_For_Mode_Change
              (My_Mode)(New_Mode);
                -- Mode changed, set new local mode
                -- and loop around
            My_Mode := New_Mode;
        in
                -- Switch on current task mode and do
                -- appropriate processing
            case My_Mode is
                when Normal =>
                    ... -- Do Normal Mode processing
                when Mode2 =>
                    ... -- Do Mode 2 processing
                when Mode3 =>
                    ... -- Do Mode 3 processing
            end case;
        end select;
    end loop;

end Typical_Task;
```

The protected record *Mode_Manger* keeps track of the current mode. It exports a protected procedure to change it and a query function. In addition, an entry is defined with a barrier which becomes true whenever the current mode does not equal the mode of the caller. (We use an entry family here, so that the caller's mode can be tested in the barrier expression.)

A *Typical_Task* will do its regular processing for a mode while at the same time be sensitive to a mode change. When this is signaled, it will switch to the new processing.

4.4. Recoverable Operations

```
select
    Input_Device.Wait_For_Cancel;
in
    Database.Begin_Transaction;
    Database.Read(...);
    Database.Write(...);
    ...
at end
    when exit =>
        -- Commit transaction, with abort deferred:
        Database.Commit_Transaction;
        Final_Status := Succeeded;
    when abort =>
        --Operation canceled, abort transaction:
        Database.Abort_Transaction;
        Final_Status := Canceled;
    when exception =>
        -- Operation failed, report it and abort transaction:
        Put_Line
            ("Operation failed: Unhandled Exception");
        Database.Abort_Transaction;
        Final_Status := Failed;
end select;
```

In this example, a task is operating on a database. If the transaction is finished normally, it is committed. However, if an exception is raised or an abort is sent to that task, the database update is stopped and the last transaction is aborted. While the task is in the *Commit/Abort* phase, it is protected from further aborts.

5. Implementation Issues

In this section we discuss certain implementation issues of the proposed change. Whenever applicable, we will concentrate on the real-time aspects of the problems. It is beyond the scope of this paper to discuss the general implementation issues of protected records and selective entry calls. We will mention these only within the context of the select-in discussion.

5.1. Multiple Queues

One of the major elements of implementing the select-in construct is the recognition that a task may now exist on multiple queues. This is not an entirely new property of Ada 9X; even in Ada 83 a task could exist on an entry queue and a delay queue at the same time. The simplification there was that the maximum number of queues was always two, that the case was easily recognizable and handled specially, and more importantly, simple rules could be defined by the implementation as to what happens if a delay expires just when an entry call is accepted. (The language could not specify exactly the rules here, so most implementations have chosen to simply ignore the delay expiration). With the proposed change to Ada, an arbitrary number of alternatives may be present in a selective entry call, and furthermore, select-in's may be nested to an arbitrary depth. (As is clear from this discussion, the problem of multiple queues is not unique to the select-in construct, but exists also for the selective entry call). This fact, prevents an implementation from using the task itself (or its TCB) as the queue element. Instead, a number of queue elements have to be created and initialized for each concurrent call. This is no different than in any operating system which supports asynchronous functions.

There are several approaches to allocating these queue elements. Each has different trade-offs in terms of space, predictability, and separation of the generated code from the RTS. One approach is for the compiler to allocate the queue elements on the stack when a **select** statement is encountered. This is clearly the simplest approach with regard to memory management (there is no heap usage) and initialization of the data structures. It does suffer, however, from the need for the generated code and the RTS code to be very intimately connected, and it complicates things for protected architectures when the application and the RTS are separated by a boundary. Another approach is to let the RTS allocate queue elements whenever necessary. This is clearly the simplest to design, but it does require the RTS to depend on dynamic memory management, a fact which is usually considered undesirable for real-time systems. If predictability of memory usage and the latency of RTS operations is of the uppermost importance, then the RTS could pre-allocate a number of queue elements (per task or per system), and raise an exception when this limit is reached. (This behavior is permitted by the proposed change.) Of course, the number of pre-allocated queue elements could be parameterized and controlled by the user.

To summarize, while asynchronous capabilities present a level of added complexity to implementations, there are a number of approaches to solve the memory management problem, with different trade-offs.

5.2. The Race Among Alternatives

The rules of the selective entry call require that only one alternative be selected, and when selected, all others will be cancelled. This is true also for the *else* part; when it is selected, no *real* alternative may start executing. The select-in construct is no different. The final part does start while the other alternatives remain pending, but it cannot complete without ensuring that all pending interrupting events have been cancelled, since the language guarantees that when a select-in construct completes, either the final part has completed normally, *or* an alternative has been chosen and aborted the final part. Unlike the case in Ada 83, when the race was between at most two events and the winner could be determined arbitrarily, here the number of alternatives is unknown statically.

A mechanism is required to arbitrate among events which occur concurrently, to choose a winner, and to make sure that no other alternatives are allowed to proceed. (We refer to the normal completion of the abortable final part or to the choosing of the else part as alternatives in the following discussion.) We call this mechanism the *CLAIM* mechanism. Fortunately, this mechanism is fairly simple and straightforward to implement. All that is required is an indivisible instruction such as test-and-set, but not a lower layer of locks. (In the design of the proposed changes, we have tried to ensure that no such lower level locking is needed even in multi-processor environments. The locks which are associated with each protected record are sufficient.)

All queue elements are connected (or pointing) to a data structure which describes the corresponding select construct. This data structure can have a *claim* bit which serves as the arbitrator. When an alternative is selected it attempts to claim the bit, and if successful it may proceed. If the bit is already set (i.e., claimed), it understands that it has lost the race and simply gives up. It is therefore crucial that no *real work* and no action with side effects (such as executing the entry body) is performed before the claim is successful. Thus only one alternative in a selective entry call may be selected, and for an abortable final part, it is guaranteed that the abortable region will not complete normally. The fact that this data structure is located in a shared memory, which is accessible to multiple processors, ensures that the above algorithm works even if more than one processor attempts to operate on an alternative of the same select construct at the same time.

5.3. Aborting a Sequence of Statements

Delay alternatives (and in particular the user-defined ones) are modeled as entry calls. The expiration of the delay is similar to a barrier of an entry becoming true and the execution of the entry body. After the delay expires, the selected alternative may proceed. Since entry bodies (or delay queue manipulation) may be done by a task other than the *owning* one, the latter may be suspended waiting for one of the alternatives to be selected. Also, if the entry call was issued from a select with an abortable final part, the task may actually be executing (or may later be suspended for unrelated reasons).

There is a common thread here: when a caller on an entry queue reaches the top of the queue, an attempt is made to claim its corresponding bit. If unsuccessful, the entry body is *not* executed, and the next caller on the queue is examined. However, if the claim is successful, the state of the task (running or not) and the kind of select construct are checked. After the entry body has completed, the affected task may either be resumed or interrupted. The task or the interrupt handler do not have to bother with checking the state of the affected task regarding protected regions, deferral of aborts, or pending finalization. This will all be taken care of by the aborted task itself after it is resumed or interrupted. Only the appropriate "nudging" should be done. If the task is in a protected or an abort-deferred region, it will continue to execute until it exits that region. Then, it will check for pending abort requests and act accordingly. After abandoning its normal thread of control, the task will begin finalizing nested scopes (if finalization code exists) until all scopes have been unwound up to the level associated with the aborted select construct. Tasks which are dependent on nested masters will be aborted as part of the finalization process.

There are several approaches to implementing the abort deferral. Similar to exceptions, they have different time/space trade-offs. Since finalization in general is beyond the scope of this paper, we only mention these approaches briefly. One is the *pc-map* method. The compiler prepares a map of code segments (sorted by PC values) for each segment which defers abort. The linker combines all these maps and establishes the global addresses. At runtime, this map is consulted whenever an abort is requested. The other approach is to generate a call to the RTS upon each entrance and exit from abort-deferred regions, and to let the RTS record and handle this as a special task state.

5.4. Selective Waits and Selective Calls

The suggestion to provide a symmetric select construct in Ada, one which would combine **accept** and entry call alternatives [6] (ARR numbers 152, 498, 612, 658, 697), has raised concerns [3, p. 100] regarding the implementability of such a construct and the need for a complex, distributed hand-shake algorithm to make sure that only one alternative is chosen in each select construct when a number of them are engaged in a rendezvous (not necessarily directly).

There was some concern that similar problems would arise with the introduction of selective entry calls, and with allowing task entry calls to be included among the alternatives. This problem does not exist however. The act of opening a number of entries in a selective wait is atomic as is closing them when one is selected. (In fact, a fairly simple transformation exists between a selective wait and protected record entries.) Just like any other entry call, whose selection is dependent on the successful claim of the associated select construct, such is the case when the entry call is used to choose one of the open entries in the selective wait. (The barrier of this internal entry could be *wait_until_a_caller_appears_on_ANY_of_the_open_entries*.) Since the processing of the selective entry call proceeds sequentially, based on the lexical order of the alternatives, the selection process is deterministic and there is no need for a complex handshake algorithm.

6. Summary

In this paper we have described the proposed change for Ada 9X to support asynchronous transfer of control. We have presented the basic behavior of the construct and discussed the alternatives that we have rejected and the reasons behind those rejections. We have also analyzed some of the implementation issues concerning this feature. Finally, we have provided some examples which show how the proposed construct may be used to address the problems which it was intended to solve. Since the revision process of the language is not yet complete, not all of the details are final and we would appreciate early feedback regarding the usability of the proposals and any potential problems or omissions.

Acknowledgement: I would like to acknowledge the help of Bill White and Rich Hilliard from Intermetrics without whose help I would never be able to master the English and Scribe languages.

References

[1]   Patrick De Bondeli. Session Summary Asynchronous Transfer Of Control. In *Proceedings of the Second International Workshop on Real-Time Ada Issues*, pages 43-49. Ada UK and United States Air Force Office of Scientific Research, Association for Computing Machinery, New York, NY, June 1-3, 1988. Appeared in *Ada Letters*, VIII(7).

[2]   Patrick De Bondeli. Asynchronous Transfer of Control and Scheduling Problems. In *Proceedings of the Second International Workshop on Real-Time Ada Issues*, pages 57-60. Ada UK and United States Air Force Office of Scientific Research, Association for Computing Machinery, New York, NY, June 1-3, 1988. Appeared in *Ada Letters*, VIII(7).

[3]   A. Burns, A. M. Lister, and A. Wellings. *Lecture Notes in Computer Science: A Review of Ada Tasking*. Springer-Verlag, Berlin, 1987.

[4]   A. Burns and A. Wellings. *International Computer Science Series: Real-Time Systems and Their Programming Languages*. Addison-Wesley, Reading, Massachusetts, 1989.

[5]   Office of the Under Secretary of Defense for Acquisition. *Ada 9X Requirements*. Technical Report, United States Department of Defense, Washington, D.C., December, 1990.

[6]   Office of the Under Secretary of Defense for Acquisition. *Ada 9X Project Revision Request Report.* Technical Report, United States Department of Defense, Washington, D.C., January, 1990.

[7]   Ada 9X Mapping/Revision Team. *Ada 9X Mapping Volume II Mapping Specification Version 3.1.* Technical Report, Intermetrics, Inc., Cambridge, MA, August, 1991.

[8]   Ada UK and United States Air Force Office of Scientific Research. *Proceedings of the Second International Workshop on Real-Time Ada Issues,* Association for Computing Machinery, New York, NY, 1988.Appeared in *Ada Letters,* VIII(7).

[9]   Software Engineering Institute and United States Office of Naval Research in Cooperation with Ada UK and ACM SIGAda. *Proceedings of the Third International Workshop on Real-Time Ada Issues,* Association for Computing Machinery, New York, NY, 1989.Appeared in *Ada Letters,* X(4).

[10]   Ada UK in cooperation with ACM SIGAda. *Proceedings of the Fourth International Workshop on Real-Time Ada Issues,* Association for Computing Machinery, New York, NY, 1990. Appeared in *Ada Letters,* X(9).

[11]   Ted Baker. Improving Immediacy In Ada. In *Proceedings of the Second International Workshop on Real-Time Ada Issues,* pages 50-56. Ada UK and United States Air Force Office of Scientific Research, Association for Computing Machinery, New York, NY, June 1-3, 1988. Appeared in *Ada Letters,* VIII(7).

[12]   *Preliminary Ada Reference Manual* United States Department of Defense, Washington, D.C., 1979. Appeared as SIGPLAN Notices, vol. 14, no. 6.

[13]   Threads Extension for Portable Operating Systems. IEEE: Posix P1003.4a/D5. December, 1990 Unapproved Draft.

[14]   A. Burns, A.J. Wellings and G.L. Davies. Asynchronous Transfer of Control. In *Proceedings of the Fourth International Workshop on Real-Time Ada Issues,* pages 75-84. Ada UK in cooperation with ACM SIGAda, Association for Computing Machinery, New York, NY, July 16-20, 1990. Appeared in *Ada Letters,* X(9).

[15]   *Reference Manual for the Ada Programming Language* ANSI/MIL-STD-1815A edition, 1983.

[16]   W.J. Toetenel, J. van Katwijk. Asynchronous Transfer of Control in Ada. In *Proceedings of the Second International Workshop on Real-Time Ada Issues,* pages 65-79. Ada UK and United States Air Force Office of Scientific Research, Association for Computing Machinery, New York, NY, June 1-3, 1988. Appeared in *Ada Letters,* VIII(7).

[17]   Thomas J. Quiggle. Ramifications of Re-introducing Asynchronous Exceptions to the Ada Language. In *Proceedings of the Third International Workshop on Real-Time Ada Issues,* pages 25-31. Software Engineering Institute and United States Office of Naval Research in Cooperation with Ada UK and ACM SIGAda, Association for Computing Machinery, New York, NY, June 26-29, 1989. Appeared in *Ada Letters,* X(4).

[18]   Thomas J. Quiggle. Asynchronous Transfer of Control, Session Summary. In *Proceedings of the Third International Workshop on Real-Time Ada Issues,* pages 15-20. Software Engineering Institute and United States Office of Naval Research in Cooperation with Ada UK and ACM SIGAda, Association for Computing Machinery, New York, NY, June 26-29, 1989. Appeared in *Ada Letters,* X(4).

Towards Ada 9X
A. Burns, Ed.
IOS Press, 1992

Hard Real-time HOOD: A Design Method for Hard Real-time Ada9X Systems†

A. Burns and A.J. Wellings

Real-time Systems Research Group
Department of Computer Science
University of York, UK

ABSTRACT

This paper presents a structured design method which is tailored towards the construction of real-time systems in general, and hard real-time systems in particular. The method is based on HOOD, which has been modified so that it is possible to express explicitly the characteristics and properties of hard real-time systems. In particular new object types have been introduced which represent periodic, sporadic and resource control objects. The new method, called HRT-HOOD (Hard Real-time HOOD), also distinguishes at the design level the difference between an object which has an active thread of control and an object which is used to synchronise and pass data between active objects.

One of the motivations for choosing HOOD as the base method is that it has a systematic mapping of the detailed designs into Ada. In the paper we therefore also consider how HRT-HOOD can be mapped to Ada9X.

Finally, we illustrate how HRT-HOOD can be used in a modified system life cycle to ensure that the real-time requirements of a system are addressed early on in the design process.

1. Introduction

The most important stage in the development of any real-time system is the generation of a consistent design that satisfies an authoritative specification of requirements. Where real-time systems differ from the traditional data processing systems is that they are constrained by certain non-functional requirements (e.g. dependability and timing). Typically the standard structured design methodologies do not have adequate provision for expressing these types of constraints.

The objective of this paper is to present a structured design method which is tailored towards the construction of real-time systems in general, and hard real-time systems in particular. Rather than developing a new method from scratch, the HOOD method is used as a baseline. HOOD (Hierarchical Object Oriented Design) has been chosen because it has a systematic mapping of the detailed design into Ada. The new method is called HRT-HOOD (Hard Real-time HOOD).

In section 2 of this paper a brief overview of HOOD is presented in order to place the work in context. Section 3 and 4 discuss why and how HOOD has been modified. A detailed description of the main modifications is given. Section 5 then describes how HRT-HOOD can be systematically mapped to Ada9X, and Section 6 considers HRT-

† The work has been supported, in part, by the European Space Agency (ESTEC Contract 9198/90/NL/SF).

HOOD's place in the software life cycle. Finally in section 7 we summarise the current work and present our conclusions.

2. HOOD Overview

HOOD attempts to combine the advantages of object-oriented design and hierarchical decomposition. It therefore supports three basic software engineering principles:[1]

1) Abstraction, information hiding and encapsulation

    An object is defined by the service it provides to its users; the internal details are hidden. The services it provides are described in *OPeration Control Structure* (OPCS) procedures, and its behaviour in an *OBject Control Structure* (OBCS). An OBCS is normally implemented using an Ada task.

2) Hierarchical decomposition

    Parent objects may be decomposed into child objects; HOOD uses the term "include" to represent the parent child relationship.

3) Control structuring

    Operations on objects are activated by control flows (threads). In general there may be several threads operating simultaneously in an object.

2.1. Objects and the operation concept

A HOOD object has *static* and *dynamic* properties. The static properties are defined to be the object's interface, and the internal components of the object which implements the functionality implied by the interface. HOOD defines the dynamic properties of an object by describing the effect on the *calling* object of calling another object's interface. These are:

- *Sequential* flow: where control is transferred directly to the required operation. The flow of control is described within the internals of the operation (the OPCS). After completion, control is returned in the calling object.

- *Parallel* flow: where control is *not* transferred directly to the called object but an *independent* flow is activated in the OBCS of the called object. This activation takes the form of an execution request for the required operation. The reaction of the object to this request will depend on the internal state of the called object. As with sequential flow, the OPCS for each operation defines the logic of the sequential nature of the operation.

HOOD distinguishes between two basic types of an object: PASSIVE and ACTIVE.

- PASSIVE objects have no control over the time at which their operations are executed. That is, whenever an operation on a passive object is invoked, control is immediately transferred to that operation (sequential flow). Each operation contains only sequential code which does not synchronise with any other object. A PASSIVE object therefore has no OBCS.

- ACTIVE objects do have the ability to control access to their operations. They do this by having an independent thread of control (the OBCS) which executes the operations on behalf of the caller (parallel flow). Such operations are called *constrained* operations. ACTIVE objects may also have non-constrained operations, which are executed in the same manner as PASSIVE operations.

    An operation of an ACTIVE object may be constrained either by *functional activation constraints*, or by constraints associated with the *type of request*. HOOD defines a functional activation constraint on an operation to be where "the semantics of an operation depend on the logical conditions set by execution of other operations of the object".

For constraints associated with "request type" HOOD defines several different classes of constrained operations. Each class indicates the effect on the calling object of requesting an execution of the called operation. These are *Highly Synchronised Execution Request* (HSER), *Loosely Synchronised Execution Request* (LSER), and *Asynchronous Execution Request* (ASER). An HSER and LSER operation can have an associated timeout, in which case they are labelled with TOER (*Timed-out Execution Request*). These classes are maintained by HRT-HOOD and will be fully defined in the next section. Note that the TOER operations are separate operations and not attributes of the invocation.

HOOD does define other object types which are derived from the ACTIVE and PASSIVE types. For example a VIRTUAL_NODE type of object is an object used as a unit of distribution; it is a form of ACTIVE object. There is also a CLASS type of object which is used to define generic objects of the ACTIVE, PASSIVE or VIRTUAL_NODE type. The objects are generic in the Ada-sense, that is the parameters to their interfaces are generic.

2.2. The HOOD use relationship (control flow)

A HOOD object is allowed to "use" another object if the former requires one or more of the operations provided by the latter. ACTIVE objects may use operations of any other objects freely, but PASSIVE objects should only use non-constrained operations of other objects.

2.3. The HOOD include relationship (decomposition)

In order to support top-down decompositions HOOD allows a parent object to be decomposed into a set of child objects etc. The "include" relationship specifies this decomposition. A PASSIVE object may include ACTIVE objects as long as this does not violate the passive properties of the parent. An ACTIVE object may include other ACTIVE and PASSIVE objects.

A design starts from a *root* object and progresses until all objects have been fully decomposed into their children. An object which has no children object is called a *terminal* object. The group of terminal objects fully defines the system under consideration. From the group it is possible to determine for all objects the client objects which call each defined operation in every server's interface. HOOD does not support the run-time creation of objects.

2.4. Representation of HOOD Designs

HOOD provides both a graphical and a textual representation of program designs. The textual representation is called the Object Description Skeleton (ODS).

3. The Motivation for Hard Real-time HOOD

As HOOD is a design method supposedly for real-time systems, it is first necessary to justify why this paper proposes non-trivial changes to it. There are two main reasons, which are now discussed.

It is increasingly recognised that the role and importance of non-functional requirements (such as timing and dependability) in the development of complex real-time safety critical applications has hitherto been inadequately appreciated. Specifically, it has been common practice for system developers, and the methods they use (such as HOOD), to concentrate primarily on functionality and to consider non-functional requirements comparatively late in the development process. Experience shows that this approach fails to produce dependable systems. For example, often timing requirements are viewed simply in terms of the performance of the completed system. Failure to meet the required performance often results in ad hoc changes to the system.

Non-functional requirements, and the constraints imposed by the execution environment, need to be taken into account throughout the system development life cycle.[4] During development an early binding of software function to hardware component is required so that the analysis of timing and reliability properties of a still unrefined design can be carried out.[6]

Hard real-time systems exhibit several timing characteristics. In particular they consist of periodic and aperiodic activities which often share resources. In order to analyse these activities for their timing properties it is necessary that:

- periodic, aperiodic(sporadic) and resource control objects be explicitly supported by the design method, and directly visible;
- all activities have deterministics execution times; and
- all resource allocation is carefully controlled so that the worst case time that an activity can be blocked waiting for a resource can be bounded.

Furthermore, it is necessary that deterministic fault tolerance techniques be used in order that the timing characteristics of the failure properties of the system can be analysed. Currently HOOD does not provide adequate support for expressing these non-functional requirements, and therefore HRT-HOOD has been developed.

Although HOOD attempts to be language independent it is heavily biased towards the facilities provided by Ada. Ada's lack of expressive power in its model of concurrency has led to a similar lack of expressive power in HOOD. For example Ada83 uses the task concept for both concurrency and synchronisation; to provide mutually exclusive access to a resource shared between two processes requires the introduction of a third process. HOOD suffers from the same problem. Other implementation languages (sometimes supported by real-time operating systems), distinguish between communication and synchronisation based on shared resources and communication based on "message passing". For example in Ada9X, the former will be supported by a monitor-like language construct called a protected record, the latter by the Ada83 rendezvous. The mapping of terminal ACTIVE objects to Ada appears only to use a task for synchronising the execution of its operations (which could in Ada9X be handled by a protected record).

With HRT-HOOD there is the need to support concurrent threads which do not necessarily have operations to control. It is not clear where or how concurrent threads of execution should be created if only HOOD object types are available. In general, a HOOD terminal passive object maps to an Ada package without tasks, although it is possible to envisage a task contained within the package as long as the task does not violate the passive nature of the object's interface.

HRT-HOOD is therefore based on the premise that:

1) it should be possible to distinguish at the design level the difference between an object which has an active thread of control and an object which is used to synchronise and pass data between active objects; and

2) it should be possible to express explicitly the characteristics and properties of hard real-time systems in the design method.

HRT-HOOD attempts to be independent of any scheduling theory that might be used to guarantee the timing properties of programs. Instead it provides a framework within which the properties of real time applications can be expressed. Similarly it does not prescribe the approach by which fault tolerance is achieved (other than by the provision of exception handlers and the possible replication of objects).

4. HRT-HOOD Overview

HRT-HOOD has the following objects:

- PASSIVE — objects which have no control over the time at which requested invocations of their operations are executed, and do not spontaneously invoke operations in other objects
- ACTIVE — objects which may control the time at which requested invocations of their operations are executed, and may spontaneously invoke operations in other objects
- PROTECTED — objects which may control the time at which requested invocations of their operations are executed, and do not spontaneously invoke operations in other objects; PROTECTED objects should not have arbitrary synchronisation constraints in a hard real-time system, and must be analysable for their blocking times
- CYCLIC — objects which represent periodic activities, they may spontaneously invoke operations in other objects, but the only operations they have are requests which demand immediate attentions (they represent asynchronous transfer of control requests)
- SPORADIC — objects which represent sporadic activities; SPORADIC objects may spontaneously invoke operations in other objects; each sporadic has a single operation which is called to invoke the thread, and one or more operations which are requests which demand immediate attentions (they represent asynchronous transfer of control requests)

A hard real-time program will contain at the terminal level only CYCLIC, SPORADIC, PROTECTED and PASSIVE objects. ACTIVE objects, because they cannot be fully analysed, will only be allowed for background activity.

HRT-HOOD distinguishes between the synchronisation required to execute the operations of an object and any internal independent concurrent activity within the object. The synchronisation agent of an object is called the Object Control Structure (OBCS) (in Ada9X this will normally be a protected record). The concurrent activity within the object is called the object's THREAD. The thread executes independently of the operations, but when it executes operations the order of the executions is controlled by the OBCS.

HRT-HOOD also has the concept of object attributes — which allow the expression of real-time attributes such as deadline, worst-case execution time etc.

In the following sections the details of the HRT object types and their attributes are discussed.

4.1. HRT-HOOD Objects

4.1.1. PASSIVE

PASSIVE objects have no control over the time at which their operations are executed. That is, whenever an operation on a passive object is invoked, control is immediately transferred to that operation. Each operation contains only sequential code which does not synchronise with any other object (i.e. it does not block). A PASSIVE object has no OBCS and no THREAD.

4.1.2. ACTIVE

The operations on an ACTIVE object may be constrained or unconstrained. Unconstrained operations are executed as soon as they are requested, similar to the operations on a PASSIVE object.

Constrained operations are executed under the control of the OBCS. As with HOOD, there are two classes of constraints that can affect the time at which requested operations are executed and their effect on the calling object.

1) *Function activation constraints* impose constraints on the time at which a requested operation can be executed according the object's internal state. An operation is said to be "open" if the object's internal state allows the operation's execution (for example: a buffer object would allow a "put" operation if its internal storage was not full). An operation is said to be "closed" if the object's internal state does not allow the operation's execution (for example: a buffer object may not allow a "put" operation if its internal storage is full; an operation requesting an object to stop operation can only follow a start operation request). An operation which has no functional activation constraints is considered to be "open". However, the OBCS still controls the time at which open operations are invoked.

2) *Type of request* constraints indicate the effect on the caller of requesting an open operation. The following request types are supported:

Asynchronous Execution Request — ASER

> When an ASER operation is called, the caller is not blocked by the request. The request is simply noted and the caller returns. In a process/message-based design method this would be equivalent to asynchronous message passing.

Loosely Synchronous Execution Request — LSER

> When an LSER operation is called, the caller is blocked by the request until the called object is ready to service the request. In a process/message-based design method this would be equivalent to the occam/CSP synchronous style of message passing.

Highly Synchronous Execution Request — HSER

> When an HSER operation is called, the caller is blocked by the request until the called object has serviced the request. In a process/message-based design method this would be equivalent to the Ada extended rendezvous style of message passing (or remote invocation[3]).

Both LSER and HSER may have an associated timeout in which case they are termed TOER LSER (Timed Operation Execution Request LSER) or TOER HSER.

In general a constrained operation may have a functional activation constraint, and will always have a type of request constraint.

4.1.3. PROTECTED

PROTECTED objects are used to control access to resources which are used by hard real-time objects. The intention is that their use should constrain the design so that the run-time blocking for resources can be bounded (for example by using priority inheritance,[7] or some other limited blocking protocol such as the immediate priority ceiling inheritance associated with the Ada9X protected records[5]). Although HRT-HOOD does allow arbitrary synchronisation constraints to be placed on access to PROTECTED objects, in general only simple mutual exclusion constraints can currently be analysed. Application specific arguments must be made to show that blocking times are bounded, or timeouts must be associated with blocking calls.

PROTECTED objects are objects which are able to control access their operations, but (unlike ACTIVE objects) they do not necessarily require independent threads of control. A PROTECTED object does have an OBCS but this is a monitor-like construct: operations are executed under mutually exclusion, and functional activation constraints may be placed on when operations can be invoked. For example, a bounded buffer might be implemented as a PROTECTED object.

A single type of constrained operations is available on PROTECTED objects. It is a:

- *protected synchronous execution request* (PSER).

A constrained operation can only execute if no other constrained operation on the PROTECTED object is executing; it has mutually exclusive access to the object. In general the schedulability analysis will determine how long a thread might be blocked whilst waiting for access to the PROTECTED object. It is not possible for the application designer to place a timeout on the PSER request.

An PSER type of request can have a functional activation constraint which can imposes any required application-level synchronisation. A timeout may be associated with this request, in which case it is a "timeout PSER request" (TOER_PSER).

PROTECTED objects may also have non-constrained operations, which are executed in the same manner as PASSIVE operations.

4.1.4. CYCLIC

CYCLIC objects are used to represent periodic activities. They are active objects in the sense that they have their own independent threads of control. However, these threads (once started) execute irrespective of whether there are any outstanding request for their objects' operations. Furthermore, they do not wait for any of their objects' operations at any time during their execution. Indeed, in many cases CYCLIC objects will not have any operations.

In general CYCLIC objects will communication and synchronise with other hard real-time threads by calling operations in PROTECTED objects. However, it is recognised that some constrained operation may be defined by a CYCLIC object because:

- other objects may need to signal a mode change to the cyclic object — this could be achieved by having CYCLIC objects polling a "mode change notifier" PROTECTED object but this is inefficient if the response time required from the CYCLIC object is short (if mode changes can occur only at well defined instances then "mode change notifier" objects would be appropriate)

- other objects may need to signal error conditions to the cyclic object — this could again be achieved by having CYCLIC objects polling an "error notifier" PROTECTED object but this is again inefficient when the response time required from the CYCLIC object is short

Several types of constrained operations are therefore available on CYCLIC objects (each may have functional activation constraints). All of these, when open, require an immediate response from the CYCLIC's thread. The OBCS of a CYCLIC object interacts with the thread to force an asynchronous transfer of control. Available operations include an:

- *Asynchronous, asynchronous transfer of control request* (ASATC). This is similar to the ASER for active objects except that it demands that the CYCLIC object responds "immediately". The request will result in an asynchronous transfer of control in the CYCLIC object's thread.

A CYCLIC object may start its execution immediately it is created, it may have an offset (that is a time before which the THREAD should be delayed before starting its cyclic execution), or it may synchronise its start via a PROTECTED object.

All CYCLIC objects have a thread, whereas only those with operations have an OBCS.

4.1.5. SPORADIC

SPORADIC objects are active objects in the sense that they have their own independent threads of control. Each SPORADIC object has a single constrained operation which is called to invoke the execution of the thread. The operation is of the type which does not block the caller (ASER), it may be called by an interrupt, in which case the label becomes ASER_BY_IT. The operation which invokes the sporadic has a defined minimum arrival interval, or a maximum arrival rate.

A SPORADIC object may have other constrained operations but these are requests which wish to affect immediately the SPORADIC to indicate a result of a mode change or an error condition. As with CYCLIC objects ASATC operations are possible. A SPORADIC object which receives a asynchronous transfer of control request will immediately abandon it current computation.

All SPORADIC objects have a thread, whereas only those with operations have an OBCS.

4.2. Real-time Object Attributes

HOOD does not explicitly support the expression of many of the constraints necessary to engineer real-time systems. In the object description skeleton language (ODS) there is a field in which the designer can express "implementation and synchronisation" constraints. Rather than use this to express an object's real-time attributes, a separate REAL-TIME ATTRIBUTES field has been added. These attributes are filled in by the designer normally at the *terminal* object level. It is anticipated that many of the values of the attributes will be computed by support tools.

The following attributes represent the type of information a designer might wish to express about an application. Some of them may depend on the scheduling theory being used or the approach to fault tolerance.

- DEADLINE

  Each CYCLIC and SPORADIC object must have a defined deadline for the execution of its thread.

- OPERATION_BUDGET

  Each externally visibly operation of a PASSIVE, PROTECT, CYCLIC and SPORADIC object must have a budget execution time defined.

  An operation of a PASSIVE, CYCLIC and SPORADIC object which overruns its budgeted time may be terminated (if desired by the application designer); in this case each externally visibly operation of an object must have an internal operation which is to be called if the operation's budget execution time is violated.

- OPERATION_WCET

  Each externally visibly operation of an object must have a worst case execution time defined. The worst case execution time for the external operation is the operation's budget time plus the budget time of the internal error handling operation.

- THREAD_BUDGET

  Each CYCLIC and SPORADIC object must have a budget execution time defined for each activation of its thread of execution. An overrun of the budgeted time may result in the activity being undertaken by the thread being terminated. Each CYCLIC and SPORADIC object may therefore have an internal operation which is to be called if its thread's budget execution time is violated.

- THREAD_WCET

Each CYCLIC and SPORADIC object must have a worst case execution time defined for its thread of execution. The worst case execution time for the thread is the thread's budget time plus the budget time of the internal error handling operation.

- PERIOD

Each CYCLIC object must have a defined period of execution.

- OFFSET

Each CYCLIC object may have a defined offset which indicate the time that the THREAD should delay before starting its cyclic operations.

- MINIMUM_ARRIVAL_TIME or MAXIMUM_ARRIVAL_FREQUENCY

Each SPORADIC object must have either a defined minimum arrival time for requests for its execution, or a maximum arrival frequency of request..

- PRECEDENCE CONSTRAINTS

A THREAD may have precedence constraints associated with its execution.

- PRIORITY

Each CYCLIC and SPORADIC object must have a defined priority for its thread. This priority is defined according to the scheduling theory being used (we are currently using deadline monotonic scheduling theory[2]).

- CEILING_PRIORITY

Each PROTECTED, CYCLIC or SPORADIC object must have a defined ceiling priority. This priority is no lower than the maximum priority of all the threads that can call the object's constrained operations.

- EXECUTION_TRANSFORMATION

A CYCLIC or a SPORADIC object may need to be transformed at run-time to incorporate extra delays. This may be required, for example, as a result of period transformation during the schedulability analysis phase of the method.

- IMPORTANCE

Each CYCLIC and SPORADIC object must have a defined importance (criticality) for its thread. This importance represents whether the thread is a hard real-time thread or a soft real-time thread.

This list may be extended - for example some hard real time scheduling theories require minimum/average execution times, utility functions etc. Others may require the replication of objects for fault tolerant purposes.

5. Translation into Ada9X

In this section we consider the systematic translation of HRT-HOOD designs to Ada9X. The structure of the mappings given is based on the structure given for HOOD.[1] In them we assume:

1) Preemptive priority based run-time scheduling is to be used and that priorities have been assigned after some appropriate scheduling analysis.

2) That no replication of objects is required for fault tolerance.

3) That operations and threads which overrun their allocated CPU budgets are to be

terminated and error handlers are to be run. PROTECTED operations are assumed to short and overruns are not detected.

Other mappings are possible.

The Ada programming language was designed to provide support for programming real-time distributed applications within a unified language framework, but it is now commonly accepted that the language has not totally succeeded in achieving all its stated design goals. Ada (as defined by ANSI/MIL-STD 1815A), with an appropriate project support environment, has successfully addressed many of the software engineering issues associated with the production of large real-time software. It has failed, however, to satisfy the requirements of hard real-time applications.[8] There is now strong expectation in the real-time community that Ada9X will provide the extra needed expressive power. Give the current status of the Ada9X project it is not possible to know for certain what the actual syntax and semantics of any new facilities will be. We use the Draft Ada9X Mapping Document dated August 1991[5] which addresses many of the real-time issues. In particular we assume the following:

1) Ada9X will provide a fast mutual exclusion primitive. This will take the form of a protected record. This approach can also be used for asynchronous communication.

2) Ada9X will provide a mechanism for asynchronous transfer of control. This is an extension to the select statement allowing an "in" clause.

3) Ada 9X will provide access to a monotonically increasing clock, and a FINE_DURATION type which has a finer delta than DURATION (as defined by STANDARD.DURATION).

4) Ada9X will provide a mechanism to give an accurate representation of a period task; in particular a delay until statement which takes a MONOTONIC.TIME (or CALENDAR.TIME) parameter will be provided.

We have also assumed that Ada9X will provide a mechanism for monitoring the execution time used by a task. Although it is not clear exactly how this will be achieved. Furthermore it is not clear that Ada9X will provide a mechanism whereby a task can be interrupted if it overruns its allocated execution time. We have assumed a special "budget delay" arm of the above Select-in.

Ada9X has also specified many changes to the type model of Ada83 in an attempt to make it more object oriented. It has also introduced a more flexible separate compilation facility in the form of library hierarchies. Considerations of these changes are beyond the scope of this paper.

5.1. Translation Process

The translation to Ada9X consists of two stages:

— the generation of the Object Description Skeletons incorporating the OPCS, thread and OBCS code; this generation can easily be automated

— the refinement of operations and object control structures from the pseudo code into Ada9X by the designer/programmer.

In general, an object is mapped to a group of packages, and an operation is mapped to a subprogram. The OBCSs are mapped either to an Ada task or to a protected record, and each thread is mapped to a task. The mapping of each object type to Ada9X is summarised below.

Object	Ada9X entity
PASSIVE	one or more packages
ACTIVE	one or more packages with a one or more tasks and
	a protected record (for asynchronous communication)
PROTECTED	one or more packages with a protected record
CYCLIC	one or more packages with a task and
	a protected record (for asynchronous transfer of control)
SPORADIC	one or more packages with a task and
	a protected record

The packages which can potentially be generated by an object <Name> during its translation into Ada9X are:

<Name>	-- the specification of which give the subprogram
	-- interface to the object
<Name_TYPES>	-- specification only, gives the object's interface
	-- type declarations and constants
<Name_INTYPES>	-- specification only, gives the internal types and
	-- object declarations
<Name_RTATT>	-- definition of the real-time attributes for the object

The structure of the package giving an object's real-time attributes is given below. First it is necessary to define some system-wide types (we assume that there is only one mode of operation).

```
with SYSTEM; use SYSTEM;
with MONOTONIC; use MONOTONIC;
package RTA is

   type importance is (hard, soft, background);-- for example

   type operation_attributes is
   record
      budget   : FINE_DURATION;
      wcet     : FINE_DURATION;
   end record;

   type thread_attributes is
   record
      pri      : PRIORITY;
      trans    : FINE_DURATION;
      imp      : importance;
      deadline : DURATION;
      budget   : FINE_DURATION;
      wcet     : FINE_DURATION;
   end record;

   DEFAULT_PRIORITY : constant PRIORITY;
               -- set to some low value

end RTA;
```

```
with RTA; use RTA;
with SYSTEM; use SYSTEM;
package Name_RTATT is

    -- for each operation
    Op_name : operation_attributes;   -- :=  .. ;

    -- for PROTECTED, SPORADIC and CYCLIC objects
    ceiling :  PRIORITY;     -- :=  .. ;

    -- for each CYCLIC and SPORADIC object
    thread : thread_attributes;  -- := ( .. );

    -- for each CYCLIC object
    period : DURATION; -- :=  .. ;
    offset : DURATION; -- :=  .. ;

    -- for each SPORADIC object
    MAT   : DURATION;; -- :=  .. ;
    start : operation_attributes; -- := ...;

end Name_RTATT;
```

In the following subsections we give some example mappings for PROTECTED, CYCLIC and SPORADIC objects. We consider only main packages and not the packages for the visible and internal types. For clarity we also omit the context clauses from the mapping, referring to them simply as:

---
with clause box

Note that it is assumed that once elaborated, all task delay until an initial time. This allows the program to startup before deadline must be met. The variable INITIAL_TIME : MONOTONIC.DURATION is assumed to be initialised and in scope for the remainder of this section.

5.2. Ada9X mapping for a PROTECTED terminal Object <Name>

Let such an object have the following:

Op_name for a non-constrained operation.

PSER   for a mutual exclusion operation.

FPSER   for a mutual exclusion operation with a functional activation constraint.

TOER_FPSER for an operation which may be blocked due to a functional activation constraint, and which has a timeout associated with its acceptance.

The specification of the package defining the provided operations etc is:

```
+--------------------------------------------------------------+
|                                                              |
|                        with clause box                       |
|                                                              |
+--------------------------------------------------------------+
```

package <Name> **is**

    -- for each non-constrained operation
    procedure Op_name(<parameter part>);

    protected OBCS **is**
        pragma CEILING_PRIORITY <Name>_RTATT.ceiling;
        -- for each constrained operation
        procedure PSER(<parameter part>);
        entry FPSER(<parameter part>);
    private record
        -- implementation synchronisation objects only
        -- PROTECTED data is stored in the Name_INTYPES package
    end OBCS;

    procedure PSER(<parameter part>) **renames** OBCS.PSER;
    procedure FPSER(<parameter part>) **renames** OBCS.FPSER;
    procedure TOER_FPSER(<parameter part>;
                Timeout_delay : DURATION;
                Timedout : **out** BOOLEAN);

    -- for each exception
    <Exception_Name> : **exception**;
        -- indication of which operations
        -- can raise the exception

end <Name>;

Note that the protected record is used purely to obtain mutual exclusion. The data to be protected is actually held in a separate compilation (Name_INTYPES); the mapping guarantees that the data will only be accessed from within the protected subprograms. This mapping has been chosen to be consistent with the mapping of other objects. The package body is:

```
┌─────────────────────────────────────────────────────────────────┐
│                                                                   │
│                         with clause box                           │
│                                                                   │
└─────────────────────────────────────────────────────────────────┘
```

```
package body <Name> is

    -- comments giving real-time attributes

    procedure Op_name(<parameter part>) is separate;
    procedure OPCS_FPSER(<parameter part>) is separate;

    -- the following subprograms are not given in the paper
    procedure OPCS_PSER(<parameter part>) is separate;
    procedure OPCS_OVERRUN_OF_BUDGET is separate;
    function OPCS_FPSER_FAC return BOOLEAN is separate;


    protected body OBCS is

        procedure PSER(<parameter part>) is
        begin
            OPCS_PSER(<parameter part>);
        end PSER;

        entry FPSER(<parameter part>) when OPCS_FPSER_FAC is
        begin
            OPCS_FPSER(<parameter part>);
        end FPSER;

    end OBCS;

    procedure TOER_FPSER(<parameter part>;
                         Timeout_delay : DURATION;
                         Timedout : out BOOLEAN) is
    begin
        select
            OBCS.FPSER(<parameter part>);
            Timedout := FALSE;
        or
            delay <Timeout_delay>;
            Timedout := TRUE;
        end select;
    end TOER_FPSER;

end <Name>;
```

The operations are mapped as follows:

```
┌─────────────────────────────────────────────────────────────┐
│                       with clause box                         │
└─────────────────────────────────────────────────────────────┘
```

```
separate (<Name>)
procedure Op_name (<parameter part>) is
begin
    select
        budget_delay(<Name>_RTATT.Op_name.budget);
        OPCS_OVERRUN_OF_BUDGET;
    in
        <OPCS_CODE>;
    end select;
exception
    -- for each exception handled
    -- in the OPCS
    when <Object_Name>.<Exception_Name> =>
        <Exception_Code>;
end Op_name;
```

```
┌─────────────────────────────────────────────────────────────┐
│                       with clause box                         │
└─────────────────────────────────────────────────────────────┘
```

```
separate (<Name>)
procedure OPCS_FPSER (<parameter part>) is
begin
    <OPCS_CODE>;
exception
    -- for each exception handled
    -- in the OPCS
    when <Object_Name>.<Exception_Name> =>
        <Exception_Code>;
end OPCS_FPSER;
```

5.3. Ada9X mapping for a CYCLIC terminal Object <Name>

Let such an object have the following:

Op_name   for non-constrained operation.

ASATC   for a asynchronous operation resulting in a asynchronous transfer of control.

The package specification is:

```
┌─────────────────────────────────────────────────────────────┐
│                                                               │
│                        with clause box                        │
│                                                               │
└─────────────────────────────────────────────────────────────┘
```

```
package <Name> is

    -- comments on real-time attributes

    -- for each non-constrained operation
    procedure Op_name(<parameter part>);

    -- for each constrained operation one entry
    protected OBCS is
        pragma CEILING_PRIORITY <Name>_RTATT.ceiling;
        procedure ASATC(<parameter part>);
        entry GET_ASATC(<parameter part>);
    private record
        ASATC_OPEN : BOOLEAN := FALSE;
    end OBCS;

    procedure ASATC(<parameter part>) renames OBCS.ASATC;

    -- for each exception
    <Exception_Name> : exception;
        -- indication of which operations
        -- can raise the exception
end <Name>;
```

The package body is:

```
┌─────────────────────────────────────────────────────────────┐
│                                                               │
│                        with clause box                        │
│                                                               │
└─────────────────────────────────────────────────────────────┘
```

```
package body <Name> is

    procedure OPCS_PERIODIC_CODE is separate;
    procedure OPCS_ASATC(<parameter part>) is separate;


    procedure OPCS_BUDGET_OVERRUN is separate;
    procedure Op_name(<parameter part>) is separate;
    procedure OPCS_INITIALISE(<parameter part>) is separate;
    -- Functional activation constraints
    function OPCS_ASATC_FAC return BOOLEAN is separate;

    task THREAD is
        pragma PRIORITY <Name>_RTATT.thread.pri;
    end THREAD;
```

```
protected body OBCS is

    procedure ASATC(<parameter part>) is
    begin
        -- one only, overwrites
        -- copy params
        ASATC_OPEN := TRUE;
    end ASATC;

    entry GET_ASATC(<parameter part>) when ASATC_OPEN is
    begin
        -- copy params
    end GET_ASATC;

end OBCS;


task body THREAD is
    T: TIME;
begin
    -- any initialisation code
    OPCS_INITIALISE;

    -- if the THREAD has an offset
    delay until INITIAL_TIME + <Name>_RTATT.offset;

    T:= clock;
    loop
        select
            when OPCS_ASATC_FAC =>
                OBCS.GET_ASATC(<parameter part>);
                OPCS_ASATC(<parameter part>);
        in
                OPCS_PERIODIC_CODE;
        end select;
        T := T + <Name>_RTATT.period;
        delay until T;
    end loop;

end THREAD;

end <Name>;
```

```
┌────────────────────────────────────────────────────────────────┐
│                         with clause box                         │
└────────────────────────────────────────────────────────────────┘

separate (<Name>)
procedure OPCS_PERIODIC_CODE(<parameter part>) is
begin
    select
        budget_delay (<Name>_RTATT.thread.budget);
        OPCS_OVERRUN_OF_BUDGET;
    in
        <OPCS_CODE>;
    end select;
exception
    -- for each exception handled
    -- in the OPCS
    when <Object_Name>.<Exception_Name> =>
        <Exception_Code>;
end OPCS_PERIODIC_CODE;


┌────────────────────────────────────────────────────────────────┐
│                         with clause box                         │
└────────────────────────────────────────────────────────────────┘

separate (<Name>)
procedure OPCS_ASATC(<parameter part>) is
begin
    select
        budget delay (<Name>_RTATT.ASATC.budget);
        OPCS_OVERRUN_OF_BUDGET;
    in
        <OPCS_CODE>;
    end select;
exception
    -- for each exception handled
    -- in the OPCS
    when <Object_Name>.<Exception_Name> =>
        <Exception_Code>;
end OPCS_ASATC;
```

5.4. Ada9X mapping for a SPORADIC terminal Object <Name>

Let such an object have the following:

Op_name   for non-constrained operation.

START   for an asynchronous operation which invokes the sporadic thread.

ASATC   for a asynchronous operation resulting in a asynchronous transfer of control.

The specification of the objects' provided operations is given by the following package specification:

```
+---------------------------------------------------------------+
|                                                               |
|                      with clause box                          |
|                                                               |
+---------------------------------------------------------------+
```

```
package <Name> is

    -- for each non-constrained operation
    procedure Op_name(<parameter part>);

    -- for each constrained operation
    -- one protected record entry

    protected OBCS is
        pragma CEILING_PRIORITY <Name>_RTATT.ceiling;
        -- for the ATC operations
        procedure ASATC(<parameter part>);
        entry GET_ASATC(<parameter part>);

        -- for the START operation
        procedure START(<parameter part>);
        -- interrupt address clause if RWNB_BY_INTERRUPT
    private
        entry WAIT_START(<parameter part>);
    record
        ASATC_OPEN : BOOLEAN := FALSE;
        START_OPEN : BOOLEAN := FALSE;
        FREQ_OVERRUN : BOOLEAN := FALSE;
        T : MONOTONIC.time;
        LAST_T : MONOTONIC.time := 0.0;
    end OBCS;

    procedure ASATC(<parameter part>) renames OBCS.ASATC;

    procedure START(<parameter part>) renames OBCS.START;

    -- for each exception
    <Exception_Name> : exception;
        -- indication of which operations
        -- can raise the exception
end <Name>;
```

The body is:

```
                         with clause box
```

```
package body <Name> is

   procedure OPCS_START(<parameter part>) is separate;

   -- the following subprograms are not given in the paper
   procedure OPCS_SPORADIC_FREQUENCY_OVERRUN
               (<parameter part>) is separate;
   procedure OPCS_OVERRUN_OF_BUDGET is separate;
   procedure OPCS_ASATC(<parameter part>) is separate;
   procedure Op_name(<parameter part>) is separate;
   -- Functional activation constraints
   function OPCS_ASATC_FAC return BOOLEAN is separate;

   task THREAD is
      pragma PRIORITY <Name>_RTATT.thread.pri;
   end THREAD;

   protected body OBCS is

      procedure ASATC(<parameter part>) is
      begin
         -- one only, overwrites
         -- copy params
         ASATC_OPEN := TRUE;
      end ASATC;

      entry GET_ASATC(<parameter part>) when ASATC_OPEN is
      begin
         -- copy params
      end GET_ASATC;

      procedure START(<parameter part>) do
      begin
         -- save params
         T := MONOTONIC.clock; -- log time of invocation request
         if T - LAST_T  < Name_RTATT.MAT then
            FREQ_OVERRUN := TRUE;
         end if;
         LAST_T := T;
         START_OPEN := TRUE;
      end START;
```

```
        entry WAIT_START(<parameter part>) when START_OPEN is
        begin
            -- param part now includes overrun indication
            -- write params
            OVERRUN := FALSE;
            START_OPEN := FALSE;
        end WAIT_START;


    end OBCS;


    task body THREAD is
        -- any parameter declaration including
        -- FREQ_OVERRUN and T
        NEXT_WAKEUP : MONOTONIC.TIME := 0;
    begin
        -- any initialisation code
        delay until INITIAL_TIME;
        loop
            select
                when OPCS_ASATC_FAC =>
                    OBCS.GET_ASATC(<parameter part>);
                    OPCS_ASATC(<parameter part>);
            in
                    OBCS.WAIT_START(<parameter part>);
                    -- parameters include T and FREQ_OVERRUN
                    if FREQ_OVERRUN then
                        NEXT_WAKEUP := NEXT_WAKEUP + <Name>_RTATT.MAT;
                        OPCS_SPORADIC_FREQUENCY_OVERRUN
                                    (<parameter part>);
                    else
                        NEXT_WAKEUP := <Name>_RTATT.MAT + T;
                        OPCS_START(<parameter part>);
                    end if;
                end select;
                delay until NEXT_WAKEUP;
        end loop;
    end THREAD;
end <Name>;
```

Note, with this mapping an invocation of the sporadic may be missed if an asynchronous
transfer of control request occurs after returning from OBCS.WAIT_START and before
the threads response.

```
┌─────────────────────────────────────────────────────────┐
│                      with clause box                       │
└─────────────────────────────────────────────────────────┘
```

```
separate(<Name>)
procedure OPCS_START(<parameter part>) is
begin
    select
        budget_delay (<Name>_RTATT.thread.budget);
        OPCS_OVERRUN_OF_BUDGET;
    in
        <OPCS_CODE>;
    end select;
exception
    -- for each exception handled
    -- in the OPCS
    when <Object_Name>.<Exception_Name> =>
        <Exception_Code>;
end OPCS_START;
```

If SPORADIC objects are defined in terms of a maximum arrival frequency, then it will be necessary to buffer the START operations in the OBCS.

6. HRT-HOOD in the Software Life Cycle

HOOD assumes a fairly traditional software development life cycle model in which the following phases are recognised:

- Requirements Definition — during which an authoritative specification of the system's required functional and non-functional behaviour is produced.
- Architectural Design — during which a top-level description of the proposed system is developed.
- Detailed Design — during which the complete system design is specified.
- Coding — during which the system is implemented.
- Testing — during which the efficacy of the system is tested.

For hard real-time systems this has the significant disadvantage that timing problems will only be recognised during testing, or worse after deployment.

In HRT-HOOD the Architecture Phase is split into two phases:[4]

- logical architecture;
- physical architecture design phase.

The logical architecture embodies design commitments which can be made independently of the constraints imposed by the execution environment, and is primarily aimed at satisfying the functional requirements. The physical architecture takes these and other constraints into account, and embraces the non-functional requirements.

The physical architecture forms the basis for asserting that the application's non-functional requirements will be met once the detailed design and implementation have taken place. It should be possible, for example, to prove that if all objects are built to their worst case timing and reliability constraints then the system itself will meet its safety requirements. In general, the physical architecture allows arguments to be developed that assess compliance with all the application's requirements.

Logical Architecture Design in HRT-HOOD

There are two aspects of HRT-HOOD which facilitate the logical architecture design of hard real-time systems. Firstly, unlike many structured design methodologies, HRT-HOOD explicitly supports the abstractions that are typically required by hard real-time system designers. Secondly, HRT-HOOD constrains the logical architecture so that it can be analysed during the Physical Architectural Design phase.

Physical Architecture Design

HRT-HOOD supports the design of a physical architecture by:

1) allowing timing attributes to be associated with objects,

2) providing a framework from within which a schedulability analysis of the terminal objects can be undertaken, and

3) providing the abstractions with which the designer can express the handling of timing errors.

Currently HRT-HOOD focuses on timing requirements and the necessary schedulability analysis that will ensure (guarantee) that the system once built will function correctly in both the value and time domains. To undertake this analysis it will be necessary to estimate the execution time of the proposed code, and to have available the time dependent behaviour of the target processor and other aspects of the execution environment.

Code Timing Estimations and Measurements

Once the Architectural Design Phases are complete, the detailed design can begin in

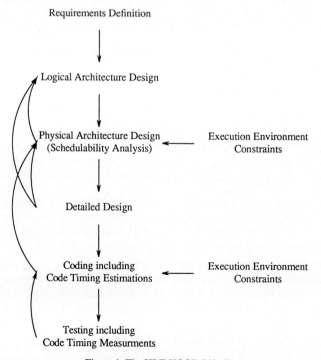

Figure 1: The HRT-HOOD Life Cycle

earnest and the code for the application produced. When this has been achieved, the execution profile of the code must again be estimated (using a worst case execution time analyser tool) to ensure that the estimated worst case execution times are indeed accurate. If they are not (which will usually be the case for a new application), then either the detailed design must be revisited (if their are small deviations), or the designer must return to the Architectural Design Phases (if serious problems exist). If the estimation indicate that all is well, then testing of the application proceeds. This should involve measuring the actual timing of code. The modified life cycle is presented in Figure 1.

Detailed Design and Coding in HRT-HOOD follows the process defined in HOOD.

7. Conclusions

In this paper we have illustrated how the structured design method of HOOD can be successfully modified to make it more appropriate for hard real-time system design. We have also shown how the proposed changes to Ada9X can be used in the systematic mapping of any HRT-HOOD design into Ada.

Acknowledgement

The authors would like to thank Eric Fyfe and Chris Bailey of British Aerospace, Space Systems, and Paco Gomez Molinero and Fernando Gonzalez-Barcia of the European Space Agency (ESTEC) for their comments on the material presented in this paper.

References

1. European Space Agency, "HOOD Reference Manual Issue 3.0", WME/89-173/JB (September 1989).
2. N.C. Audsley, A. Burns, M.F. Richardson and A.J. Wellings, "Hard Real-Time Scheduling: The Deadline Monotonic Approach", *Proceedings 8th IEEE Workshop on Real-Time Operating Systems and Software*, Atlanta, GA, USA (15-17 May 1991).
3. A. Burns and A.J. Wellings, *Real-time Systems and their Programming Languages*, Addison Wesley (1990).
4. A. Burns and A. M. Lister, "A Framework for Building Dependable Systems", *Computer Journal* **34**(2), pp. 173-181 (1991).
5. Intermetrics, "Draft Ada 9X Mapping Document, Volume II, Mapping Specification", Ada 9X Project Report (August 1991).
6. H. Kopetz, "Design Principles for Fault Tolerant Real Time Systems", MARS Report, Institut für Technische Informatik, 8/85/2 (1985).
7. L. Sha, R. Rajkumar and J. P. Lehoczky, "Priority Inheritance Protocols: An Approach to Real-Time Synchronisation", *IEEE Transactions on Computers* **39**(9), pp. 1175-1185 (September 1990).
8. A.J. Wellings, "Real-time Requirements Session Summary", *Proceedings of the 4th International Workshop on Real Time Ada Issues, Ada Letters* **10**(9) (1990).

Towards Ada 9X
A. Burns, Ed.
IOS Press, 1992

Formal Specification of Reusable Ada Software Packages

Timothy J. Read

Hi-Q Systems Limited
Hi-Q House
Ancells Court
Fleet
Hants
GU13 8UZ

Tel. 0252 815035
Fax. 0252 815022

Abstract

Formal notations for specifying computer systems, such as Z [1], promise to improve software quality and to reduce development costs. These benefits are due to the clear, unambiguous description of the system that is generated and the better understanding of the requirements this gives. To date, users of formal specifications have concentrated on producing specifications of entire systems. This of course benefits the system that is specified, however it can be difficult to re-use parts of the system in future developments. This is because the structure of Z specifications can be very different to the structure of Ada programs, making it hard to identify the parts of the specification that describe a particular package. This paper describes a new approach to using Z which yields a specification with a one-to-one correspondence to the Ada packages that implement it. This enables an individual package to be extracted together with its formal specification for re-use in future systems. This paper is based on research undertaken by the author whilst with Siemens Plessey Defence Systems.

1. Introduction

Formal specifications, written using mathematical notations such as Z, offer many benefits to software developers. The behaviour of a system can be defined precisely at an early stage in development. This can highlight potential problems and misunderstandings, enabling corrections to be made before the expense of coding and testing. Furthermore, a formal specification can be mathematically analysed to prove properties of the behaviour of the specified system, such as the upholdance of safety or security policies.

The Z specification language has been used to good effect on real projects to describe entire computer systems (notably on the IBM CICS development [2]). However, it can be difficult to re-use parts of those systems in future developments. The conventional approach to writing a Z specification gives a good description of the behaviour of the whole system but does not aim to define the behaviour of individual parts of the software. This is because the notations provided by Z for structuring specifications are fundamentally different to the facilities provided by Ada for structuring programs. The main unit of specification in Z is the schema. This consists of a signature, which introduces typed variables and a predicate which defines the relation between the variables. Schemas are used to describe operations, using the predicate to define the properties of the operation. At the bottom level, a schema corresponds well with an Ada procedure. The variables declared in the signature are implemented by the parameters and local variables of the procedure. The procedure body implements the behaviour specified by the predicate. The following example illustrates this (techniques for developing programs from unit specifications are covered in depth elsewhere (for instance [3]) and are not considered further in this paper).

$$
\begin{array}{|l}
\hline
\text{LARGEST} \\
\hline
X?, Y?, R! : \mathbb{Z} \\
\hline
X? \geqslant Y? \Rightarrow R! = X? \\
X? \leqslant Y? \Rightarrow R! = Y? \\
\hline
\end{array}
$$

```
procedure LARGEST(X, Y : in INTEGER; R : out INTEGER) is
begin
   if X > Y then
      R := X;
   else
      R := Y;
   end if;
end;
```

At this level, the schema and the procedure correspond well, however the mechanisms for combining low-level units are significantly different. The Z notation uses the schema calculus to construct specifications of larger units from smaller components. The calculus operators conjunction ($\wedge$, logical and) and disjunction ($\vee$, logical or) are often used. Both construct a new schema with a signature containing every variable declared in the signatures of the constituent schemas (if a variable is declared in both constituents, the declarations must be type-compatible) and a predicate formed by combining the predicate parts with the appropriate logical connector. The main features of Z are described in the glossary in appendix A .

The schema calculus provides a powerful facility for developing specifications of large systems using the specifications of components however it is very different to the mechanisms used by Ada to combine procedures. In Ada, the procedure call mechanism is used to incorporate a subprogram into a larger unit. At the point of call, formal parameters are replaced by the corresponding actual parameters and local declarations elaborated, creating a new scope which exists for the duration of the call. Several procedures may be combined using sequential composition. The user of the procedures need not be concerned with avoiding clashes between the names of their parameters and local variables since the scope rules of the language resolve these automatically. In contrast, the Z schema calculus combines scope and has no concept of formal and actual parameters (in this respect, schema calculus is analogous to textual inclusion). It is therefore difficult to develop specifications of subsystems in isolation and then combine then at a later stage.

Ada provides several other structuring mechanisms which have no direct counterpart in Z. The package allows data and procedures to be grouped together. Using a package, the visibility of data can be further controlled, limiting access to the procedures defined in it. Private types can be defined, which restrict manipulation of variables of the type to the operations defined in the package. More fundamental is the provision of the task, for implementing concurrent programs. Z has no notation designed for describing the interaction of concurrent processes.

Clearly, there are significant incompatabilities between the Z notation and Ada. Any attempt to develop an Ada program with the same structure as a Z specification is not likely to lead to a well-structured Ada program. This poses two problems. First, to implement the specification the implementor must identify a suitable program structure and determine how the specification maps on to it. Second, it is difficult to develop a library of re-usable Ada packages, each with its own specification.

To overcome these problems, the correspondence between the formal specification and the Ada program must be improved. This means that the formal specification must have the same structure as an Ada program. Ways to use formal notations to describe individual packages are needed. In this paper an alternative approach to producing Z specifications is suggested to do this. It was decided that any approach should not require extensions to the Z notation, so that specifications may be produced and analysed with existing tool support and remain universally understood. Combinations of Z facilities and restrictions on the use of Z are employed to obtain the desired effect.

For an approach to specification to be suitable for describing an Ada package, it must meet the following criteria :

1. it provides a good description of the behaviour of the package;
2. it can be easily incorporated into the specification of program units that use the package;
3. it is simple to check that specifications meet any restrictions on the use of Z that need to be imposed.

The remainder of the paper begins by considering different ways in which Ada package facilities can be used. Four classes of Ada package are identified which require different treatment. Each of these is considered and an approach to specification proposed that meets the above criteria. Finally, some experiences of applying these techniques and their place in the development lifecycle is discussed.

2. Classes of Ada Package

An Ada package can declare new data types, local variables, procedures, functions and tesks (concurrent programs are beyond the scope of this paper and are not considered further). These may be visible to the package user (because they are declared in the package specification) or hidden (because they are declared in the package body). Packages may restrict visibility of the representation of a new type by declaring private types and may be parameterised by generic types, values and subprograms.

Using combinations of these facilities, different kinds of packages can be produced which require different treatment for specification. Four classes are considered here.

1. *Service Package* - A service package defines one or more types and operations on those types (for example, a package to process complex numbers).
2. *Restricted Service Package* - A restricted service package limits the use of its types to the operations defined in the package (by declaring private types).
3. *Generic Service Package* - A generic service package is parameterised by types and/or constants to provide the same service for different objects (for example, a generic stack).
4. *State-based Package* - A state-based package declares variables either in the package specification or package body.

Each of these classes of package is considered in turn and an approach to specification suggested.

3. Services Packages

A service package introduces data types and provides operations to manipulate variables of those types, such as a package to process complex numbers (from [4]).

```
package COMPLEX_NUMBERS is

   type COMPLEX is record
      RL, IM : REAL;
   end record;

   function ADD(X, Y : COMPLEX) return COMPLEX;

   . . .

end COMPLEX_NUMBERS;
```

A service package does not declare any variables, so there is no need for the specifier to model the state of the package. Each operation is specified by defining the relation between the input and output variables. Using the conventional Z style, operations are specified as schemas.

```
 ┌ COMPLEX ────┐
 │ RL, IM : REAL │
 └──────────────┘
```

```
 ┌ ADD_COMPLEX ─────────┐
 │ X?, Y? : COMPLEX       │
 │ R! : COMPLEX           │
 ├───────────────────────┤
 │ R!.RL = X?.RL + Y?.RL  │
 │ R!.IM = X?.IM + Y?.IM  │
 └───────────────────────┘
```

The schema COMPLEX defines a data type with two named components (this is analogous to an Ada record). The ADD operation takes two input complex numbers X? and Y? (by convention inputs are decorated with a ? and outputs with a ! in Z) and returns a complex number R!. The predicate part of the schema defines the properties of the operation showing that the parts of the result are calculated by summing the appropriate parts of the two inputs. This approach provides a good description of the operation however it can be difficult to use it in subsequent specifications. The Z schema cannot be used in a procedural or functional style, so it is not possible to write predicates like A = ADD_COMPLEX(P,Q) or ADD_COMPLEX(P, Q, A). The desired effect can be achieved using the Z schema calculus however the resulting specification is long-winded and difficult to comprehend. If however, the add operation is specified as a mathematical function, use becomes much easier.

```
 │ ADD : (COMPLEX × COMPLEX) → COMPLEX
 ├────────────────────────────────────
 │ ∀ X, Y : COMPLEX •
 │   (ADD(X, Y)).RL = X.RL + Y.RL ∧ (ADD(X, Y)).IM = X.IM + Y.IM
```

The specification above defines a function that takes a pair of complex numbers (the inputs) and returns a complex number (the result). Again, the lower half of the specification formally defines the properties of the function. Function application can be used to apply this operation with much simpler notation. It is now possible to write A = ADD(P,Q) or more complicated equations such as A = ADD(P,ADD(Q, R)) (Z also allows the definition of infix functions if preferred). However, the actual specification of the operation has suffered and is not as easily comprehensible as the original. The solution proposed is to combine the two notations, using a schema to describe the operation and defining a functional interface to it. This is easy to do in Z using set comprehension terms. The following definition specifies a functional interface to the ADD_COMPLEX schema operation.

$$\begin{array}{|l}
\hline
\text{ADD} : (\text{COMPLEX} \times \text{COMPLEX}) \longrightarrow \text{COMPLEX} \\
\hline
\text{ADD} = \{\, \text{ADD\_COMPLEX} \bullet (X?, Y?) \mapsto R! \,\} \\
\end{array}$$

This approach can be generalised to operations that are more naturally expressed as procedures, using an abbreviation for set membership provided by Z. The membership test $x \in P$ can be written $P(x)$. By defining a set containing every combination of values that meet the specification of an operation, a procedure-like notation for applying that operation can be used. Again, set comprehension terms can be used to define such a set in terms of a schema definition of the operation, as the following example shows.

$$\begin{array}{|l}
\hline
\text{ADD\_PROCEDURE} \_ : \mathbb{P}\,(\text{COMPLEX} \times \text{COMPLEX} \times \text{COMPLEX}) \\
\hline
(\text{ADD\_PROCEDURE} \_) = \{\, \text{ADD\_COMPLEX} \bullet (X?, Y?, R!) \,\} \\
\end{array}$$

These techniques can be used to specify a complete service package. Appendix B contains a specification of the directed graph package described by Booch in [5].

4. Restricted Service Packages

A restricted service package is a variation of the service package in which the use of the new types is restricted to the operations provided in the package. Z has no facility for hiding the representation of a type so there is no easy solution for specifying private types. One approach is to ignore the fact that the type is private when specifying the package and to rely on specifications that use the package to respect this. This however is difficult to check, as there are many ways in which a specification can depend on the representation of a type.

Although Z cannot hide the representation of an existing type, it does provide a facility to define a new type without any representation: a given set. A given set is suitable for specifying a private type outside the package however it is not suitable for defining the behaviour of the package where a type with representation is needed.

The approach proposed introduces one type for defining the interface and a separate type for defining the behaviour. When defining the behaviour of the package, a type with the appropriate representation is used and the package specified as before. When the interface to the package is defined, a given set is introduced representing the visible private type. In order to define the Z interface functions and sets in terms of the behaviour specifications, the correspondence between the given set and the representation type must be defined. The details of this mapping are not important however it must guarantee that there is a one-to-one correspondence between the two types : for every element in the given set there is exactly one corresponding value in the representation type and vice versa. This is achieved in Z by defining a bijection between the two types.

The following example shows how the complex number example can be re-specified to define a private complex number type. First the interface is defined in terms of the given set PRIVATE_COMPLEX.

[PRIVATE_COMPLEX]

> ADD_PRIVATE :
>   (PRIVATE_COMPLEX × PRIVATE_COMPLEX) →
>   PRIVATE_COMPLEX

The behaviour is defined as before (the definitions of COMPLEX and ADD_COMPLEX given earlier are assumed). Finally, to complete the interface definition, the mapping bijection is declared and this is used to define the value of the function ADD_PRIVATE.

> map : COMPLEX ⤖ PRIVATE_COMPLEX

ADD_PRIVATE = { ADD_COMPLEX • (map X?, map Y?) ↦ map R! }

Using this approach to define private types, it is much easier to ensure that a specification using the type does not violate the restrictions on the use of private types. It is sufficient to ensure that the specification does not refer to the mapping function to convert the private type into its representation type. The use of a bijection ensures that the interface operations behave as expected. For instance, it is possible to prove properties such as the following.

⊢ ∀ X, Y, Z : COMPLEX • ADD(X, ADD(Y, Z)) = ADD(ADD(X, Y), Z)

If a limited private type is required, then further trust must be placed in the user of the specification not to define operations which depend on equality or assignment to implement them.

5. Generic Service Packages

A generic service package is parameterised by data types, constants and operations. Users of the package must instantiate these parameters to specific types/values to provide the required variation of the service. Z provides a generic type mechanism which can be used to parameterise individual operations. It is not possible to parameterise a group of operations as it is with Ada so each Z operation must be individually instantiated (the user of the package must ensure that each operation is instantiated with the same type(s)). The same generic parameters should be applied to both the interface and the behaviour specifications. The example below specifies a generic stack. First the generic stack data type is defined and the interface for a push operation.

$\underline{\quad}$ STACK [ITEM] $\underline{\quad\quad\quad\quad\quad}$
CONTENTS : 1 .. 100 $\rightarrow$ ITEM
TOP : 0 .. 100

$\underline{\quad}$ [ITEM] $\underline{\quad\quad\quad\quad\quad\quad}$
PUSH _ : $\mathbb{P}$ (STACK$_{[ITEM]}$ × ITEM × STACK$_{[ITEM]}$)

Next, the behaviour of the push operation is specified and the interface set defined in terms of this.

$\underline{\quad}$ PUSH_BODY [ITEM] $\underline{\quad\quad\quad\quad}$
st?, st! : STACK$_{[ITEM]}$
i? : ITEM
$\underline{\quad\quad\quad\quad}$
st?.TOP < 100
st!.TOP = st?.TOP + 1
st!.CONTENTS = st?.CONTENTS $\oplus$ {st!.TOP $\mapsto$ i?}

$\underline{\quad}$ [ITEM] $\underline{\quad\quad\quad\quad\quad\quad}$
(PUSH _)$_{[ITEM]}$ = {PUSH_BODY$_{[ITEM]}$ • (st?, i?, st!)}

To instantiate the package, the type and operations must be individually instantiated.

[MY_ITEM]

MY_ITEM_STACK $\hat{=}$ STACK$_{[MY\_ITEM]}$

MY_ITEM_PUSH == (PUSH _)$_{[MY\_ITEM]}$

Z has no similar facility for defining generic constants, however they are easily simulated. An additional variable representing the constant is added to each type and operation. When the types and operations are instantiated, this variable is constrained to the particular value of the constant. For instance, a generic matrix package might be parameterised according to the size of the matrix.

```
┌─ MATRIX ──────────────────┐
│  X, Y : ℕ
│  DATA : (ℕ × ℕ) ⇸ ℕ
├──────────
│  dom DATA = (1 .. X × 1 .. Y)
└──────────────────────────┘
```

When the package is instantiated, the particular values of the generic constants are constrained.

MY_MATRIX ≙
    [MATRIX |
        X = 2
    ∧
        Y = 4]

Generic subprograms are not considered further in this paper.

6. State-Based Packages

A state-based package declares local variables, either in the package specification or the package body. For the specifier, the most significant difference between state-based packages and service packages is that the state must be modeled. In the conventional Z style, the state is defined as a schema. Operations are defined in terms of the relation between initial and final states, inputs and outputs using the schema notation. The following example illustrates a state-based stack package specified in the conventional style.

[ITEM]

```
┌─ STACK_STATE ──────────────┐
│  CONTENTS : 1 .. 100 → ITEM
│  TOP : 1 .. 100
│
└────────────────────────────┘
```

```
┌─ PUSH_BODY ──────────────────────┐
│  ΔSTACK_STATE
│  I? : ITEM
├──────────────
│  TOP < 100
│  TOP' = TOP + 1
│  CONTENTS' = CONTENTS ⊕ {TOP' ↦ I?}
└──────────────────────────────────┘
```

This provides a good description of the behaviour of operations but again it can be difficult to use in subsequent specifications, particularly when sequential composition of operations or iteration is needed.

A simple extension to the approach used for specifying service packages improves use to a certain extent. The initial and final state are treated as an input to and output from the operation respectively as illustrated below (note that the Z schema operator θ is used to refer to the entire state in the set comprehension term).

PUSH _ : ℙ (STACK_STATE × ITEM × STACK_STATE)

(PUSH _) = {PUSH_BODY • (θ STACK_STATE, I?, θ STACK_STATE)}

This approach provides the required parameter passing mechanism, however it remains difficult to sequentially compose operations because additional variables must be introduced to denote the state between operations as is illustrated below.

```
┌─ PUSH_A_PAIR ──────────────────────────┐
│ ΔSTACK_STATE
│ X?, Y? : ITEM
│ ───────────────────────────────────────
│ ∃ MID : STACK_STATE •
│     PUSH (θ STACK_STATE, X?, MID) ∧
│     PUSH (MID, Y?, θ STACK_STATE')
└─────────────────────────────────────────┘
```

To overcome the need for explicit variables denoting intermediate states, operations must be defined in a different way. It must be possible to separate the state components so that a Z operation can be applied to unify the final state of one operation with the initial state of the next. For instance, if operations are represented by state transition functions, relation composition can be employed to combine operations.

OP1, OP2 : ST ⇸ ST

---

st' = (OP1 ⨾ OP2) st

In fact, a relation between states is required, as operations may be non-deterministic (for given parameters and initial state, more than one final state may be reached). The state transition for an operation depends upon the values of the operations parameters. This is modeled by treating an operation as a function from parameter values to the corresponding state transition relation (a similar approach is used by Whysall in [6]).

OP [PARAMS, STATE] == PARAMS ⇸ STATE ↔ STATE

To apply these operations conveniently, two Z operations similar to function application are defined. Because the state transition is described by a relation rather than a function, a non-deterministic choice is required when there is more than one possible final state for a given initial state. This is specified by stating that the final state is a member of the set of possible final states for the given initial state. Thus the operation application functions must return a set of values for the final state. Two Z operations are defined. The : operator takes an individual input state and a transition relation and returns the set of possible result state values. The ; operation does the same for a set of input states.

$$[X]$$

$$(\_ : \_) 2 : (X \times X \leftrightarrow X) \nrightarrow \mathbb{P}\, X$$

$$\forall x : X;\ f : X \leftrightarrow X \mid x \in \mathrm{dom}\, f \bullet x : f = \mathrm{ran}\, (\{x\} \lhd f)$$
$$\mathrm{dom}\, (\_ : \_) = \{x : X;\ f : X \leftrightarrow X \mid x \in \mathrm{dom}\, f\}$$

$$[X]$$

$$(\_ ; \_) 2 : (\mathbb{P}\, X \times X \leftrightarrow X) \nrightarrow \mathbb{P}\, X$$

$$\forall x : \mathbb{P}\, X;\ f : X \leftrightarrow X \mid x \subseteq \mathrm{dom}\, f \bullet x ; f = \mathrm{ran}\, (x \lhd f)$$
$$\mathrm{dom}\, (\_ ; \_) = \{x : \mathbb{P}\, X;\ f : X \leftrightarrow X \mid x \subseteq \mathrm{dom}\, f\}$$

Because the membership operation is not the most natural way to write the constraint specifying that the result state is in the set of states, a further Z operator is defined.

$$[X]$$

$$\_ \to \_ : \mathbb{P}\, X \leftrightarrow X$$

$$\forall s : \mathbb{P}\, X;\ x : X \bullet s \to x \Leftrightarrow x \in s$$

Using this approach, the push operation can be redefined in a form that is much easier to apply. A further function, make_operation, is required to convert the relation defined by the set comprehension term into a function.

$$[X, Y]$$

$$\mathrm{make\_operation} : (X \leftrightarrow Y) \to X \nrightarrow \mathbb{P}\, Y$$

$$\forall R : X \leftrightarrow Y \bullet$$
$$\mathrm{make\_operation}\, R =$$
$$\{x : X \mid x \in \mathrm{dom}\, R \bullet x \mapsto \{y : Y \mid (x, y) \in R\}\}$$

PUSH : OP[ITEM, STACK_STATE]

PUSH =
make_operation
{ PUSH_BODY • I? ↦ (θ STACK_STATE ↦ θ STACK_STATE')}

The example below shows how these definitions can be used to specify the PUSH_A_PAIR operation.

PUSH_A_PAIR
ΔSTACK_STATE
X?, Y? : ITEM

θ STACK_STATE : PUSH X? ; PUSH Y? -> θ STACK_STATE'

This approach is easily extended to cope with packages with variables declared in the package body. These can be treated using the same techniques as private types (the only limitation on the approach discussed below is that as with limited private types, the specification cannot prevent the user from changing the state). To illustrate this, the stack package will be respecified with the variable MAX in the visible part of the state and the variables S and TOP in the hidden part. A schema defining the visible part of the state is defined in the usual way. A given set denoting the hidden part is introduced and a further schema defined containing a single component of this type. The entire state is defined to be the conjunction of these two components.

STACK_VISIBLE
MAX : ℕ

MAX = 100

[HIDDEN]

STACK_HIDDEN
hidden : HIDDEN

STACK ≙ STACK_VISIBLE ∧ STACK_HIDDEN

Operations are then declared using this state.

PUSH : OP$_{[Z, STACK]}$

To define the behaviour of the operations, the hidden part of the state must be specified. A schema defining these variables is introduced.

```
┌─ STACK_BODY ─┐
│ S : ℕ ↦ ℤ
│ TOP : ℕ
└──────────────┘
```

As with private types, a conversion bijection is defined, relating values of the actual state to values of its visible representation. The CONVERT schema uses this function to relate the two state components in a schema.

convert : STACK_BODY ↠ HIDDEN

```
┌─ CONVERT ─────────────────┐
│ STACK_BODY
│ STACK_HIDDEN
│ ────────────────────────
│ hidden = convert (θ STACK_BODY)
└───────────────────────────┘
```

Because there may be constraints relating the values of these variables with the values of the visible variables, another schema is defined which describes the entire state as seen in the package body.

```
┌─ STACK_STATE ──┐
│ STACK_VISIBLE
│ STACK_BODY
│ ───────────────
│ S ∈ 1 .. MAX → ℤ
│ TOP ∈ 0 .. MAX
└────────────────┘
```

The operations on the stack may now be defined in the usual way. These definitions can be used to define the visible operations using the CONVERT schema.

```
┌─ PUSH_BODY ─────────┐
│ ΔSTACK_STATE        │
│ I? : ℤ              │
├─────────────────────┤
│ TOP < MAX           │
│ TOP' = TOP + 1      │
│ S' = S ⊕ {TOP' ↦ I?}│
└─────────────────────┘
```

PUSH =
make_operation
{PUSH_BODY; ΔCONVERT • I? ↦ (θ STACK ↦ θ STACK')}

This completes the specification of the package. To ensure that the package is used correctly, specifications using it must be inspected to ensure that the conversion function is not used to access the hidden components of the state directly and that the visible component representing the hidden components (the variable hidden) is not copied or changed.

7. General Issues

The Z notation has no facility for dividing a specification into packages or modules. Every schema, given set and global variable must have a unique name. Additionally, overloading is not permitted, so a name cannot be re-used for a different purpose. This presents a problem for large specifications constructed from parts developed at different times, as name clashes are inevitable. Clearly there is a need for some discipline in the choice of names when writing specifications of re-usable components. A simple but effective approach is to precede each definition with the name of the package that implements it, for example STACK_PUSH, STACK_POP. This has the advantage of resembling Ada's use of a preceding package name to identify declarations from a specific package (for example, STACK.PUSH).

8. Experience of Application

The techniques described in this paper have been applied at Siemens Plessey Defence Systems to specify existing library packages formally. The aim of this effort was to assess the practicality of the techniques and to investigate the benefits of formal specifications.

Because the specification was of existing software, the package structure was already known. Producing the specifications involved representing the data types and structures and defining the behaviour of the operations. Whenever possible, the original English specifications were used to determine the purpose of operations, with the source code only used when necessary to resolve ambiguities.

Because of the reverse engineering nature of this work, it initially proved difficult to identify the right level of abstraction in the specification (there was a tendency to produce a formal statement of the source code line by line). Further abstraction problems arose from the use of low level facilities in some packages such as access types and representation clauses. In order to obtain a good formal specification (one that clearly describes the behaviour of the package and is amenable to analysis), a higher level of abstraction is needed.

For the purposes of the exercise, it was decided not to produce formal specifications of the lowest level packages (including pre-defined packages). Instead, a base-line was established by defining the interface definitions only for these packages. Having done this it was possible to construct the specifications of higher level packages on top of these. This proved successful, and confirmed that the techniques can be applied to realistic examples.

Inevitably, formal specifications produced using these techniques are more implementation-oriented, as a particular program structure is suggested. This raises the question of how the techniques can be incorporated into a formal development cycle. The program structure is usually identified towards the end of the design phases and certainly after requirements analysis and specification. Producing a program-oriented specification therefore conflicts with the expectation that a specification is implementation-independent. This suggests that such specifications may not be appropriate for a top-level formal specification, but be better suited as a target for specification refinement. However, if software is to be re-used, design cannot be a purely top-down process (in fact no design method is, as all are guided by implementation constraints even if the design is ultimately presented in a top-down fashion). If re-use is to be successful, methods must ensure that a design is developed from the specification which gives full consideration to the opportunity to re-use existing software packages. The availability of formal specifications of the packages makes it easier to establish which packages are appropriate so should complement such a method.

The full implications of this approach to specification and its role in formal development remain to be investigated. Experience to date suggests has already shown that the techniques described in this paper provide the technical foundations for a formal development method.

9. Future Developments

There are two directions in which this work can be developed : enhancing the specification techniques and improving development methods.

The specification styles can be extended to improve the correspondence with Ada programs. The most important area for attention is the specification of concurrent programs. This is likely to require the use of additional notation, such as CSP [7] and is an important research area in its own right. A mechanism for specifying exceptions, defining the circumstances in which exceptions are raised in units and specifying the handling and propogation of exceptions is needed. A formal definition of the semantics of exceptions is required to do this effectively. Additionally, formal definitions of predefined Ada packages and theories of language features such as dynamic memory allocation are needed.

Development of methods, incorporating these techniques is required. Further research is needed to address this issue. Particular consideration should be given to identifying a suitable package structure including whether specification refinement is needed and to determining which packages can be re-used.

10. Conclusions

This paper presents an approach for using Z specifications to define different classes of Ada packages. The specifications produced provide clear descriptions of the individual packages and can easily be combined for use in subsequent specifications. This enables the developer to produce re-usable software packages with formal specifications. The benefits of this are twofold :

a)   the quality of an individual package is improved through the application of formal methods ;

b)   re-use should be encouraged, because the function of a package is clearly defined, making it easier to determine whether or not it is suitable as a component of a new application.

The techniques provide a technical foundation on which a formal development method for use with Ada can be built.

References

[1]   Spivey JM, The Z Notation : A Reference Manual, Prentice Hall International, 1989.
[2]   Collin BP et al, Introducing Formal Methods : the CICS experience with Z, TR 12.260, 1987.
[3]   Morgan C, Programming from Specifications, Prentice Hall International, 1990.
[4]   Barnes JGP, Programming in Ada, Addison-Wesley, 1984.
[5]   Booch G, Software Components with Ada, Benjamin Cummings, 1987.
[6]   Whysall PJ, McDermid JA, An Approach to Object-Oriented Specification in Z, In Proceedings of the 5th Annual Z User Meeting, Springer Verlag, 1991.
[7]   Hoare CAR, Communicating Sequential Processes, Prentice Hall International, 1985.

Appendix A : Z Glossary

Logic

$\wedge$ - logical and
$\vee$ - logical or
$\Rightarrow$ - logical implication
$\forall$ - universal quantifier (for all)
$\exists$ - existential quantifier (there exists)

⊢ - theorem

Sets

∈ - set membership
ℙ - powerset (set of all subsets)
⊆ - subset
♯ - size of a set

Relations and Functions

× - cartesian product
↔ - relation
→ - total function
↛ - partial function
⤖ - bijection (one to one mapping)
dom - domain of a relation
ran - range of a relation
◁ - domain restriction
⊕ - functional overriding

Sequences

seq - sequence
head - head of a sequence
tail - tail of a sequence
⁀ - sequence concatenation

Appendix B

This appendix contains a specification of the Queue_Nonpriority_ Nonbalking_Sequential_Unbounded_Unmanaged_Noniterator package described in [5] pp142-153. The package is an example of a restricted generic service package.

First, the interface to the package is defined. A set or function is supplied for each operation in the package. Note that the Queue data type (which is limited private in the Ada implementation) is defined as a generic parameter to the definitions rather than as a given set. This is because the actual type is dependent on the generic parameter Item.

```
[Queue, Item]
  Copy _  : ℙ (Queue × Queue × Queue)
  Clear _ : ℙ (Queue × Queue)
  Add _   : ℙ (Item × Queue × Queue)
  Pop _   : ℙ (Queue × Queue)
  Is_Equal _ : ℙ (Queue × Queue)
  Length_of : Queue → ℕ
  Is_Empty _ : ℙ Queue
  Front_Of : Queue ↛ Item
```

Next, the representation of the private type is defined. The Z type chosen for this has been selected for its suitability for specification, rather than to correspond exactly with the Ada implementation.

Queue_private [Item] == seq Item

Z schemas for each of the operations can now be defined. Each of these is parameterised with the generic type Item.

```
┌─ Copy_body [Item] ════════════════════════════╗
│ From_The_Queue?, To_The_Queue?, To_The_Queue! :
│     Queue_private[Item]
├────────────────
│ To_The_Queue! = From_The_Queue?
└──────────────────────────────────────────────┘
```

```
┌─ Clear_body [Item] ═══════════════════════════╗
│ The_Queue?, The_Queue! : Queue_private[Item]
├────────────────
│ The_Queue! = ⟨⟩
└──────────────────────────────────────────────┘
```

```
┌─ Add_body [Item] ═════════════════════════════╗
│ The_Item? : Item
│ To_The_Queue?, To_The_Queue! : Queue_private[Item]
├────────────────
│ To_The_Queue! = To_The_Queue? ⌢ ⟨The_Item?⟩
└──────────────────────────────────────────────┘
```

```
┌─ Pop_body [Item] ═════════════════════════════╗
│ The_Queue?, The_Queue! : Queue_private[Item]
├────────────────
│ The_Queue! = tail The_Queue?
└──────────────────────────────────────────────┘
```

```
┌─ Is_Equal_body [Item] ════════════════════╗
│ Left?, Right? : Queue_private[Item]
├────────────────
│ Left? = Right?
└───────────────────────────────────────────┘
```

```
┌─ Length_Of_body [Item] ══════════════════╗
│ The_Queue? : Queue_private[Item]
│ return! : ℕ
├────────────────
│ return! = #The_Queue?
└──────────────────────────────────────────┘
```

```
┌─ Is_Empty_body [Item] ═══════════════════╗
│ The_Queue? : Queue_private[Item]
├────────────────
│ The_Queue? = ⟨⟩
└──────────────────────────────────────────┘
```

```
┌─ Front_Of_body [Item] ─────────────┐
│ The_Queue? : Queue_private[Item]
│ return! : Item
├─────────────────
│ The_Queue? ≠ ⟨⟩
│ return! = head The_Queue?
└─────────────────────────────────┘
```

The interface definitions are completed by defining the mapping between the representation of the private type and the visible type, and using this to define the interface sets and functions in terms of the schema operations.

```
┌─ [Queue, Item] ════════════════════════
│ map_queue : Queue_private[Item] ⤖ Queue
│
```

```
┌─ [Queue, Item] ═══════════════════════════════
│ (Copy _)[Queue, Item] =
│ {Copy_body[Item] •
│       (map_queue From_The_Queue?, map_queue To_The_Queue?,
│       map_queue To_The_Queue!)}
│
```

```
┌─ [Queue, Item] ═══════════════════════════════
│ (Clear _)[Queue, Item] =
│ {Clear_body[Item] •
│       (map_queue The_Queue?, map_queue The_Queue!)}
│
```

```
┌─ [Queue, Item] ════════════════════════════
│ (Add _)[Queue, Item] =
│ {Add_body[Item] •
│       (The_Item?, map_queue To_The_Queue?,
│       map_queue To_The_Queue!)}
│
```

```
┌─ [Queue, Item] ═══════════════════════════════
│ (Pop _)[Queue, Item] =
│ {Pop_body[Item] • (map_queue The_Queue?, map_queue The_Queue!)}
│
```

```
┌─ [Queue, Item] ═══════════════════════════════
│ (Is_Equal _)[Queue, Item] =
│ {Is_Equal_body[Item] • (map_queue Left?, map_queue Right?)}
│
```

```
┌─ [Queue, Item] ═══════════════════════════════
│ Length_of[Queue, Item] =
│ {Length_Of_body[Item] • map_queue The_Queue? ↦ return!}
│
```

[Queue, Item] ─────────────────────────

$(\text{Is\_Empty} \underline{})_{[\text{Queue, Item}]} =$
$\{\text{Is\_Empty\_body}_{[\text{Item}]} \cdot \text{map\_queue The\_Queue?}\}$

[Queue, Item] ─────────────────────────

$\text{Front\_Of}_{[\text{Queue, Item}]} =$
$\{\text{Front\_Of\_body}_{[\text{Item}]} \cdot \text{map\_queue The\_Queue?} \mapsto \text{return!}\}$

To illustrate the use of this specification, an instantiation of the package is given, using the Airplane example from [5].

Airplane ::= Glider | Transport | Commercial | Fighter | Reconnaissance

[Airplane_Queue] ─────────────

$\text{Airplane\_Queue\_Copy} == (\text{Copy} \underline{})_{[\text{Airplane\_Queue, Airplane}]}$

$\text{Airplane\_Queue\_Clear} == (\text{Clear} \underline{})_{[\text{Airplane\_Queue, Airplane}]}$

$\text{Airplane\_Queue\_Add} == (\text{Add} \underline{})_{[\text{Airplane\_Queue, Airplane}]}$

$\text{Airplane\_Queue\_Pop} == (\text{Pop} \underline{})_{[\text{Airplane\_Queue, Airplane}]}$

$\text{Airplane\_Queue\_Is\_Equal} == (\text{Is\_Equal} \underline{})_{[\text{Airplane\_Queue, Airplane}]}$

$\text{Airplane\_Queue\_Length\_Of} == \text{Length\_of}_{[\text{Airplane\_Queue, Airplane}]}$

$\text{Airplane\_Queue\_Is\_Empty} == (\text{Is\_Empty} \underline{})_{[\text{Airplane\_Queue, Airplane}]}$

$\text{Airplane\_Queue\_Front\_Of} == \text{Front\_Of}_{[\text{Airplane\_Queue, Airplane}]}$

Towards Ada 9X
A. Burns, Ed.
IOS Press, 1992

118

LOTAda: Design and Implementation of a LOTOS to Ada Compiler

J.A. Mañas, M. Veiga, J. Salvachúa, A. Alvarez

Dpt. Telematics Engineering

Technical University of Madrid

E–28040 Madrid, Spain

Abstract

This paper describes the design and implementation of LOTAda[1], a LO-TOS to Ada translator which not only translates LOTOS specifications into Ada, but also allows the integration of LOTOS and Ada code into a single program. The translator developed is an adaptation of a previous LOTOS to C translator already in existence. Back-end code generators for both behaviour and data have been modified to generate Ada code. The paper reports major design decisions taken in the course of the project, gives an overview of the architecture of the translator, describes some experience on the performance of the generated code, and offers some conclusions on the experience gained with the project.

1 Introduction

LOTOS, a *formal description technique based on the temporal ordering of observational behaviour*, reached its International Standard status (ISO 8807) in 1989. This was the result of last decade's efforts for developing this FDT (Formal Description Technique), partly funded by the European Community through its SEDOS-ESPRIT project (ST-410) [1].

---

[1]Work done for the European Space Agency (European Space Research and Technology Center) under contract number 103290

DIT, the Department of Telematics Engineering of the Technical University of Madrid, later developed two compilers under the name of TOPO [2], one for the data part of LOTOS, and a separate one for the behavioural part. "El Prado" [3], a system based on non-circular attributed grammars [4], was used as a development tool to build a collection of boxes that may be fitted together around a common representation with the form of a coloured abstract syntax tree [5]. TOPO is a package of DIT–UPM[2] that also includes a LOTOS front-end, a static semantics analyser, and support tools such as a cross reference generator.

This paper describes briefly the LOTOS to Ada translator that has been built under contract number 103290 for the European Space Agency (European Space Research and Technology Center). The translator produced is an adaptation of the previous LOTOS to C translator already in existence. We give an overview of the software architecture of the translator, making reference to specific LOTOS features that guided the major design decisions. Then we present some conclusions on the experience gained.

2   Software Architecture

LOTOS is a complicated language, both in syntactic and in semantic terms. Generation of executable code out of a LOTOS specification is a task that must be tackled in several stages to keep complexity under control. It is composed of two clearly distinguishable parts: data and behaviour.

The data part is complex due to the overloading and structuring facilities, as well as the scope (visibility) rules. Furthermore, a unique canonical object has to be produced comprising all the types in the specification, and a rewrite system is to be produced from it. Code for a specialized rewrite machine is generated that provides equality resolution in the initial semantics model of it. The great complexity of these tasks may be mastered by means of a virtual machine, $\Lambda\delta$-machine, that isolates the identification of the rewrite engine from the actual code generation.

For the behaviour part, a clear operational semantics is provided in ISO-8807, strongly based on the n-way symmetrical rendezvous paradigm. But it is compli-

---

[2] *Departamento de Ingeniería de Sistemas Telemáticos—Universidad Politécnica de Madrid*

cated in itself, and any complete implementation of the language will have to deal with complex run-time synchronisation facilities.

L O T O S is able to specify highly concurrent systems, where very many activities may be involved at any moment. In this framework, code generation is an enormous task, and plenty of implementation decisions have to be taken to move from very high level L O T O S to very low level machine code. Furthermore, as experience is gained on the understanding of the language and its implementation, these decisions may be subject to severe changes. In order to keep complexity under control while allowing for easy maintenance, it is of paramount importance to identify intermediate stages, and keep them clearly isolated. If this isolation is achieved, the complexity of each of the stages can be kept under control, and each of them can be easily replaced without disturbing the others.

2.1   Structure of the translator

In T O P O an intermediate stage is identified. It is a level of virtual machines, both for behaviour and data. $\Lambda\beta$-machine is a virtual machine for the behavioural part [6, 7], while $\Lambda\delta$-machine provides a virtual machine for the data part [8]. These provide abstract implementation models, while being open to diverse concrete implementations.

Later on, T O P O translates from these virtual machines into code for a systems programming language. Previously, T O P O had relied on the widely available C language. The existence of this stage has benefited from the very many C compilers in existence, providing portability of code to many target machines. Now similar remarks can be made regarding Ada. The translation of the L O T O S behavior therefore follows the scheme shown in figure 1.

An important feature of our implementation is that T O P O accepts L O T O S specifications that may be extended with **annotations**. These annotations are, syntactically, an identifiable class of comments, and their contents are expressions or statements in some programming language. They may appear in a few predefined productions of the language, thus becoming a syntactically fixed extension of L O T O S. Semantically, annotations go unprocessed through both the $\Lambda\beta$-machine and the $\Lambda\delta$-machine, and are only interpreted when code for a systems programming language is produced, thereby being passed to the appropriate compiler. Currently,

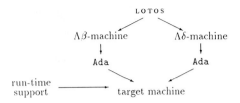

Figure 1: Overall translation framework

these annotations can contain expressions and statements in C and Ada. They are also used to link internal to external names, in order to refer to user provided code (e.g. user libraries).

2.2   Translator Components

The system is designed as a collection of tools which share a common internal representation of the LOTOS specification under consideration. This method allows for simple modularisation of the complete system, as well as for sharing of common parts between them. Thus, the distinction between Ada and C is delayed as far as possible, that is, until the very last stages of the translator.

The object of TOPO is, at every moment, a single specification written in LOTOS. Eventually, the need may arise to access a shared library of data types, the so called *the standard library*. Despite the definite article in its naming, there may be a number of such libraries accessible, but only one is considered for each user specification.

LOTOS specifications can be in one of several alternative formats:

text Textual form.

Plain ASCII representation of the specification.

CAST Coloured Abstract Syntax Tree.

A representation adequate to apply attributed grammar techniques for the manipulation of the specification. It is basically an internal representation, in which tree navigation is simple and efficient; this internal representation can be written onto an external file, and read back in memory, in order to exchange information between tools. CAST exchange is based on a linear traversing of the tree, and can be supported by either files or pipes.

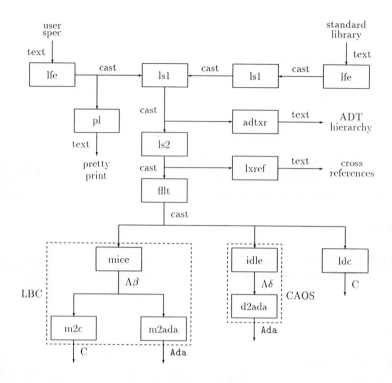

Figure 2: Individual tool components

$\Lambda\beta$-**machine** Virtual machine that holds the behaviour. It is an intermediate stage between CAST representation, and generation of code for the target language.

$\Lambda\delta$-**machine** Virtual machine that holds the data. It is an intermediate stage between CAST representation, and generation of code for the target language.

The textual representation is needed for users to write their specifications using any conventional or specific editor. The CAST representation allows for simple semantics analysis of the specification, as well as for adequate traversing to generate code. And the $\Lambda\beta$-machine and $\Lambda\delta$-machine are needed to decouple semantics stages from any concrete target language; thus permitting late binding between LOTOS and the target language.

The translator is made out of the following components (see figure 2):

1. LFE: LOTOS Front End.

2. LS1: LOTOS Static semantics analysis, phase 1.

3. LS2: LOTOS Static semantics analysis, phase 2.

4. FFLT: Full FLaTtener.

5. MICE: Machine Independent Code gEnerator (for behaviour).

6. M2C: Mice to C (code generation).

7. M2ADA: Mice to Ada (code generation).

8. CAOS: Compilador de Act One Simplificado (flattened ACT ONE compiler).

9. IDLE: Intermediate Data LanguagE generator.

10. D2ADA: LOTOS Data language to Ada.

11. KAOS: Kernel of cAOS.

12. LDC: LOTOS Data Compiler onto C (code generation).

13. PL: Pretty Printer.

14. ADTXR: ADT hierarchy (structural cross reference).

15. LXREF: Cross references (between identifiers).

2.3   Brief functional definition of each component

LFE LOTOS Front End.

Reads plain ascii, and generates the corresponding CAST. It is a purely syntactic stage. The resulting CAST is minimally coloured: it contains a table of lexical values (i.e. identifiers), and references to it, and to source line numbers for later error reporting.

LS1 LOTOS Static semantics analysis, phase 1.

Reads CAST and generates a transformed and enriched CAST (i.e. with more colouring). It is devoted to data types preprocessing, resolving library references, and data hierarchies. "Standard" libraries are preprocessed by this component. Data types in the resulting CAST are "semi–flattened", that is each type is self contained. A preliminary semantics analysis is performed on data objects, leaving this information on an "object table".

LS2 LOTOS Static semantics analysis, phase 2.

Reads CAST and generates an enriched CAST (i.e. with more colouring). It is devoted to identifier association: it resolves overloading and scopes. In the output, every object is in an Object Table that relates declarations and references. There are 7 kinds of objects: specification, process, gate, type, sort, operation, and variable.

FFLT Full FLaTtenner.

Reads CAST and generates a transformed CAST where there is a single data type: the canonical data type of the specification. It performs the union of all the data types.

MICE Machine Independent Code gEnerator (for behaviour).

Reads CAST and generates code for $\Lambda\beta$-machine.

M2C Mice to C (code generation).

Reads $\Lambda\beta$-machine code and generates C code.

M2ADA Mice to Ada (code generation).

Reads $\Lambda\beta$-machine code and generates Ada code.

CAOS Compilador de Act One Simplificado (flattened ACT ONE compiler).

CAOS = IDLE + D2ADA.

IDLE Intermediate Data LanguagE generator.

Reads CAST and generates code for $\Lambda\delta$-machine.

D2ADA LOTOS Data language to Ada.

Reads $\Lambda\delta$-machine code and generates Ada code.

KAOS Kernel of cAOS.

Data run time support.

LDC LOTOS Data Compiler onto C (code generation).

Reads CAST and directly generates C code. It is an old piece of software that will be replaced by some D2C (LOTOS Data language to C) in the near future.

PL Pretty Printer.

Reads a CAST representation of an specification, and generates *source* text in a systematic layout. Any CAST is a valid input since no semantics information is strictly needed and, therefore, any stage after **ls1** is adequate to feed **pl**. Nevertheless, there is an option to print also the unique reference associated to an identifier, an option that only works after semantics analysis is performed (i.e. **ls2**).

ADTXR ADT hierarchy (structural cross reference).

Reads a CAST representation of the specification, and generates a tree representation of the data types hierarchy. It recursively lists inter data dependencies. Some analysis is needed on the data types: it works after **ls1** stage.

LXREF Cross references (between identifiers).

Reads a CAST representation of the specification, and generates a listing that relates every identifier to a binding declaration, and very occurrence (usage) of it. Semantics information is convenient (e.g. on overloading resolution), but it may as well work on earlier stages, although the information provided may be less accurate.

The modules that have been written as part of the new translator are M2ADA and D2ADA, that is, the back-end translators from $\Lambda\beta$-machine and $\Lambda\delta$-machine code into `Ada`. The run-rime support packages for both behaviour and data parts, have also been written in `Ada`.

3   Performance Experiments

Let's consider a collection of specifications of the classical sieve of Eratosthenes, a procedure to obtain prime numbers. Eratosthenes algorithm implies a linear growth of the number of processes involved, thus being an example for which run-time complexity continuously grows, and which permits to derive conclusions as a function of it.

The objective is to evaluate the influence of the specification style and run-time complexity on the overall performance of the code automatically generated by a compiler. It is usually assumed that the style used to write a LOTOS specification will influence the efficiency of derived implementations. This assumption stems from years of experience in programming, where dramatic benefits may derive from changing the organization of the program.

When a specification language is used in the life cycle of a software engineering project, the goal is to cover a number of stages, from user requirements capture, thru a number of refinements, down to an implementation. This evolution may be done in LOTOS, but it costs time, effort, and money. Although there are (or may be some day) tools to preserve properties of the specification during the transformation process (e.g. proving that successive steps conforms to the reference specification), there is still a large need for human creativeness.

The cost of greatly transforming a specification must be balanced against the expected benefits. We are tryning to provide quantitative figures to help in that decision. We just consider one compiler that is able to cope with the whole language. It is applied to a collection of specification styles, and the results are compared.

3.1   Informal Specification

Eratosthenes, a Greek wise man [275?–194 B.C.], devised a working procedure to obtain a list of prime numbers sorted in ascending order. It starts by writing down as many positive numbers as you may need, beginning with the number 3, and goes on by increments of 2, skipping even numbers:

$$3, 5, 7, 9, 11, 13, 15, 17, 19, 21, 23, 25, 27, 29, 31, 33, 35, \ldots$$

The first number in the list is a prime number. Any multiple of it is not, and may be removed from the list

$$\underline{3}, 5, 7, \not{9}, 11, 13, \not{15}, 17, 19, \not{21}, 23, 25, \not{27}, 29, 31, \not{33}, 35, \ldots$$

As more primes are identified, more multiples are removed from the list

$$\underline{3}, \underline{5}, 7, \not{9}, 11, 13, \not{15}, 17, 19, \not{21}, 23, \not{25}, \not{27}, 29, 31, \not{33}, \not{35}, \ldots$$

$$\underline{3}, \underline{5}, \underline{7}, \not{9}, 11, 13, \not{15}, 17, 19, \not{21}, 23, \not{25}, \not{27}, 29, 31, \not{33}, \not{35}, \ldots$$

$$\underline{3}, \underline{5}, \underline{7}, \not{9}, \underline{11}, 13, \not{15}, 17, 19, \not{21}, 23, \not{25}, \not{27}, 29, 31, \not{33}, \not{35}, \ldots$$

$$\ldots$$

We shall slightly modify this ancient procedure. Instead of putting down a list of numbers, and then removing out some of them, we shall consider one number at a time (starting with 3, and then proceeding by increments of 2). At each step we check whether any of the primes found so far divides exactly the current number. If anyone does, we go for the next number; if none does, it becomes a new prime.

3.2 Formal Specifications

Six *specifications* will be considered below. Of course many more might be devised. We have chosen five LOTOS specifications that seem significant enough, and a direct implementation in `Ada`.

eratos1	constraint oriented
eratos2	constructive oriented
	full LOTOS
eratos3	concurrent programming
	`Ada` style: two way unidirectional rendezvous, without
	rendezvous predicates
eratos4	single task programming
	C style: no rendezvous, single control flow
eratos5	extended automata
	C style: no rendezvous, single control flow; balancing
	data and behaviour parts
eratos6	direct implementation in `Ada`

We shall mostly consider control aspects. `Ada` will be used for the data part (i.e. ADTs are compiled manually in `Ada`). We need natural numbers, for which `Ada` integers are used. Furthermore, we shall eventually need lists of integers to hold prime numbers. Lastly, in `eratos5`, list traversal will be moved from explicit behaviour into an ADT. All these data types are coded in `Ada`. The details are not shown since they are pretty obvious.

3.2.1 Constraint Approach

Although there is no widely accepted definition of *constraint approach style*, let's try one:

A specification is said to be written according to the constraint oriented paradigm when the number of effective/potential partners involved in a synchronization is higher than 2 for a significant number of events.

Specification is organized as an AND conjunction of constraints (N partners involved in successful synchronizations), and/or as an OR disjunction of constraints (2 partners are involved in each successful synchronization, but there are N potential pairs to succeed). There are typically very few gates.

Our constraint oriented specification will be based on two gates, good, and bad. An event on either of these gates has a single experiment: the number under consideration. A synchronization good!n models that all the constraints for n to be a prime number hold. A synchronization bad!n models that any of the constraints for n to be a prime number fails[3].

Let $\mathcal{P}(n)$ be the predicate on natural numbers that is true if and only if n is prime.

Let P_n be the set of prime numbers smaller than n:

$$P_n = \{p | \mathcal{P}(p) \wedge p < n\}$$

Let N_n be the number of primes smaller than n, that is $N_n = \text{card}(P_n)$

For a new number n to be tagged as prime, it is required that no previous prime number p divides it, thus the constraint on good involves N_n partners

$$\mathcal{P}(n) = \text{true} \Leftrightarrow \forall p, n \bmod p \neq 0$$

where $p \in P_n$.

On the other hand, for a new number n to be tagged as non-prime, it suffices that some previous prime number p divides it, thus the constraint on bad involves 2 partners, but there are N_n potential candidates

$$\mathcal{P}(n) = \text{false} \Leftrightarrow \exists p, n \bmod p = 0$$

where $p \in P_n$.

The specification may be organized as follows:

---

[3]Since LOTOS is unable to "capture" constraint failure, the specification will positively state the conditions for N not to be a prime number. Those conditions are ORed.

Constrained Oriented Specification _____

```
specification Eratosthenes_Sieve : noexit
  << booleans := int of Ada >>
  << natural numbers := int of Ada >>
behaviour
  hide good, bad in
    ( generate [good, bad] (3)
    |[good, bad]|
      mkfilter [good, bad]
    )
    |[good]|
      listen [good]
  where
    << number generator >>
    << organize filters >>
    << environment folding >>
  endspec
```

Basically, we have a *generator* that offers odd numbers for consideration: $3, 5, 7, 9, 11, 13, \ldots$ Each one may be prime or not, that being decided by a series of filters.

In order to get a working program that produces something, an environment is folded into the specification: any event on gate good denotes a new prime number. There is a process that "hears" it, and prints the number out. C(ode) annotations are used to achieve this side–effect:

Environment folding _____

```
process listen [good] : noexit :=
    good ?d: nat
    (*| C  put_line ("-> " &  pint (success(0).n)); |*) ;
    listen [good]
  endproc
```

The generation of a series of numbers for consideration is straightforward:

Number generator _____

```
process generate [good, bad] (n: nat): noexit :=
    good !n;
    generate [good, bad] (n+2)
[] bad !n;
    generate [good, bad] (n+2)
endproc
```

Lastly, a collection of filters has to be set up. This is dynamic: new filters are added, as new prime numbers are found.

At the beginning, `mkfilter` is ready to accept any number as prime: any number is prime until it is proved otherwise. As soon as a prime is found, a `filter` is started for it. It works in synchronization for gate `good`, and in interleaving for gate `bad`. This organization of parallelism strictly reflects the conjunctive constraint on gate `good`, and the disjunctive constraint on gate `bad`:

Organize filters _____

```
process mkfilter [good, bad] : noexit :=
  good ?n: nat;
  ( mkfilter [good, bad]
  |[good]|
    filter [good, bad] (n))
where
  << filter multiples of n >>
endproc
```

`mkfilter` just waits for new prime numbers to be discovered. The real task of detecting multiples is for the `filters`. Its specification is straightforward: a number may be good if this filter cannot divide it. It is bad if this filter can divide it. The specification of each filter is obvious:

Filter multiples of n _____

```
process filter [good, bad] (n: nat) : noexit :=
    good ?d: nat [(d % n) <> 0];
        filter [good, bad] (n)
    [] bad ?d: nat [(d % n) = 0];
        filter [good, bad] (n)
endproc
```

It is enough that one **filter** say it is bad, for an event on gate **bad** to succeed. But it is required that every **filter** says it is good, for an event on gate **good** to succeed. This organization of constraints is (dynamically) achieved in **mkfilter**.

3.2.2 Constructive Approach

There is no widely accepted definition of what constitutes a constructive approach either, so let's attempt again a definition of our own:

> A specification is said to be written according to the constructive paradigm when the number of effective/potential partners involved in a synchronization is exactly 2 for most of the events.

> The specification is organized as a collection of boxes and a large number of gates to connect those boxes in pairs.

We shall use the classical "data flow" model to specify Eratosthenes' sieve according to a constructive paradigm. It is a very common way of writing functional programs (e.g. in LISP).

The basic idea is to have a series of boxes. Each box is a concurrent task parameterized by a prime number. Each box is devoted to filter out multiples of its parameter. Boxes are connected according to a waterfall pattern. A number generator feeds the first box with an endless stream of odd numbers. The first box removes those numbers that may be divided by 3, and feeds the remaining stream of data to the next box. The second box removes multiples of 5, and so on.

The last box in the chain detects prime numbers: any number able to reach it has successfully passed all the filters known so far: it is selected as prime, and a new box is created to filter out multiples of this new prime number.

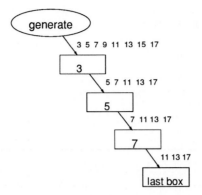

The chain of filters grows dynamically as new primes are discovered. Nevertheless, gates just connect a predecessor and a successor box. Therefore every synchronization is 2–way, and this specification may be called "constructive".

The specification starts by offering 3 as a prime number. Initially there is no filter, but a last box.

In order to get some printing, the environment is folded into the specification, as in the specification of the previous section.

```
Constructive Specification
    specification Eratosthenes_Sieve : noexit
      << booleans := int of Ada >>
      << natural numbers := int of Ada >>
      behaviour
        hide good, channel in
          ( generate [channel] (3)
          |[channel]|
            last_box [channel, good])
          |[good]|
            listen [good]
      where
        << number stream generator >>
        << last box in the chain >>
        << environment folding >>
      endspec
```

The box producing an endless stream of numbers is pretty direct to specify:

Number stream generator ⎯⎯⎯⎯⎯⎯⎯⎯⎯⎯⎯⎯⎯⎯⎯⎯⎯⎯

```
process generate [channel] (n: nat) : noexit :=

channel !n ;

generate [channel] (n+2)

endproc
```

The last box in the chain is slightly more complicated. It processes sequentially the input stream of numbers. Any number that reaches it is a prime number: the number is tagged as prime, and communicated to the environment. Then, the box unfolds itself into a filter for the last prime found, and a new last box. A new gate is "created" for local communication between these boxes.

Last box in the chain ⎯⎯⎯⎯⎯⎯⎯⎯⎯⎯⎯⎯⎯⎯⎯⎯⎯⎯⎯⎯⎯⎯⎯⎯⎯⎯⎯⎯⎯

```
process last_box [channel, good] : noexit :=

channel ?d: nat ;

good !d ;

( hide next in

        filter [channel, next] (d)

    |[next]|

        last_box [next, good])

where

    << intermediate box in the chain >>

endproc
```

Intermediate boxes are simpler: numbers from the input stream are considered one by one. If the parameter divides the first item in the stream, the box goes to consider the next item. If the parameter does not divide the first item, it is passed forward to the output stream (into the next box in the chain), and the box goes for then next input item.

Intermediate box in the chain _____

```
    process filter [cin, cout] (n: nat) : noexit :=
        cin ?d: nat [(d % n) = 0];
        filter [cin, cout] (n)
    [] cin ?d: nat [(d % n) <> 0];
        cout !d;
        filter [cin, cout] (n)
    endproc
```

3.2.3 Concurrent Programming Approach

Both specifications above require a large number of concurrent processes able to communicate between them. Although expensive, there are programming languages able to cope with this paradigm. Here we shall use `Ada` as a target language. We do not plan to make any `Ada` implementation, but we shall try to identify to which extent the `Ada` model of process cooperation influences the LOTOS specification style.

When considering the specification above, we may easily identify one construct that `Ada` doesn't support: predicates on rendezvous.

`Ada` imposes several requirements on inter–process communication such as two partners per rendezvous, one–way data flow, no value matching, no value negotiation, and no predicate on value acceptance. A small modification of `filter` is enough to meet all these requirements:

Intermediate box in the chain (for `Ada`) _____

```
    process filter [cin, cout] (n: nat) : noexit :=
        cin ?d: nat ;
        (   [(d % n) = 0]->
            filter [cin, cout] (n)
        [] [(d % n) <> 0]->
            cout !d;
            filter [cin, cout] (n))
    endproc
```

We shall apply another modification to the last box. It is not strictly required by Ada but it is a usual decision of implementers (still questionable, of course). We shall remove the synchronization with the environment via gate good, and substitute it by an Ada annotation.

Last box in the chain (for Ada)

```
process last_box [channel] : noexit :=
  channel ?d: nat
  (*| C put_line ("-> " & pint (success(0).n)); |*) ;
  ( hide next in
        filter [channel, next] (d)
     |[next]|
        last_box [next])
  where
     << intermediate box in the chain (for Ada) >>
  endproc
```

Resource Oriented Specification (concurrent)

```
specification Eratosthenes_Sieve : noexit
  << booleans := int of Ada >>
  << natural numbers := int of Ada >>


behaviour
  hide channel in
     generate [channel] (3)
    |[channel]|
     last_box [channel]
  where
     << number stream generator >>
     << last box in the chain (for Ada) >>
  endspec
```

3.2.4 Single Task Programming Approach

We may further restrict the available means to implement our LOTOS specification, and try to use as target a more conventional (non-concurrent) programming language. For instance, a C or Pascal paradigm of computation.

By the way, we are coming closer to a conventional assignment in programming courses.

Now the modifications are larger since we were heavily using dynamic process creation, and now there is one single process. By close inspection of the specification so far it may easily be discovered that we are using a chain of processes to distribute the manipulation of a (virtual) list of data. It must be easy to collapse all those processes into a single process that is parameterized by the list of data, and traverses it. Instead of having data traversing a chain of processes, we now have one single process traversing a list of data.

Basically we have two loops, one to step over odd numbers, and the other to step over primes found so far. It approximately matches the following Ada structure

```
n:= 3;
loop
  p:= last_prime;
  while (p /= empty) loop
    -- decide if n is prime w.r.t. p
    p:= p.next;
  end loop;
  n:= n+2;
end loop;
```

LOTOS process `findprime` models the outer loop, and LOTOS process `isprime` models the inner one.

Resource Oriented Specification (single task) ──────────

```
specification Eratosthenes_Sieve : noexit
  << booleans := int of Ada >>
  << natural numbers := int of Ada >>
  << lists of natural numbers := int lists in Ada >>
behaviour
  findprime (3, empty)
  where
    << find next prime number >>
    << check previous primes >>
  endspec
```

Here follows the outer loop. Since LOTOS lacks iterators, recursion is used. Nevertheless, tail recursion optimization can be applied at compile time, thus becoming equivalent to a for loop.

Find next prime number ──────────

```
process findprime (n: nat, primes: natlist) : noexit :=
    isprime (n, primes)
  >> accept valid: bool in
       [valid]->
         i (*| C put_line ("-> " & pint (F.var(0).n)); |*) ;
         findprime (n+2, add (primes, n))
    [] [not (valid)]->
         findprime (n+2, primes)
  endproc
```

Here follows the inner loop. Once again we need to use recursion as a replacement for iteration. Tail recursion optimization may be applied again. Notice that this LOTOS process closely models a boolean function in C (a predicate):

Check previous primes _____

```
    process isprime (n: nat, primes: natlist) : exit (bool) :=
        [primes = empty]->
           exit (true)
    [] [hasany (primes)]->
        [(n % hd (primes)) = 0]->
           exit (false)
    [] [hasany (primes)]->
        [(n % hd (primes)) <> 0]->
           isprime (n, tl (primes))
    endproc
```

3.2.5   Extended Automata

The last specification was based on two nested loops:

```
n:=3;
loop
  p:= last_prime;
  while (p /= empty) loop
    -- decide if n is prime w.r.t. p
    p:= p.next;
  end loop;
  n:= n+2;
end loop;
```

We were using LOTOS behaviour to model both of them. But this mapping of Ada loops into "active" LOTOS processes is not mandatory: other opportunities do exist.

Let's here apply a very usual design tradeoff between data and control. Algorithms are very often suitable for balancing the part that is implemented by means of data structures, and the part that is implemented by means of control flow (i.e. loops, function calls, procedures, ...)

When we apply a data oriented design criteria to the Eratosthenes' sieve, we may easily move the traverse of the list of prime numbers into a predicate on data. The inner loop goes into data. The only part that remains under behaviour responsibility is the scanning of odd numbers, i.e. the outer loop.

Data Based Specification ─────────────────────

```
specification Eratosthenes_Sieve : noexit

  << booleans := int of Ada >>

  << natural numbers := int of Ada >>

  << lists of natural numbers := int lists in Ada >>

  << data based implementation of isprime() >>

behaviour

  findprime (3, empty)

  where

    << find next prime number (data based) >>

  endspec
```

Here follows the ADT specification of the predicate `isprime`.

Data based implementation of isprime() ─────────────────

```
type IsPrime is Booleans, Naturals, Lists

  opns

    isprime  (*| extern |*) : nat, natlist -> bool

  eqns

    forall n, p: nat, ll: natlist

    ofsort bool

      isprime (n, empty) = false;

      n % p = 0 =>

        isprime (n, add (ll, p)) = false;

      n % p <> 0 =>

        isprime (n, add (ll, p)) = isprime (n, ll);

  endtype
```

And the outer loop is straightforward:

```
Find next prime number (data based) _____

    process findprime (n: nat, primes: natlist) : noexit :=
      let valid: bool= isprime (n, primes) in
          [valid]->
              i (*| C put_line ("-> "& pint (F.var(0).n)); |*) ;
              findprime (n+2, add (primes, n))
         [] [not (valid)]->
                findprime (n+2, primes)
    endproc
```

3.2.6   Implementation in `Ada`

One step more in the direction of an efficient implementation will forget about automatic compilation of LOTOS specifications, and go for a direct implementation in `Ada`.

We shall use this last case as a reference for comparison purposes. It may be reasonably expected that a direct implementation in `Ada` establishes a lower bound of achievable performance.

The implementation below doesn't need a big presentation. It is a very con-

```
Ada Implementation _____

    package the_types is
     type intlist_rec;
     type intlist is access intlist_rec;
     type  intlist_rec is
       record
         i : integer;
         next : intlist;
       end record;
    end the_types;


    with the_types; use the_types;
    << predicate isprime >>
    with the_types; use the_types;
    with isprime;
    with text_io; use text_io;
    << main loop: findprime >>
```

ventional assignment for students in programming courses. There are several optimizations that may apply for better performance, but we have tried to reflect the
last LOTOS specification as precisely as possible. We do not want to compare algorithms, but to estimate the overhead due to the use of an automatic tool to derive
code.

Main loop: findprime

```
procedure eratos is
    n: integer;
    primes: intlist:= NULL;
    begin
    n:= 3;
     loop
      if (isprime (n, primes)) then
        put_line ("-> " & integer'image(n));
        primes:= new intlist'(n, primes);
      end if;
     n:= n+2;
    end loop;
   end eratos;
```

Predicate isprime

```
    function isprime (n: integer; primes: intlist)
     return boolean is
       p : intlist := primes;
     begin
      while (p /= NULL) loop
       if (n mod p.i = 0) then
         return FALSE;
       end if;
       p := p.next;
      end loop;
      return TRUE;
     end isprime;
```

3.3   Performance Evaluation

The previous specifications/implementations of the sieve of Eratosthenes were used
to generate as many executable images on a Sun–4/260 machine (a SPARC based
model). More precisely, the target machine had 10 MIPS, and run at 16.67 MHz.
Main memory was 16 Mb, plus 128 Kb for cache. The operating system was SunOS
4.0.3.

The examples where run at working hours with an average load of 1-2 processes
waiting in the ready queue. No special action was taken to get any privilege in
competing for resources.

TOPO 1R7, `Ada` version 1R1, was used for generating code, and its run time
support was used. The `Ada` code was compiled with Verdix 6.0 `Ada` compiler. Executable images were stripped.

Some extra code was also added to the main loop in the kernel to log statistics
about number of synchronizations, and partners involved in each rendezvous. Some
extra code was also added to dynamically measure the consumption of resources:
time and memory space. This modifications imposed some overhead, and the results
may be slightly biased. In a real situation the figures should be better, but it is
difficult to estimate how much better they can be.

There is a touchy question about the order to scan previous primes. The first
specification (constraint oriented) is quite abstract, and the probing order is non
deterministic. The second and third specifications (data flow) add filters as new
primes are found, and these filters are added to the end of the chain: previous
primes are scanned in ascending order. The other specifications (4th, 5th, and 6th)
probe previous primes in a *last found – first tried* manner.

Probing order makes a significant difference: there are many more multiples of
(say) 3, than of (say) 7, and trying 3 before 7 speeds up the process. It is difficult
to estimate the influence of this fact on the performance figures: for `eratos1` it is
random; `eratos2` and `eratos3` are in the best situation. The figures for the rest
would improve if probing order were reversed.

3.3.1   Total Elapsed Time

Figure 3 shows the recorded elapsed time as a function of the number of primes
found. The time is the sum of user and system time, as reported by SunOS function

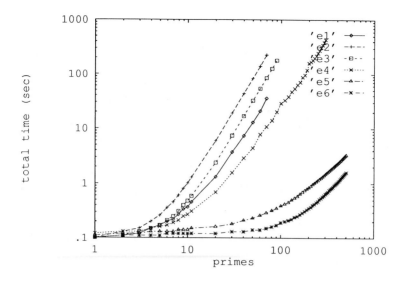

Figure 3: Total elapsed time as a function of runtime complexity.

`getrusage(2)`.

As it might be reasonably expected, as run-time complexity grows, execution time time grows as well. Please notice it is a log–log plot.

There are, basically, two groups of specifications, as it regards total time performance:

A first group includes the constraint approach and the three constructive approaches. Still there are differences between them. It must be noticed that the constraint specification is not the worst approach, and it is comparable to the others. The worst performance is for eratos2, the constructive approach based on predicates, that is roughly three times slower than the constraint oriented. Performance doubles for the constructive approach based on guards (**Ada** paradigm). Lastly, there is a higher improvement for the single task paradigm.

The second group puts together the two implementations based on the single task paradigm. The LOTOS specification is roughly two times slower than a direct implementation in **Ada**, both of them being of the same order of complexity.

All the remarks made so far in this subsection apply only to the upper part of figure 3, that is for large run-time complexity. For low run-time complexity, figure 3 is hard to read. Figure 4 zooms on the lower part of it.

The conclusions in this complexity zone are slightly different from those that apply to large run-time complexity. Now all the specifications behave within the

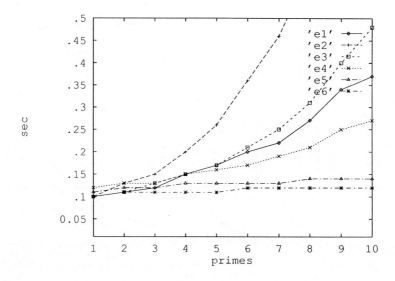

Figure 4: Total elapsed time as a function of runtime complexity: zoomed on the small complexity zone.

same order of magnitude, and it does not make a significant difference the specification paradigm used. It is not even significant the advantage of direct coding in `Ada`.

There are basically two factors to take into consideration when comparing constraint oriented and constructive oriented approaches: the number of events, and the complexity of the events. For the constraint style, there are few but complex events. For the constructive style, there are many simple events. As far as runtime complexity is small, it is better to have few events, even if they are complex. When complexity grows (see graph   ), each event starts being too expensive.

3.3.2   Events

Figure 5 shows the number of successful events plotted against the number of primes found. Every kind of event is recorded, including internal events `i`. There is no concept of event in the `Ada` implementation.

The small difference between `eratos2` and `eratos3` is due to the removal of gate `good`.

Do not feel confused by the erratic figures in specs 2 and 3: data flow on the

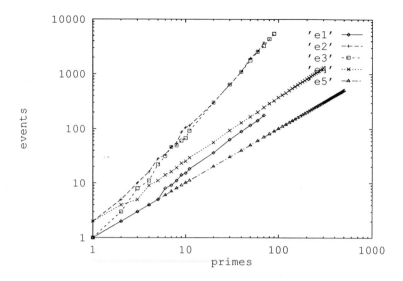

Figure 5: Number of successful events as a function of runtime complexity

chain of filters is non deterministic. The figures above are recording the arrivals to the last box, but it is unknown how many numbers have been generated by generate, and at which filter have they arrived.

3.3.3   Overall Analysis

There are basically two dimensions to read the previous graphs: specification paradigm, and run-time complexity. Each of the examples uses a different paradigm, from constraint oriented in eratos1.lot to direct Ada coding in eratos6.a.

Although specifications are finite, the algorithm implies a continuously growing complexity at run-time. As more prime numbers are known, more constraints, processes, data in the lists, ... are active. Run-time complexity grows as the number of primes grows. That is the reason for the graphs to be plotted against the number of prime numbers found so far.

Looking at a single curve, it may be estimated for a given paradigm, how performance evolves as complexity grows. If an abscissa is fixed on the x–axis, performance dependency on specification paradigm may be estimated.

One major conclusion to be derived from the previous data is that for a small number of constraints/processes, a constraint oriented specification may run faster than a constructive oriented alternative. However, when complexity (either con-

straints or processes) grows up, the cost of N-way rendezvous overtakes the benefit
of few events.

Another conclusion is that a data oriented specification (as `eratos5`) is competitive in time and space with a direct implementation in `Ada`. With respect to size
figures, they are identical for small complexity.

4   Conclusions

In general, retargetting the LOTOS translator to generate `Ada` code has been a positive experience. As the previous version of the translator generated `C` code, the task
has been simplified by the fact that it is relatively simple to find a "C-equivalent"
subset of `Ada`. However, the experience has not been without problems.

A number of significant conclusions may be derived from the experience of implementing the sieve of Eratosthenes using different specification styles. Most of
them have been pointed out as the data were presented. Let's just revise here the
most significant ones.

One important conclusion is that intuition can easily fail when foreseeing the
cost of specification styles in time and space. For instance, it is surprising that a
constructive specification performs worse than a constraint one. There is a moral to
derive: do not make intuitive assumptions, but carefully profile the product, before
going for a refinement.

Careful profiling of concrete cases is mandatory to decide whether the effort of
transforming a very abstract specification into a more implementation oriented one
is worthwhile. Of course, more examples are needed, and conclusions derived from
the case shown in this paper must be confirmed by other experiments.

It is important to assess to which extent are the results applicable to real protocols. It may be reasonably estimated that a real specification of a communication
protocol may have a limited number of constraints, even if specified in a constraint
oriented style. Then, the figures for a small number of primes in our experiments
apply. They suggest that transforming into a constructive specification may even
degrade performance. It is important to notice as well that imposing `Ada` paradigms
for concurrent process modeling may mean recovering some performance benefits.
However, dramatic benefits must be expected from sensible balancing of data and

behaviour: an old recipe in protocol engineering, widely used in extended automata.

Another relevant conclusion to be derived is that measuring the number of events per second is a risky figure for comparison purposes. There are expensive events and cheap events. Overall time and space consumption seem much better indicators.

As a technical detail, there are some features of C which are not present in Ada, in spite of being a much larger language than C. One of these features, which happens to be of much use in generating code by our translator, is allowing subprogrammes as (subprogramme) parameters. Not having this feauture in Ada obliged us to make some significant changes in the way code is generated.

More important is the fact that Ada is a sophisticated high level language with very powerful constructs. As such, Ada is very well suited for the design of large and complex software systems. A judicious use of the different Ada features makes it possible for designers and coders to produce programs which are easily understood, tested, and maintained. However, these powerful features of Ada become largely irrelevant when generating code automatically by a translator. They cannot be used while others, whose main purpose is to help users spot logical errors (i.e., strong typing) only get in the way making code generation more cumbersome. In summary, Ada is not an "assembly-like" target language, but a high level design language.

The last problem encountered has been determined by the relative lack of maturity of current Ada compilers. Working with four different Ada compilers in order to produce as much portable code as possible, we have found that in general the code produced by current Ada compilers is still significantly larger and slower than expected. Although redesigning some parts of our LOTOS translator backend would certainly improve the generated code, we are convinced that most of the differences in speed and memory performance between the new LOTOS/Ada translator and the previous LOTOS/C one are due to the code finally generated by the Ada compilers. At any rate, we expect this performance problems to disappear as the quality of Ada implementations improves.

On the positive side (which we still believe is more significant than the negative), generating Ada code directly from LOTOS allows us to easily link with Ada implemented abstract data types as well as with Ada procedures.

Our LOTOS translator permits the integration of libraries containing already implemented abstract data types, with the code produced. This is particularly important as it regards the speed and size of running code, for it is well known how inefficient implementations of abstract data types by means of rewrite techniques can be. Having the data types already implemented in a programming language means an improvement in execution time of one or two orders of magnitude.

The fact that Ada is very well suited for the development of libraries of abstract data types makes it very attractive to use (fast) implementations of the data types together with LOTOS specifications. Already existing packages of abstract data types such as [9] and [10] show that in Ada this option can be pursued even with widely available software.

Perhaps of much more significance than the libraries of abstract data types implemented in Ada, the new translator allows for simple integration of Ada actions —procedures— into LOTOS specifications. This can be done by using the TOPO mechanism of annotations, which permits to associate procedures in a different programming language —Ada in this case— with LOTOS events. These procedures are then automatically invoked when the corresponding LOTOS events occur. What makes this way of integrating Ada and LOTOS so attractive is that LOTOS can then be used to specify complex synchronisation constraints of software systems — something where LOTOS excels— while the algorithmic part can still be programmed in Ada.

References

[1] ISO. *Information Processing Systems – Open Systems Interconnection – LO-TOS - A Formal Description Technique Based on the Temporal Ordering of Observational Behaviour.* IS-8807. International Standards Organization, 1989.

[2] José A. Mañas and Tomás de Miguel. From LOTOS to C. In Ken J. Turner, editor, *Formal Description Techniques, I,* pages 79–84, Stirling, Scotland, UK, 1989. IFIP, North-Holland. Proceedings FORTE'88, 6–9 September, 1988.

[3] José A. Mañas and Tomás de Miguel. A Tutorial on El Prado. Technical report, Dpt. Telematics Engineering, Techinal Univ. Madrid, Spain, October 1986.

[4] Donald E. Knuth. Semantics of Context-free Languages. *Matematical Systems Theory.* 2(2):127–145, June 1968.

[5] Tomás de Miguel, José A. Mañas, and Tomás Robles. Generación de Her-

ramientas para Software de Comunicaciones. In *Jornadas de I+D en Teleco-municaciones*, Madrid (ES), Noviembre, 12–13 1991. In Spanish.

[6] José A. Mañas and Joaquín Salvachúa. $\Lambda\beta$: A Virtual LOTOS Machine. In Gordon Rose and Ken Parker, editors, *Formal Description Techniques, IV*, Sydney (AU), 1992. IFIP, Elsevier Science B.V. (North-Holland). Proceedings FORTE'91, 19–22 November, 1991.

[7] José A. Mañas and Joaquín Salvachúa. The $\Lambda\beta$-machine in TOPO. Technical report, Dpt. Telematics Engineering Technical Univ. Madrid, Spain, June 1990.

[8] Tomás Robles, Marcelino Veiga, and José A. Mañas. The $\Lambda\delta$-machine in TOPO. Technical report, Dpt. Telematics Engineering Technical Univ. Madrid, Spain, January 1991.

[9] G. Booch. *Software Components with Ada: Structures, Tools, and Subsystems.* Benjamin-Cummings, Menlo Park, 1987.

[10] D. R. Musser and A. A. Stepanov. *The Ada Generic Library: Linear List Processing Packages.* Springer-Verlag, New York, 1989.

Towards Ada 9X
A. Burns, Ed.
IOS Press, 1992

US NAVY
NEXT GENERATION COMPUTER SYSTEMS
PROGRAM
POSIX, REAL-TIME, AND Ada

Daniel Juttelstad
Naval Underwater Systems Center
Newport, Rhode Island, USA

James Oblinger
Naval Underwater Systems Center
Newport, Rhode Island, USA

Abstract

The US Navy has an ongoing program for Next Generation Computer Resources (NGCR) which is intended to establish the future standards for the development of Navy projects. NGCR has several working areas that address components for standardization. This paper presents a brief overview of the NGCR program with concentration in the area of operating systems. This is followed by a cursory discussion of the Institute of Electrical and Electronics Engineers (IEEE) Portable Operating System Interface (POSIX) with emphasis in the areas of Real-Time and Ada work that POSIX is addressing.

1   Next Generation Computer Resources Program Background

The US Navy Next Generation Computer Resources (NGCR) Program sponsor is the Space and Naval Warfare Systems Command, Washington D.C. The objective of this program is to increase the Navy's use of commercially available technology in the development of Navy computer systems rather than developing Navy components. This is being achieved by adopting commercial standards for Navy use. There is no effort to standardize on hardware components, but rather software technology. This leaves the hardware selection up to the Navy system development project and its commercial contractor.

The NGCR program is divided into working groups that address the selection and development of standards within their respective areas. The working groups consist of individuals from industry, academia, and U.S. Navy Laboratories.   Each area is responsible for defining the requirements, and selecting acceptable, commercially available standards that meet these requirements. The intent is that the standards should be first adopted, secondly (if required) adapted, and finally (if required) developed. The strongest emphasis is on the adoption of a standard. It is believed that the greater the acceptance of the standards for the development of commercial products, the greater the benefits to the Navy. The benefits include simplifying vendor selection, development cost reduction, and maintenance cost reduction. The areas that standards development working groups address are depicted in Table 1 along with their respective standards where applicable.

TABLE 1 NGCR STANDARDIZATION AREAS	
BACKPLANE[1,2] (Future Bus II)	1992
LOCAL AREA NETWORK[1,2] (SAFENET)	1992
HIGH PERFORMANCE NETWORK[3]	1993
HIGH SPEED DATA TRANSFER NETWORK[3]	1994
OPERATING SYSTEM[1,2] (POSIX)	1995
HIGH PERFORMANCE BACKPLANE[3]	1997
DATA BASE MANAGEMENT[3]	1998
PROJECT SUPPORT ENVIRONMENT[2]	1998
GRAPHICS LANGUAGE/INTERFACE[3]	1998
1 Certification of products through NGCR 2 In progress 3 FY 91/92 startup	

The NGCR area of standardization that is applicable to this paper is the Operating System. The work in this area is performed by the Operating System Standard Working Group (OSSWG). Their effort is to establish the Navy standard operating system interface. The OSSWG went through an extensive evaluation of available candidate operating system interfaces to select the Navy standard. This evaluation was performed by first defining the Navy system needs and operating system services requirements [1]. In 1990 this evaluation process was completed with the selection of the IEEE Technical Committee for Operating Systems (TCOS) standard 1003, POSIX.

2   POSIX (Portable Operating System Interface) Overview

When referring to the POSIX standard, you are usually referring to one of the group of standards being developed by the IEEE. The goal of these standards is to define a portable user and application environment. POSIX, is currently divided into separate working groups, called "dot groups", numbered from 1003.0 to 1003.18. The goals of each of the working groups is documented in a Project Authorization Request (PAR). The efforts of the dot groups are coordinated by the Standards Coordination Committee (SCC) and the Standards Activities Board (SAB).

Not every dot group is involved in developing a standard. Each dot group will be one of several types depending of the goals of the group. The most common type is the standards group, whose goal is to write a standard. A second dot group type is the Application Environment Profile (AEP) where the goal is to define, for a particular class of applications, such as supercomputing, realtime etc, a subset of all standards in order to achieve interoperability or applications portability to meet the requirements of that application class. This derived set of standards is called a Profile. Another type is the Application Program Interface (API) where the goal is to define the interface between the applications software and the applications platform, across which all services are provided. The complete and formal definitions of these terms can be found in the documents from reference [2].

The remainder of this section gives a brief description of several of the dot groups [3].

2.1   POSIX 1003.0 Guide to POSIX-Based Open System Environment

As the title implies this is a guide document rather than a standards document. It identifies many different standards and specifications which cover the full range of a complete information processing system. The guide can be used by a computer user interested in applying standards to an information processing system or seeking information for generating a Profile.

2.2   POSIX 1003.1   System Services and C Language Binding System Application Program Interface

ISO/IEC 9945-1:1990 (POSIX.1) defines a standard operating system interface and environment originally based on the UNIX Operating System. It supports applications portability at the source-code level between multivendor computer systems.

POSIX.1 establishes a set of basic services fundamental to the efficient construction of applications programs. Access to these services is provided through an operating system using the C programming language. The OS interface establishes standard semantics and syntax, and allows for application developers to design portable applications.

2.3   POSIX 1003.2 Shell and Utilities Interface

POSIX.2 is the base standard and deals with the basic shell programming language and a set of utilities required for the portability of shell scripts. POSIX.2a, the User Portability Extension (UPE) supplements the base standard. It standardizes commands, such as vi, that might not appear in the shell scripts but are important enough to be expected to be available on any real system. POSIX.2b, is a newly approved group covering extensions and requests from other POSIX groups, such as POSIX.4 (Real-Time) and POSIX.6 (Security).

Together POSIX.2 and 2a will make up the International Standards Organization's ISO 9945-2.

2.4   POSIX 1003.3 Test Methods

This standard defines the general requirements and test methods for measuring conformance to POSIX standards. In addition there is description on how to write test assertions. The purpose of this standard is to define general rules for developing test assertions and related test methods for measuring conformance of an implementation to POSIX standards.

The IEEE Standard 1003.3-1991 was published by the IEEE on April 17, 1991.

2.5   POSIX 1003.4 Real-Time Extensions

This standard defines systems interfaces to support the source portability of applications with real-time requirements. The system interfaces are all extensions or additions to ISO/IEC 9945-1:1990(E). The interfaces included in this standard were the minimum set required to make IEEE Std 1003.1-1988 minimally usable to realtime applications on single processor systems.

POSIX 1003.4a "Thread Extensions for Portable Operating Systems" POSIX provides standardized interfaces as extensions or additions to POSIX 1003.1 and POSIX 1003.4 interface standards. This standard provides interfaces to support multiple threads within POSIX 1003.1 processes in order to support the requirements of tightly coupled realtime applications.

2.6   POSIX 1003.5 Ada Bindings

This standard defines an Ada Language binding to the "Portable Operating System Interface for Computing Environments, ANSI/IEEE Std 1003.1-1988 (POSIX.1), for the Ada language.

POSIX 1003.5a This standard defines an Ada Language binding to the "POSIX Realtime Extensions 1003.4a.

2.7   POSIX 1003.6 Security

This standard, as the name implies, defines an interface for security functions. The scope of this interface includes the definition of new system functions and commands for the additional security mechanisms supported by the standard, as well as new, security-related constraints and requirements for the functions and commands defined by the other POSIX standards.

Since the purpose of this standard is to provide for application portability between conforming systems, security requirements in areas that do not pertain to application portability are not addressed.

2.8   POSIX 1003.7 System Administration

The standard defines interfaces for use by the System Administration function. The current set of functions being defined are Print Management, Software Management and User Environment Management.

2.9   POSIX 1003.8 Transparent File Access

This standard is a specification of system services including file behavioral characteristics. It provides a file use specification permitting the use of the widest possible kinds of file systems which can resemble ISO/IEC 9945-1:1990, allowing an application to determine the behavior which it can expect when manipulating a file, and providing the means for an application to simultaneously manipulate files whose access characteristics may differ since they reside in different file systems.

2.10   POSIX 1003.11 Transaction Processing Application Environment Profile

This profile specifies the transaction processing requirements for platforms supporting transaction processing applications and platforms which support transaction processing systems.

2.11   POSIX 1003.12 Network Independent Interfaces

This standard defines an interface which allows portable applications to communicate in a network independently of the underlying protocols.

2.12   POSIX 1003.13 Real-Time Application Environment Profile

This document, a project of the POSIX.4 group, specifies the set of standards and requirements needed for portability of Real-Time applications, users, and system administrators.

2.13   POSIX 1003.14 Multiprocessing Application Environment Profile

This profile specifies the set of standards and requirements needed for portability of multiprocessing applications, users, and system administrators.

3   POSIX, Real-Time, and Ada

Two POSIX areas of standardization of major concern to the US Navy are 1003.4 Real-Time, and 1003.5 Ada Binding. These are of major concern because the primary applications that the US Navy NGCR program are targeting for are their air, surface, and submarine platforms. These platforms have a combination of real-time applications ranging from "soft real-time" to "hard real-time". "Soft real-time" is defined as when the failure to meet a deadline results in a degradation of system performance or functionality. "Hard real-time", on the other hand, implies that failure to meet the deadline results in a system failure. Hard real-time requirements are kept to a minimum in system design as Navy systems are designed to be fault tolerant. Ada bindings are naturally a concern of the US Navy NGCR program because Ada is the US Department of Defense standard language.

3.1 Real-Time and NGCR

The POSIX 1003.4 Real-time working group is investigating real-time extensions to the POSIX 1003.1 standard. Prior to NGCR, and other special interest groups, involvement with POSIX 1003.4 Real-time work area, the groups efforts were mostly in the area of "soft real-time." With these new groups representation "hard real-time" issues are being addressed.

Some of the considered extensions to Real-time POSIX are defined in the following paragraphs.

Binary Semaphores provide a facility for synchronization among multiple processes contending for access to a shared resource. This method appears to be more efficient than the traditional UNIX approach of locking files which is too time consuming and disk intensive to be useful in high performance real-time systems.

Process Memory Locking provides an API which allows the user to designate certain program and/or data memory to be excluded from the normal UNIX virtual memory management paging/swapping algorithms.

Shared Memory interfaces enable a high bandwidth and high performance form of interprocess communication when there is hardware support for this.

Priority Scheduling interfaces permit real-time applications to override the de-facto "time-sharing" UNIX style process scheduling policy with various priority based scheduling policies more appropriate to real-time multitasking. It appears that by doing this can hard real-time deadlines are more able to be guaranteed.

Asynchronous Event Notification extends the classic UNIX signal concept by allowing arbitrary user defined events to be attached to user initiated actions and external events, and subsequently notifying the user process (synchronously or asynchronously) when the event is triggered.

Clocks and Timers provide interfaces to various resolution clocks and interval timers which provide better granularity and more flexibility than the traditional UNIX 1/hz second clock (time) and 1 second interval timer (alarm, sleep). Real-time systems usually have tight timing tolerances that are best met by higher resolution, low jitter clocks and timers.

3   POSIX, Real-Time, and Ada

Two POSIX areas of standardization of major concern to the US Navy are 1003.4 Real-Time, and 1003.5 Ada Binding. These are of major concern because the primary applications that the US Navy NGCR program are targeting for are their air, surface, and submarine platforms. These platforms have a combination of real-time applications ranging from "soft real-time" to "hard real-time". "Soft real-time" is defined as when the failure to meet a deadline results in a degradation of system performance or functionality. "Hard real-time", on the other hand, implies that failure to meet the deadline results in a system failure. Hard real-time requirements are kept to a minimum in system design as Navy systems are designed to be fault tolerant. Ada bindings are naturally a concern of the US Navy NGCR program because Ada is the US Department of Defense standard language.

3.1 Real-Time and NGCR

The POSIX 1003.4 Real-time working group is investigating real-time extensions to the POSIX 1003.1 standard. Prior to NGCR, and other special interest groups, involvement with POSIX 1003.4 Real-time work area, the groups efforts were mostly in the area of "soft real-time." With these new groups representation "hard real-time" issues are being addressed.

Some of the considered extensions to Real-time POSIX are defined in the following paragraphs.

Binary Semaphores provide a facility for synchronization among multiple processes contending for access to a shared resource. This method appears to be more efficient than the traditional UNIX approach of locking files which is too time consuming and disk intensive to be useful in high performance real-time systems.

Process Memory Locking provides an API which allows the user to designate certain program and/or data memory to be excluded from the normal UNIX virtual memory management paging/swapping algorithms.

Shared Memory interfaces enable a high bandwidth and high performance form of interprocess communication when there is hardware support for this.

Priority Scheduling interfaces permit real-time applications to override the de-facto "time-sharing" UNIX style process scheduling policy with various priority based scheduling policies more appropriate to real-time multitasking. It appears that by doing this can hard real-time deadlines are more able to be guaranteed.

Asynchronous Event Notification extends the classic UNIX signal concept by allowing arbitrary user defined events to be attached to user initiated actions and external events, and subsequently notifying the user process (synchronously or asynchronously) when the event is triggered.

Clocks and Timers provide interfaces to various resolution clocks and interval timers which provide better granularity and more flexibility than the traditional UNIX 1/hz second clock (time) and 1 second interval timer (alarm, sleep). Real-time systems usually have tight timing tolerances that are best met by higher resolution, low jitter clocks and timers.

Inter Process Communications (IPC) Message Passing addresses the need for a form of interprocess communication interface that is not inexorably tied to any specific implementation, but which supports loosely coupled, heterogenous, LAN based communications. The traditional UNIX IPC mechanisms, such as pipes, signals, and files, are often too restrictive or heavyweight for use in real-time systems.

Synchronized Input and Output provides interfaces whereby an application can guarantee that a set of data recorded in mass storage is current and self consistent. Traditional UNIX I/O assumes that the "OS knows best," but fails to address the need for embedded real-time systems to more closely control the reading and writing of data which might be needed for recovery purposes or might be written and read by different components of the system.

Asynchronous Input and Output provides alternative I/O interfaces that allow a single process to initiate I/O to one or several devices simultaneously and continue processing while awaiting I/O to complete. This approach appears to be more amenable to real-time systems than the conventional UNIX approach which is to create separate processes to perform each I/O operation as well as queuing and notification functions. Real-time systems often cannot tolerate the extra process context switching overhead associated with the conventional method.

Real-time Files interfaces provide additional information to the OS file system so that the OS can optimize file access for real-time applications by reducing latency, preventing fragmentation, and increasing addressability speed. This serves to improve performance and eliminate non-determinism typically associated with UNIX file access.

POSIX Threads provide a complete API set for lightweight processes that can co-exist with the heavier POSIX process model. Threads within a single POSIX process share a considerable amount of state information (including memory); thus context switching among threads experiences lower overhead, and inter-thread IPC can take advantage of the inherent shared memory. Additionally, threads provide a second level of concurrency model that matched quite nicely with the two levels implicit in the Ada programming language. As an example several tightly coupled Ada tasks per Ada program, several loosely coupled Ada programs per system.

Other real-time extensions that will soon be incorporated into POSIX draft standards include timeouts on blocking interfaces, interrupt handling, memory allocation from differing types of memory, synchronization harmonized between processes and threads, ROMability, dynamic creation of interface objects, and time synchronization between processes.

3.2   Ada and NGCR

UNIX based systems have been popular platforms for Ada language implementations, but there has been a great deal of difficulty, misunderstanding, and controversy surrounding such implementations. UNIX implementations have typically been a poor fit for the services required by the Ada language. This is in part due to the fact that the Ada paradigm is in conflict with the UNIX paradigm. Ada as a language has included many of the components that were normally provided by the operating systems such as

UNIX. Generally, the outcome of this poor fit is that portable Ada programs do not work exactly as might be expected, either from the Ada perspective or from the UNIX perspective. Vendors, realizing this, typically provide additional non-standard libraries to allow Ada programs to be more "UNIX like." Unfortunately, this does very little for portability, even from one Ada compiler implementation to another on the same UNIX operating system.

POSIX has been supporting Ada through the P1003.5 working group, the product of which is to be a standard which makes the functionality of ISO/IEC 9945-1:1990 (1003.1) available to the Ada programmer. There is a new PAR being started within the same working group to do the same for the evolving Real-time Extensions (1003.4 and 1003.4a).

It is important to note what P1003.5 does and does not attempt to do. In particular, P1003.5 provides an Ada language binding to POSIX interfaces; i.e., an Ada like way to invoke POSIX services. It does NOT attempt to define POSIX interfaces suitable for supporting all the Ada run-time capabilities. Generally speaking, the POSIX community seems to feel that the latter is not in its scope. Nonetheless, recent activity in 1003.4 (i.e., concern that Pthreads be usable as Ada tasks) indicates that there is increasing sentiment toward supporting the Ada run-time environment in POSIX. When 1003.5 starts working in the context of the new (Real-time) PAR, and is confronted with a number of 1003.4 capabilities which do map nicely onto Ada run-time requirements, this issue will be once again revived.

It is essential that NGCR OS support not only an Ada language binding to all defined OS interfaces, but also the implicit interfaces that are required by the Ada run-time and the standard Ada library packages. These latter requirements are effectively detailed in OSSWG requirements for service class 16 while the language binding requirements appear in service class 1 [1].

4 Conclusion

Although POSIX interfaces differ substantially from most conventional real-time operating systems used heretofore in Navy systems, the substantial progress achieved by P1003.4 coupled with increased industry impetus toward real-time UNIX implementations would indicate that POSIX will eventually be an acceptable OS interface for all but the smallest and most time critical Navy applications.

Real-time profiles being developed by P1003.13 will stress the need for high performance OS implementations for real-time systems. The interfaces themselves cannot generally be evaluated with respect to performance because performance is a characteristic of an implementation, not an interface. However, performance metrics are being developed as part of the standards, and substantial effort has been expended to ensure that the real-time interfaces do not preclude efficient implementations. Thus, it is reasonable to expect that the Navy will be able to purchase good real-time operating system implementations compliant with the POSIX interface standards. This means that, in spite of the fact that POSIX interfaces are quite unlike those found in conventional real-time operating systems, NGCR OS based on POSIX will support real-time applications once real-time programmers understand and accept the POSIX like interfaces.

With respect to Ada, in cases where an OSSWG requirement is satisfied directly within the language, or from a standard Ada library package, and an explicit binding to the underlying service interface adds no functionality, the explicit binding is not necessary. In support of the goals of application portability and reusability, NGCR applications must avoid the practice of substituting non-standard language constructs and library packages for standard Ada capabilities. Toward this goal, it is essential that the NGCR OS implementations support standard Ada capabilities with very high performance, since performance requirements of real-time systems often take precedence over software engineering goals. Hopefully, as Ada matures into Ada-9x, new standard capabilities will be added to compensate for some of the architecture and OS dependent problems that have previously forced use of non-standard interfaces.

5   Acknowledgements

The authors would like to express their appreciation to the members of the NGCR OSSWG for their contributions which were used in the preparation of this paper. Without the combined industrial, academic, and government effort to establish the methods for selecting and adopting commercially available standards, the NGCR program would not have experienced the success it has to date.

The authors would especially like to acknowledge Mr. Frank Prindle of the Naval Air Development Center (NADC) for his contributions to the OSSWG documentation that was heavily utilized in section 3 of this paper.

References

[1] Juttlestad, D. P. (compiler for Operating System Standards Working Group), Operational Concept Document for the Next-Generation Computer Resources (NGCR) Operating Systems Interface Standard Baseline, Naval Underwater Systems Center Technical Document 6998, 1 April 1991.

[2] IEEE Computer Society. POSIX Standards (Working drafts of the POSIX standards that are currently under development). IEEE Computer Society, 1730 Massachusetts Avenue NW, Washington, DC 20036-1903; Tel: +1 202-371-0101; FAX +1 220 728-9614.

[3] IEEE Computer Society. A "Standards Status Report" that lists all current IEEE Computer Society Standards Projects is available from the IEEE Computer Society, 1730 Massachusetts Avenue NW, Washington, DC 20036-1903; Tel: +1 202 371-0101; FAX: +1 220 728-9614.

Towards Ada 9X
A. Burns, Ed.
IOS Press, 1992

The Development of Secondary Ada Language Bindings

Ms M G Edwards
Royal Military College of Science, Cranfield Institute of Technology, UK

Mrs G Atkinson
Defence Research Authority (Maritime Division), UK

Mr M P Griffiths
Royal Military College of Science, Cranfield Institute of Technology, UK

Abstract

For reasons of lack of availability or finance an Ada language binding
to a chosen commercial utility package may not be available, and the
application programmer may have to consider writing an Ada interface
to a binding provided for another language. Development of such a
"secondary" language binding is a labour intensive task, particularly if
it is to be carried out in a shareable and portable way. This paper
outlines the experiences gained in such an attempt, the major decisions
to be made and the techniques which can be employed.

1   Introduction

It is a regrettable fact that Ada application programmers are still less likely to
find an appropriate language binding for their chosen commercial utility package than
their colleagues using FORTRAN or C. Apart from abandoning use of Ada or of the
utility, such application programmers are faced with the choice of developing an interface
between Ada and the language of the provided binding, herein called a "secondary
binding" - a labour intensive and non-trivial task. This paper is about the experiences of
developing one such binding, and of installing another, of the problems encountered,
solutions found, and recommendations for others who may attempt similar tasks. The
binding developed was for the FORTRAN version of Graphical Kernel System (GKS) as
provided by UNIRAS for VAX VMS under the name UNIGKS. The binding merely
installed was for the UNIX C version of X Windows.

The majority of the work on which this paper is based was carried out by Mrs
Giselle Atkinson and Mr Robert Pratt as part of their respective third year undergraduate
projects [1] [2].

2   Secondary Ada Language Bindings

2.1   Nature and Implications

As provided by utility package suppliers, a language binding enables the application programmer to invoke the facilities of the utility in the syntax of the application language. This binding represents a mapping from the application language to the underlying set of functions made available by the utility. The implementor of such a "primary" binding is concerned only with the features of the application language which can and should be employed in this. In contrast, the implementor of a secondary binding is concerned with mapping between two high level languages, sometimes with widely differing degrees of structure. Some interesting problems arise in creating a mapping from a highly structured language such as Ada to a lesser structured one such as Fortran. (It may be impossible to achieve full functionality in the reverse direction, particularly if the more advanced features of Ada are employed.)

Although the necessary syntax could be written on an "as needed" basis, for extensive software development it is preferable to develop a full secondary binding in a shareable and portable form. The architecture of a suitable software development environment is represented in Figure 1.

Since the resulting system will be a mixed language one, and will require the support of the operating system for language intercommunication, this will inevitably introduce some non-portability, principally because of non-standard features of the provided primary binding, the use of implementation dependent pragmas for the association of languages and names, the representation of some scalar data types and, in some cases, the use of data structure descriptors.

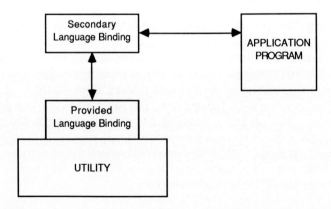

Figure 1: Structure of a System Employing a Secondary Language Binding

2.2   Standard Language Binding Specifications

An early decision to be made by the secondary Ada language binding developer is whether or not to follow an existing standard Ada binding specification, provided that one exists, and that its form does not pose insurmountable problems of implementation. Where it does exist, there must be a strong motivation to follow the standard in the interests of ease of communication within the application community.

GKS itself exists as a standard [3] [4], specified as a set of functions and states in a language independent way.   Also, international standard language binding specifications are available for some of the more significant application languages, including Ada [5]. The approach to the development of this particular standard binding is well described in the literature [6] [7]. Hence, for the authors of this paper, the choice of whether to follow the standard binding specification for GKS was a real one.   In contrast, X Windows is not itself a standard, so it is not yet possible to find standards for its language bindings.   Instead, the authors of this paper used the STARS Ada implementation of the Xlib bindings Version 1.0 , produced jointly by UNISYS and SAIC.

Of interest to the application programmer is whether, in designing the syntax of an Ada binding specification, those responsible have or have not choosen to exploit the particular strengths of Ada. The committee responsible for the ISO Ada/GKS binding specification took the former course, employing a richness of types, generics and names intended to make GKS programming much more robust and visible than it would be in Fortran or C. Interestingly, a different philosophy appears to have been adopted by the committees working on the Ada/SQL binding specifications [8], who set out to make the bindings to various application languages as similar as possible, keeping closely to the structure of the underlying SQL standard. Not surprisingly, this seems to have been of concern within the Ada community, with the result that a model was developed for Ada/SQL of two layers of binding, a "concrete" layer corresponding closely to the underlying utility, and an "abstract" model which fully exploits the Ada typing facilities. Using this terminology, the ISO Ada/GKS binding is an "abstract" one, whereas the Ada/X Windows binding is closer to being a "concrete" one.

The decision was made to follow standard language binding specifications wherever possible, mainly for pedagogic reasons (the implementations were required for use on an undergraduate course which strongly festures the use of Ada). The authors of this paper were thus faced with an interesting contrast between the challenge of developing a "rich" secondary language binding to FORTRAN for GKS, and the relative ease of installing a tailor-made minimal binding to C for X Windows.

2.3   Motivations for the Development of a Syntactically Rich Secondary Ada Binding for Graphics Programming

At the authors' college Ada is the principal programming language used on undergraduate Computing degrees, and it is desirable for it to be employed in specialist final year subjects such as Computer Graphics. Students are encouraged to exploit Ada's typing and exception handling capabilities in their work, and they are not enthusiastic when faced with the need to transfer to structurally weaker languages. The Graphics environments provided for the students by proprietary products include UNIGKS from UNIRAS, with a Fortran binding running under VMS (which conforms closely to the ISO FORTRAN/GKS binding specification [9]), and GKS and PHIGS from SUN Microsystems, with C bindings running under UNIX.

The advantages of having a rich Ada interface to GKS may be summarized as follows, where illustrations conform to the ISO standard Ada/GKS language binding specification:

a)   Use of individual typing for objects of similar structure but distinct semantics aids visibility and guards against misuse. An example is the representation of a coordinate value, which may appear in any of three coordinate systems within a program - world, normalised and device coordinates. In the Ada binding specification use is made of a generic package for such types, which is instantiated for each coordinate system.

b)   When compared with the Fortran binding, visibility is greatly aided by the use of meaningful Ada names, particularly for functions, a simple example of which is "CLOSE_GKS" versus "GCLKS". The Fortran binding syntax is also replete with integer flags, used for the many switches and state settings in which GKS abounds. The Ada binding provides readable enumeration literals in their place.

c)   Ada's extensive data structuring facilities are employed in the expression of structured objects such as coordinate sets for points and polylines and for transformation matrices. This can greatly reduce the number of object references in a program, particularly in parameter lists of subprogram calls.

d)   Strong typing filters many illegal values before they reach the GKS package, so reducing the need to use the GKS error messages.

3   Techniques Employed in Creating the Secondary ADA/GKS Binding

3.1   The Architecture of the Binding

The ISO Ada/GKS Binding Specification has two main packages, one containing types, the other subprogram specifications. As implemented the topology

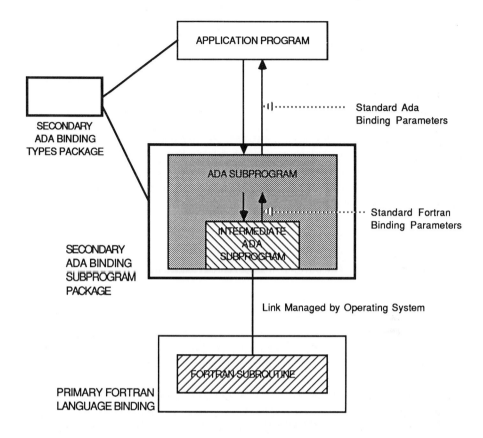

Fig 2: Topology of the Secondary Ada Language Binding to the GKS/Fortran System

of the resulting system is shown in Figure 2.   Each Fortran/GKS subprogram is represented by an Ada subprogram, the two being associated by pragmas.   The complexity of the association depends on the degree of mismatch between the structures present in the two subprogram parameter lists, and may be categorised in three classes:

3.1.1 Simple Association

Where the Fortran subprogram has no parameters or only scalar ones the association is simple and the pragmas alone would suffice e.g. for closing a workstation, assuming a VMS environment:

> *--the top level procedure visible to the application programmer*
> procedure CLOSE_WS (WS : WS_ID);

--the association between equivalent Ada and Fortran subprograms
```
        pragma   INTERFACE (FORTRAN, CLOSE_WS);
        pragma   IMPORT_PROCEDURE ( INTERNAL => CLOSE_GKS,
                                    EXTERNAL => "GCLWK" );
```

3.1.2 Simple Data Mismatch

Where the structure of the Fortran and Ada parameters differ it is necessary to modify the parameter list before the Fortran subprogram is invoked. The procedure visible to the programmer can no longer communicate directly with its Fortran equivalent, but must employ an intermediary. The latter is called following input parameter modification. Where return parameters are involved, some conversion of results may be necessary. The general structure of the procedures is shown below:

--the top level Ada procedure visible to the application programmer
```
procedure  GKS_ADA_ROUTINE    ( ADA_PARAMETER1: in ADA_TYPE);
                                ADA_PARAMETER2: out ADA_TYPE)
is
```
--an internal procedure linked to the GKS/Fortran code
```
        procedure LINK_ROUTINE
                    ( FORTRAN_PARAMETER1      : in FORTRAN_TYPE;
                      FORTRAN_PARAMETER2      : out FORTRAN_TYPE);

        pragma INTERFACE (FORTRAN, LINK_ROUTINE);
        pragma IMPORT_PROCEDURE
                    ( INTERNAL     => LINK_ROUTINE,
                      EXTERNAL     => GKS_FORTRAN_ROUTINE);
begin
```
--any manipulation of the input parameter needed prior to the Fortran call
```
        TEMP_PARAMETER := function of ADA_PARAMETER1;
```
--the call to the Fortran system
```
        LINK_ROUTINE   ( TEMP_PARAMETER,
                         FORTRAN_PARAMETER2);
```
--any manipulation of the output parameter needed following the call
```
        ADA_PARAMETER2 := function of FORTRAN_PARAMETER2;
end GKS_ADA_ROUTINE;
```

3.1.3 Close Coupled Procedures

In the process of the rationalization of types in the Ada binding, some Ada/Fortran subprogram pairs have become misaligned in respect of their parameters. A parameter value which is established in one Fortran subroutine may appear in the parameter list of an Ada procedure with which it is not directly linked. For example, the prompt echo types of virtual input devices are entered in the BUILD_DATA_RECORD procedures of the Ada binding, but in the INITIALISE subroutines in the Fortran.

Fortunately, most of this strong coupling occurs between procedures that have a common parameter whose type is implementation dependent, such as the various DATA_RECORD types. This type can then be designed to include all information needed for transfer between procedures, provided that the procedures are called in the correct order. Where no such common parameter exists it is necessary to make use of a global object. Although it does not have to be visible to the programmer it may be a constraint in that it requires certain events to occur in a prescribed order.

3.2 Data Representation

3.2.1 Numeric Types

The main numeric entities employed in GKS are the three kinds of coordinates. In the FORTRAN binding, all coordinates are represented by REALS. In the ISO Ada binding a generic package provides three distinct kinds of coordinate by instantiation. The actual generic parameter controls the precision of representation. This parameter must be set to a value which closely matches the target language representation.

3.2.2 Enumeration Types and Literals

GKS employs a large number of state variables and flags. Whereas their values are known in the underlying GKS by meaningful names, they appear in the FORTRAN standard as integers. The Ada binding employs enumeration types with literals matching the GKS names, but this means that the Ada enumeration literals must be given the appropriate integer values.

The first thought was that the values should be given by means of the enumeration type attribute POS. However, there is no guarantee that the POS value will match the required integer value so it is safer to use representation clauses e.g.

```
type    SEGMENT_VISIBILITY   is    (VISIBLE, INVISIBLE);
for     SEGMENT_VISIBILITY   use   (VISIBLE =>0, INVISIBLE =>1);
```

In some cases the FORTRAN binding standards authority, unlike their Ada counterparts, chose to alter the order in which the values were listed away from that in the underlying standard. An example is SEGMENT_VISIBILITY itself, which is enumerated as (INVISIBLE, VISIBLE) in FORTRAN, and as (VISIBLE, INVISIBLE) in Ada and in GKS. This opens up a choice of actions. We can deviate from the Ada standard, and restore the ordering to that of the FORTRAN. Alternatively, the Ada standard order can be maintained and the necessary values assigned by means of a case statement. The representation clause would not then be used. Whatever approach is taken, the Ada use of such a function and its FORTRAN counterpart should be semantically equivalent. The application programmer should be warned that violations may still be possible when using unchecked conversion or when relying on the actual ordering of the enumeration literals.

A further requirement for the representation of enumeration literals was discovered after some lengthy fault-finding. The failure of some values to affect the graphical output was finally traced to an optimising act by the Ada compiler in packing each value into 8 bits. The receiving FORTRAN procedure expected a 32 bit parameter, and did in fact receive 32 bits, but the relevant data appeared only in the first 8, the rest ensuring that the result appeared to be garbage. It is thus essential to include a further representation clause with each enumeration type declaration which, in this case was:

for   SEGMENT_VISIBILITY'SIZE   use 32;

3.2.3 Structured Types

There being no record types in FORTRAN each Ada record had to be unpacked into components to be assigned to corresponding FORTRAN parameters. This was done in the body of each relevant Ada procedure, and caused few problems.

Rather more work was involved where one or more of the record components was an array, particularly if such an array was of variable length. For example, the coordinate values of primitives such as POLYLINE are stored as an array of (X,Y) records in Ada but as two separate arrays, for X and Y coordinates respectively, in FORTRAN. In the latter case the length of an array has to be specified as an extra parameter. In carrying out the conversion, local arrays were used, constrained and indexed with the help of attribute values from the Ada parameters, as illustrated for the procedure POLYLINE, as shown below. Such copying between arrays, required for the most commonly used primitives, represents a major overhead in the use of this particular secondary binding.

```
procedure POLYLINE (POINTS : in WC.POINT_ARRAY) is
    type FIGURE_ARRAY is array (1..POINTS'LENGTH) of WC_TYPE;
    X_COORD, Y_COORD : FIGURE_ARRAY;
    procedure F_POLYLINE (NUMBER_OF_POINTS  : in INTEGER;
                    X_COORD, Y_COORD: in FIGURE_ARRAY;
    pragma INTERFACE   ( FORTRAN, F_POLYLINE);
    pragma IMPORT_PROCEDURE (   INTERNAL  => F_POLYLINE,
                    EXTERNAL => "GPL");
begin
    for COUNT in 1..POINTS'LENGTH loop
        X_COORD(COUNT) := POINTS(POINTS'FIRST + (COUNT-1)).X;
        Y_COORD(COUNT) := POINTS(POINTS'FIRST + (COUNT-1)).Y;
    end loop;
    F_POLYLINE (POINTS'LENGTH, X_COORD, Y_COORD);
end POLYLINE;
```

The above example is representative of cases where application level parameters had to be modified before being passed to the target system, and where the use of intermediate structures provided an easy mechanism. The next section is concerned with a case where the manipulation of a returning parameter is required before it can be passed to the application level.

No problems were encountered in the passing of single dimension arrays, but two dimensional arrays, such as the main structure of the output primitive CELL_ARRAY, needed care. In VAX VMS the array parameter must be passed using the correct mechanism, by reference, and the rows and columns of the array must be reversed.

3.2.4 Strings

Some work had to be done to allow user-defined Ada strings for device and channel names in place of their Fortran integer equivalents. The correspondence was made in the GKS initialization routines using case statements.

The most complex feature of string handling across the language boundary was concerned with passing an output parameter of variable length from FORTRAN to Ada. An example of where this occurs is with the GKS input procedure REQUEST_STRING. A simple but implementation dependent approach would be to let the user select one of a range of fixed length Ada string variables to receive the returning value. A more general approach is to use an intermediate string of maximum length, constrained by, for instance, STRING_SMALL_NATURAL'LAST.

4   Experiences with the Rich Ada/GKS Binding

4.1   Scope of Development

Because of the size of the Ada/GKS binding specification an early decision was made to identify a useful achievable sub-set. GKS can be roughly divided into output, input, data manipulation, workstation control, metafile and inquiry functions. Examination of previous GKS programs written in FORTRAN revealed that little use had been made of most of the inquiry functions. Since the latter represent over half the GKS procedures in the UNIRAS implementation, leaving most of them out provided a considerable saving without significantly reducing the value of the remaining subset.

Although some experimentation was carried out on the metafile functions, these were also eliminated from full development, mainly because of their non-standard representation within the UNIGKS package.

If the intended applications had not involved user interaction then the next candidate for elimination could have been the set of input functions.

Conformance testing [10] was carried out on the final product, using equivalent programs written for the Ada secondary binding and for the FORTRAN binding.

4.2   Areas of Difficulty Encountered

The major difficulties encountered were concerned with debugging in a mixed language environment, complicated by a lack of visibility of the effects of errors. It was possible for syntactically correct Ada to send inappropriate values to the GKS Fortran binding and for no error message to be generated by the Ada or Fortran language system or by GKS. The major feedback in such cases was a failure to produce the expected graphics, and in the absence of detailed evidence the ensuing debugging was sometimes time-consuming. The majority of such errors were discovered eventually to be related to incorrect presentation of data structures or data representation.

The Ada language system itself occasionally caused problems, and the solutions were in general highly installation dependent. It was to be expected that care would be needed in passing Ada unconstrained arrays and multi-dimensional arrays to the Fortran system. Other dificulties were completely unanticipated, such as the occasional need to pass array parameters of zero length, for which the method was discovered only after much trial and error.

Apart from the difficulties outlined above, there were certain things that could not be done or done fully due to the realities of the language mismatch between Ada and Fortran. Obviously one cannot translate code representing features not present in the target language such as exception handling.

5   Efficiency Considerations of the Rich Binding

Whenever a task like this is attempted, a common question is "How much does it cost?". This section assesses some of the space and time penalties which are associated with the bindings as developed.

5.1   Code Size

The additional object code produced by the intermediate Ada packages was of the order of 16kbytes. A significant fraction of this, about 15%, is elaboration code for the numerous procedures and a similar amount for the interface for OPEN_WS, where the translation from a string in Ada to an integer in FORTRAN requires a lot of comparisons. Most of the rest is devoted to parameter shuffling in order to implement the parameter mismatches as described in section 3.1.2

This amount of code is not excessive when compared to the size of the GKS package itself, and thus the code overhead is not really a problem.

5.2   Execution Time

This aspect is potentially more serious. Most of the procedures have little binding code associated with them, and those which have a significant amount are only rarely invoked e.g. OPEN_WS. However, as we all know, small code size does not necessarily imply small execution time, and a few much used procedures are potentially very expensive. These are the ones which require the format conversion of coordinate vectors by array copying e.g. POLYLINE, POLYMARKER. There seems to be no alternative to array copying. If the number of coordinate pairs is large (it may be thousands of floating point values in some applications), this will be extremely expensive both in terms of execution time, and in the necessity to create additional arrays of the appropriate size to store the intermediate FORTRAN format.

6   Experiences with the Minimal X Windows/Ada Binding

The STARS binding was designed to meet the requirements of the very environment for which we required it. Furthemore, the code for it already existed, and merely had to be copied to its new destination. It was not surprising that few problems were experienced, and that those were relatively minor. In resolving the problems the authors were greatly aided by the close match between the Ada and C functions, which made the documentation easy to follow. Before embarking on own development of a secondary binding, application programmers are recommended to explore whether such a simple solution to their needs exists and is acceptable.

7   Summary

This paper is principally concerned with some of the techniques required to develop a syntactically rich secondary Ada language binding. Such a development requires careful use of data representation techniques. It will almost certainly be somewhat implementation dependent, and may not lead to full functionality of result, particularly where error handling is concerned.

The major overhead was discovered to lie with the extensive array copying which must be done in order to convert between the variable length arrays of Ada and their fixed length FORTRAN equivalents. For applications requiring the rapid generation of large sets of coordinates this overhead may not be acceptable.

There is motivation to follow an official standard binding specification in such development work. However, standards are provided primarily for package developers, working in single programming language contexts, and may contain features which will be difficult to implement across a mixed language interface, particularly one involving Ada. Some of these difficulties could be avoided if standards developers are prepared to sacrifice a small degree of syntactic and aesthetic "richness" in favour of simplicity and lower overheads. Even then, it is doubtful whether development of rich secondary Ada bindings can be justified except in special cases.

References

[1]   G Atkinson
        The implementation of an Ada Language Binding to the Graphical Kernel
        System   1990
        42 Degree Course Student Project   RMCS (Cranfield Institute of Technology)

[2]   R Pratt
        The Installation and Documentation of an Ada Interface to the X-Windows
        System   1991
        43 Degree Course Student Project,   RMCS (Cranfield Institute of Technology)

[3]   Graphical Kernel System Functional Description ISO 7942

[4]   P R Bono, J L Encarnacao, F R A Hopgood, P J W ten Hagen
        GKS The First Graphics Standard
        IEE Computer Graphics and Applications, July 1982

[5]   GKS - Ada Binding Specification   ISO 8651/3

[6]   T M Leonard
        Ada and the Graphical Kernel System
        Ada in Use : Proceedings of the Ada International Conference 1985

[7]   B M Brosgol, G R Cuthbert
        The development of the Ada Binding of the Graphical Kernel System   Ada
        User Vol 8 Supplement 1987 (6th Ada (UK) Int. Conf.)

[8]   J W Moore
        The ANSI Binding of SQL to Ada   Ada Letters, Volume XI, No 5, 1991

[9]   GKS-FORTRAN Binding Specification   ISO 8651/1

[10]   F Kruckeberg
        Principles of Conformity Testing   Computers and Graphics, Vol 8 No 1, 1984

Towards Ada 9X
A. Burns, Ed.
IOS Press, 1992

A Real-Time Solution of Robot Inverse Kinematics using Ada and Transputers

T.M. Hamdi, S.A. Velastin

Department of Electronic and Electrical Engineering,
King's College London,
Strand, London WC2R 2LS,
United Kingdom

Abstract

Ada has been generally associated with large and very large systems. In this paper we explore its use for small-size applications, typified by a robot controller, and concentrate on the aspects of ease of design and portability.

The paper presents the implementation and testing of approximate parallel solutions for an inverse kinematics algorithm, using Ada under VAX/VMS and targeted to a multi-transputer system. The approach can be used for robots that have a closed-form solution.

1. Introduction

Most robots in current industrial use are provided with programming aids that assume that the position of each workpiece with respect to the robot is either constant or involves simple linear motion, e.g. on a conveyor system. The overall objective of our current research work is to develop both the programming methods and the equipment required to control fixed-arm robots in such a way that each individual workpiece may have a new position and orientation with respect to the robot and may even be moving in an unpredictable way while the robot is performing its task.

An important aspect in the achievement of this goal deals with mappings between vectors in two spaces: joint space θ and cartesian space x, where θ represents the position of the joints of the robot manipulator and x represents the position and orientation of the end effector of the robot manipulator. The mapping from joint space to Cartesian space is referred to as the Direct Kinematics Algorithm while the mapping from Cartesian space to joint space is referred to as Inverse Kinematics Algorithm (IKA) [1]. In an adaptive robot, tasks and on-line sensor corrections are usually specified in the Cartesian space, whereas the robot manipulator is actuated in joint space. Therefore, the execution of the IKA in real time is very important for the system to be able to react to random changes in workpiece position and orientation without hindering full-speed operation.

The characterisation of the IKA is analytically complex and closed-form solutions do not always exist, forcing the use of numerical iterative procedures [2,3]. For dextrous and adaptive operation, the IKA usually needs to be executed for every sampling period Δt along a given trajectory in a 6-D cartesian space. Even for a robot with closed-form solution, it takes typically about 8 - 10 ms [4] to obtain an inverse solution. This output rate is usually not fast enough for a control system with typical sampling period of the order of 1 ms.

To decrease execution times parallel processing supported by a multiprocessor architecture could be used. The computational time can be reduced by distributing the IKA over a number of concurrent processes. Further investigation into the means to achieve generic designs and suitable implementations led us to the selection of a combination of Ada and the transputer.

Ada has been implemented for a wide range of different systems, it does not need "extensions" for concurrent programming and its main features are not tied to a specific processor. This compares favourably with other languages such as C, Pascal or occam (the language which was developed closely to the Transputer [5]) . In addition to its advanced software safety aspects, these features are of major benefit for the rapid prototyping of concurrent systems without the need of early commitment to specific physical processing topologies. Practical issues related to the portability of Ada are explored in this paper in the context of the migration of software from VAX/VMS to a transputer-based system.

The transputer is specifically designed for the implementation of multiprocessor systems, with each transputer supporting four high speed serial links to other transputers and whose operation is, in principle, well-matched to the rendezvous synchronisation mechanism of Ada. Transputer-based systems can be upgraded in performance with relative ease by the addition of additional processing elements. Furthermore, highly concurrent applications can be tested thorough the use of time-slicing on a single transputer.

This paper presents the design, implementation and testing of approximate parallel solutions for inverse kinematics problem, with algorithms for the RTX robot as examples. In section 2 parallel solutions for inverse kinematics algorithms are reviewed, and an appropriate solution in section 3 is described for calculating the IKA for an RTX robot. Section 4 discusses the implementation of the solution using Ada under VAX/VMS and Ada under a multi-transputer system. Section 5 discusses the speed up factor from this implementation, and Section 6 describes the characteristics of the error incurred by the approximate parallel solutions.

2. A Parallel Inverse Kinematic Solution

The computation of the IKA, when a closed form solution is available, involves the evaluation of the following set of equations at each instant t_k:

$$\theta_i(t_k) = g_i (D(x_k), \theta_1(t_k), ..., \theta_{i-1}(t_k)) \qquad \text{for } i = 1, 2, ..., n \qquad (1)$$

where D is a 4 by 4 "Cartesian Demands" matrix which represents the required orientation and position of the end effector (Appendix A) and n is the total number of robot joints.

To evaluate (1), g_1 through g_n are evaluated in ascending joint number order since each g_i depends on the solutions of g_1 through g_{i-1}. In other words, the evaluation of the inverse kinematics is, as illustrated in fig. 1, intrinsically sequential and this makes it difficult to exploit the parallelism offered by a multiprocessor system.

In recent years, some robot control systems have been simulated or implemented based on multiprocessor architectures. In the context of computing the IKA, a pipelined architecture based on Coordinated Rotation Digital Computers (CORDIC) is described by Lee [6] for robot manipulators with closed form solutions. Harber [7] further revised the architecture and presented its implementation on a bit-slice VLSI chip. Although the

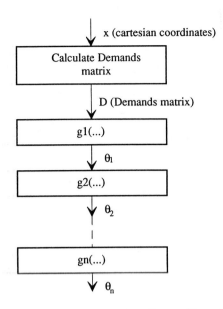

Fig. 1: <u>Sequential Computation of inverse kinematics</u>

architecture increases the throughput of the system, roughly in proportion to the number of processors, its major drawback is that it does not significantly reduced the latency of the inverse kinematics, defined as the difference between the time at which a desired x is available and the time at which the corresponding joint positions θ are computed.

2.1 An approximate parallel solution

An approximate parallel solution was proposed by Zang [8] on the assumption that robot joint positions do not change substantially from one sampling period (t_{k-1}) to the next (t_k), due to the continuity of the joint trajectories. The dependency among the joint solutions g_i can be thus removed by using joint values calculated in the previous sampling period. Analytically, (1) can be approximated by

$$\theta_i(t_k)= g_i \ (D(x_k), \theta_1(t_{k-1}),...,\theta_{i-1}(t_{k-1})) \qquad \text{for } i = 1,2, ... ,n \qquad (2)$$

Through this reformulation, all g_i in (2) can be evaluated simultaneously in parallel once D becomes available. Throughout this paper, this solution will be referred to as the "Last Value" method.

The obvious danger in the algorithm is the introduction of errors due to the approximation of $\theta_i(t_k)$ by $\theta_i(t_{k-1})$. But as discussed in [4], the errors caused by (2) do not accumulate or deteriorate over time.

2.2 A Parallel solution by linear extrapolation

The error in the Last Value solution described in the previous section is caused by the assumption that $\theta_i(t_{k-1})$ has not changed when $t=t_k$. The situation can be improved if

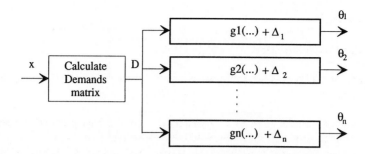

Fig. 2: <u>Parallel computations for Inverse Kinematics (Linear Extrapolation)</u>

information about the velocity in both joint space and Cartesian space is used. Analytically,

$$\theta_i(t_k) = g_i(D(x_k), \theta_1(t_{k-1}), ..., \theta_{i-1}(t_{k-1})) + \Delta_i \qquad \text{for } i = 1,2,...,n \qquad (3)$$

where the first term is the original Last Value parallel solution and Δ_i represents an error compensation term. Equation (3) is useful however, only if Δ_i can be determined from the information available at t_{k-1} and from D at t_k, as illustrated in fig. 2. Clearly, when all Δ_i are zero, this scheme is equivalent to the approximate solution described in the previous section.

Zang [4] derived a first order approximation for Δ_i (proportional to the change of velocity and of position) valid for linear motion and small sampling periods. Two questions arise from this new approximation (a) How accurate are these approximations? and (b) What is the increase in execution times due to of the additional computation of the error compensation term? Both questions will be discussed in the context of the inverse kinematics for the RTX robot.

3. Inverse Kinematics of the RTX robot

The RTX is a robot with six degrees of freedom. The first three joints are of a translation-roll-roll (TRR) type and are followed by a wrist of a roll-pitch-yaw (RPY) type. The three axes of the wrist joints intersect at a single point, which means that a closed form solution is possible [1]. In general there are three ways to solve the inverse kinematic problem, that is, the algebraic approach, the geometric approach, and the iterative approach. For this type of robot the geometric approach is specially effective. We have used the equations, with some corrections described in appendix B, derived by Song [9] using the geometric approach.

Further analysis of these equations, leads to the following conclusions:

a) The computation time of g_1 is insignificant (compared to the other joints) and can be considered to be part of the computation of matrix D
b) The computation of g_3 does not depend on g_2 and, therefore, these two expressions can be evaluated in parallel. Therefore, from (a), the values for these first three joints can be calculated without the need for approximation.

4. Implementation

4.1 Standard implementation

The IKA for the RTX was implemented and tested using Vax Ada. This took the form of two programs:

a) An strictly sequential IKA as in equation (1), fig. 1. This program is used as a reference to evaluate the errors introduced by approximate solutions.
b) A parallel program that implements the Linear Extrapolation solution as in equation (3) and the Last Value solution as in equation (2). The operator decides, at run time, which of the two methods is used. As discussed earlier, the approximate solution is obtained by setting the Δ terms to zero.

These programs were then transferred, recompiled and executed on a system with a single transputer. These required practically no changes in the source code supporting the case for the use of a fully standardised language.

4.2 Implementation on a multi-transputer system

Ideally, the migration of the software to a multi-transputer system should require little modification ins the source code except for a description of the network topology. However, there were three significant problems:

i) The Alsys Ada compiler [10], does not implement the rendezvous mechanism for inter-task communication between tasks resident on different transputers.
ii) The transputer architecture is one of a distributed memory type i.e. data cannot be easily shared between processes resident on different transputers.
iii) The Alsys Ada compiler (version 5.3) makes the Transputer think that each Ada partition is an Occam process.

Regarding the above problems the following changes needed to be made:

i) Partitionning of the Ada programs

Implementation on a multi-transputer system involved the partitioning of the parallel Ada program into a set of programs, each program running on one transputer, communicating via transputer channels.

If two or more partitions need to share a writable passive object, then the solution is either to build all these partitions into a single larger one, so that the passive object can also be incorporated within it, or to decide which partition should own the data and make other partitions access it via a "channel" mechanism (discussed later).

In practice that meant that shared variables between tasks, in the RTX parallel program, were implemented by one of the following techniques:

a) One of the tasks was designated as the owner of the data and all accesses by other tasks to had to be recoded using the CHANNELS package (see below)
b) Tasks which share the data were forced to be mapped to a common partition (program), so that the data becomes local to that partition.

ii) The Channels Communications

On a transputer, inter-process communication takes place based on "channels". Channels mapped to transputer links (for inter-processor communications) are known as hard channels. Processes communicating with each other on the same transputer use internal channels, also known as soft or "memory" channels. Alsys Ada [10], provides a CHANNELS Ada package to interface to the transputer channel facilities. Each inter-partition rendezvous (ie the entry and accept statements) must be converted into operations using the CHANNELS package. For example

CALLER   **ACCEPTOR**

Standard Ada

acceptor.RW(<params>)   accept RW(<param>)
                                    <Rendezvous code>
                                    end RW;

Transputer

write (<chan>. <params>)   read (<chan>, <params>)
.....   <Rendezvous code>
read (<chan>, <params>)   write (<chan>. <params>)

iii) The Occam harness

A set of Ada programs can be run in parallel on a single transputer or distributed across a multi-transputer network in the same way as any other transputer process [10]. To obtain this type of operation an occam process called a "harness" is used as wrapping for the Ada program. Thus each Ada program running in parallel has a small "mini-harness". A "main" harness (Fig 3) is then used to invoke each of the mini-harnesses in parallel. It is this main harness that defines the combination of soft links (within one transputer) and hard links (multi-transputer) that are used in a given multi-processing network.

5. Performance

The following is a summary of the development systems used for this application:

a) Vax Ada version 1.0 running on VAX/VMS version 5.4.
b) Paratech Sprint2 transputer board (T805 transputer @ 20MHz, 4Mbytes of 80 ns memory) installed on a PC on a Novell network.
c) Alsys Ada compiler for PC Transputer hosts version 5.3.

Table 1 shows average execution times for a set of more than 20 robot jobs (each of approximately 200 pieces of input data). For the parallel programs (last 3 columns), these values correspond to the transputer-specific versions (using the Alsys CHANNELS package) running on a single transputer.

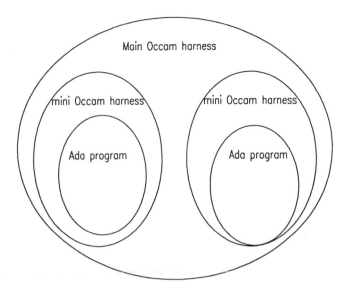

Fig. 3: The Occam harnesses required to run two Aada partitions
(on one Transputer or two)

We found that the implementation of trigonometric functions was such that computation times varied according to the value of the arguments. For example, the calculation of sine for angles over 60 degrees takes up to 10 times as much as for angles less than 60 degrees. Also taken into account was the worst case for computing the D matrix (in some cases it might be negligible). Consequently, times quoted correspond to "worst case" conditions. To illustrate the importance of this problem, we also quote "typical" computation times for one of the programs.

As expected, the values for the Sequential and Last Value programs are very close since the same equations are used except for the values for task 1 where the approximate solution requires additional computations related to the use of previous results.

For the Linear Extrapolation parallel solution, there are more initial calculations to perform (task 1) but there are no differences for tasks 2 and 3 since no error corrections are required. Differences arise for tasks 4, 5 and 6 because of the extra time taken to compute Δ_4, Δ_5 and Δ_6.

Program section (all times in milliseconds)	Sequential (worst case)	Last Value (worst case)	Linear Extrapolation (worst case)	Linear Extrapolation (typical)
Task 1 (D, g1)		22.990	24.037	4.390
Task 2 (θ_2)		1.074	1.079	1.079
Task 3 (θ_3)	55.763	0.953	0.947	0.953
Task 4 (θ_4)		8.105	8.168	1.237
Task 5 (θ_5)		8.053	8.147	1.032
Task 6 (θ_6)		15.700	15.816	4.026

Table 1: Execution times

Transputer 1	Transputer 2
procedure PARTITION_1 is	procedure PARTITION_2 is
-- task comp_theta2 --	-- task comp_theta3 --

task comp_theta4
begin
       read inputs (use $\theta_3(t_{k-1})$);
       computation of equations;
       output results;
end comp_theta4;
	begin
	       read inputs (use $\theta_3(t_{k-1})$,
	       $\theta_4(t_{k-1})$ and $\theta_5(t_{k-1})$);
	       compute theta6;
	       output results to the first
	       transputer;

-- task comp_theta5 --	end PARTITION_2
begin	
-- Input $x(t_k)$; -- computation of D matrix; -- Inter_communications; --communication with partition2; -- output results; end PARTITION_1;	

Fig4: Implementing the RTX algorithm on two transputers

From the results shown in table 1, we can conclude that the use of two processors would yield an improvement of approximately to 50% in calculation times for tasks 2 to 6. For example (Fig 4), this could be achieved if tasks 2, 4, and 5 were executed on one transputer and tasks 3 and 6 on another (the initial calculations must be performed first and thus can be executed on either processor). For the complete programs (including task 1) this would represent a 31% improvement and 29% improvement for the Last Value and the Linear Extrapolation programs respectively. A similar speed-up factor can be calculated for "typical" values (e.g. last column).

After some extra work it was found that the computation of the D matrix can be divided using two tasks running in parallel (each taking approximately 12 millisecond), which means that if three transputers were used with appropriate partitions then it is possible to reduce the execution timings to less than 20 milliseconds.

6. Error characteristics

The error between joint values obtained from the sequential (exact) program and the approximation and linear extrapolation programs, has the following characteristics:

a) As argued in [4], the error is not accumulative.
b) Fig. 5 shows the error between the exact and the approximate solutions, for joint number 4, as the end position of the robot changes. As expected, the Linear Extrapolation method produces a better result than the Last Value method.
c) The error for small end-effector speeds is small, usually less than 1 degree. The error increases as velocity increases. This can be seen by comparing figures 5 (b) and 6.

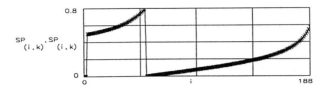

(a) Error (degrees): Last Value solution

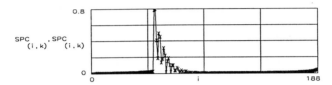

(b) Error (degrees): Linear Extrapolation solution

Fig. 5: Error results

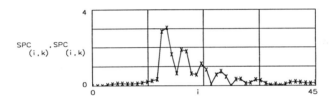

Fig. 6: Error (degrees): Linear Extrapolation solution (quadruple speed)

Conclusions

The IKA for the RTX robot was implemented in Vax Ada in sequential and parallel forms. The algorithms were then transferred successfully to a transputer system, recompiled and executed with minimal changes in the source code.

To run the parallel programs on a multi-transputer system, some extensive changes had to be made to suit the non-global memory architecture of the transputer. The inter-process communications scheme also had to be changed using the (non-standard) Alsys Ada package CHANNELS. This modification is quite straightforward because of the similarity to the entry and accept statements used in Ada. However, channel-based task synchronisation does not have the type-safe characteristics of the Ada tasking mechanism and therefore this is a major disadvantage from a software engineering point of view.

Finally, with the current Alsys implementation of Ada, writing a multi-transputer program needs some detailed knowledge of the Occam language in order to download a set of Ada programs in a transputer network. Therefore, we believe that true support for Ada tasking on multiple-transputer systems will be a major factor for the language to gain popularity in the transputer user community.

The execution timings for the programs were recorded and it was shown that a maximum of two transputers are needed to reduce the execution times by one third. The actual timings, however, fall outside application requirements. Future work will investigate other areas of potential parallelism in the algorithm, compare these execution times with pure Occam implementations and consider the use of different processing elements (e.g. DSPs).

Appendix A: Cartesian Demands Matrix

Let $x_k = [px\ py\ pz\ \phi x\ \phi y\ \phi z]^T$ be the vector of Cartesian demands where px, py and pz describe end-effector position and ϕx, ϕy and ϕz describe end-effector rotations about the x,y and z axis of a global reference frame. Then,

$$D(x_k) = \begin{matrix} n_x & s_x & a_x & d_x \\ n_y & s_y & a_y & d_y \\ n_z & s_z & a_z & d_z \\ 0 & 0 & 0 & 1 \end{matrix}$$

where,

$n_x = \cos(\phi y)*\cos(\phi z);$
$n_y = \cos(\phi z)*\sin(\phi x)*\sin(\phi y)+\cos(\phi x)*\sin(\phi z);$
$n_z = -\cos(\phi x)*\sin(\phi y)*\cos(\phi z)+\sin(\phi x)*\sin(\phi z);$

$s_x = -\cos(\phi y)*\sin(\phi z);$
$s_y = -\sin(\phi x)*\sin(\phi y)*\sin(\phi z)+\cos(\phi x)*\cos(\phi z);$
$s_z = \cos(\phi x)*\sin(\phi y)*\sin(\phi z) + \sin(\phi x)*\cos(\phi z);$

$a_x = \sin(\phi y);$
$a_y = -\sin(\phi x)*\cos(\phi y);$
$a_z = \cos(\phi y)*\cos(\phi x);$

$d_x = p_x - d_6*a_x$ (where d_6 is the wrist length)
$d_y = p_y - d_6*a_y$
$d_z = p_z - d_6*a_z$

Appendix B: Corrected RTX Inverse Kinematics Equations

Equations (21) and (23) in [9] were found to be incorrect. These should be replaced by:

$\alpha = \cos^{-1}((A_2^2+A_3^2-L^2)/(2A_2A_3))$
$\gamma = \cos^{-1}((L^2+A_2^2-A_3^2)/(2LA_2)))$

Appendix C: Examples of parallel Ada programs on the Transputer

As discussed before, the Ada programs had to be partitioned to run in parallel on the transputer. The programs in this case are divided into two partitions. he first partitions contains the computation for joints 1, 2, 3, 5 and 6. The second partition contains the computation for joint 4. There are six programs in this appendix.

1- The Ada program for partition 1. Because of lack of space only the most important parts of the program are included.

2- The Ada program for partition 2.

3- An Occam dummy loop for partition 2.

4- The Occam program for the channels description for partition 2 (this is the mini harness).

5- Partition 1 has similar programs to 3 & 4 which are not shown here. Two further occam programs, the main harness programs, are shown here to handle input and output from and to the Transputer, and to combine all the four Occam programs. For more explanations on these programs please refer to [10].

Program 1: RTXCHAN.ADA

```
-- This program implements the algorithm in the paper
-- INVERSE KINEMATICS OF THE RTX ROBOT :geometric approach & the solution
-- of non-uniqueness, to compute joints 2,3,5 and 6

with INTEGER_TEXT_IO, FLOAT_TEXT_IO, LONG_FLOAT_TEXT_IO, TEXT_IO,
    LONG_FLOAT_MATH_LIB, CALENDAR, CHANNELS, FLOAT_IO, INTEGER_IO;

procedure RTXCHAN is

use INTEGER_TEXT_IO, FLOAT_TEXT_IO, LONG_FLOAT_TEXT_IO, TEXT_IO,
    LONG_FLOAT_MATH_LIB, CALENDAR, CHANNELS, FLOAT_IO, INTEGER_IO;

    -- robot definitions

    C2: CHANNELS.CHANNEL_REF:= CHANNELS.OUT_PARAMETERS(3);
    -- output channel (link 3 on the transputer) to other partition
    C : CHANNELS.CHANNEL_REF := CHANNELS.IN_PARAMETERS (3);
    -- input channel (link 3 on the transputer) from other partition

    RESULT : FLOAT;

    task COMP_THETA2 is
      entry NEW_THETA2;
      entry RESULT2 (ANGLE2 : in out LONG_FLOAT);
    end COMP_THETA2;

    task body COMP_THETA2 is
      TIME1, TIME2      : TIME;
      INTERVAL          : DURATION;
      BETA, GAMMA, THETA2, K : LONG_FLOAT;
      LENGTH, S, SIZE, P2X   : LONG_FLOAT;

    begin
      loop
        accept NEW_THETA2;
        -- lENGTH := px;
        -- p2x:= px**2;
        -- TIME1:=CLOCK;
        LENGTH := SQRT ((PX ** 2) + (PY ** 2));
        -- put(px);new_line; put(length); new_Line;
        -- S:= (A2+A3+LENGTH)/2.0;
        --  comp_theta3.comp_alpha(L,S) ;
        ERROR2 (NO_OF_ANG) := 'f';
        if PX = 0.0 then
          if PY > 0.0 then
            BETA := PI / 2.0;
          elsif PY < 0.0 then
            BETA := - PI / 2.0;
          end if;

        else
          BETA := ARCTAN (PY / PX);
```

```
    end if;
    -- old  gamma:= abs(2.0*atan( (1.0/(S-A3))*sqrt( (S-A2)*(S-A3)*(S-L)/S)));
    -- gamma:= abs(acos((L**2+A2**2-A3**2)/(2*L*A2)));
    LENGTH := LENGTH / (2.0 * A2);
    if abs (LENGTH) > 1.0 then
       COORD_ERROR      := TRUE;
       ERROR2 (NO_OF_ANG) := 'c';
    else
       GAMMA := abs (ARCCOS (LENGTH)); -- for rtx at the university
       if PX >= 0.0 then
          K := 0.0;
       elsif PX < 0.0 then
          if PY > 0.0 then
             K := 1.0;
          elsif PY < 0.0 then
             K := - 1.0;
          end if;
       end if; -- for px
       THETA2 := BETA - POS_ARM * GAMMA + PI * K;
       if THETA2 < - PI / 2.0 or THETA2 > PI / 2.0 then
          ERROR2 (NO_OF_ANG) := 'o';
          ARM_ERROR        := TRUE;
       end if; -- for range of theta
    end if; -- for checking the cosine
    accept RESULT2 (ANGLE2 : in out LONG_FLOAT) do
       ANGLE2 := CONVD * THETA2;
    end RESULT2;
    --  time2:=clock;
    -- interval:= time2-time1;
    -- put(" time taken  ");put(long_float(interval)); new_line;
    end loop;
end COMP_THETA2;

task COMP_THETA3 is
  entry RESULT3 (ANGLE3 : in out LONG_FLOAT);
  entry NEW_THETA3;
end COMP_THETA3;

task COMP_THETA5 is
  entry NEW_THETA5 (THETA2 : in LONG_FLOAT;
             THETA3 : in LONG_FLOAT;
             THETA4 : in LONG_FLOAT);
  entry RESULT5 (ANGLE5 : in out LONG_FLOAT);
end COMP_THETA5;


task COMP_THETA6 is
  entry NEW_THETA6 (THETA2 : in LONG_FLOAT;
             THETA3 : in LONG_FLOAT;
             THETA4 : in LONG_FLOAT;
             THETA5 : in LONG_FLOAT);
  entry RESULT6 (ANGLE6 : in out LONG_FLOAT);
end COMP_THETA6;

-- main program body

begin

    -- below is the sequential part of program, which is always needed for the initial data
```

```
    if PARALLEL = FALSE then

        COMP_THETA2.NEW_THETA2;
        COMP_THETA2.RESULT2 (THETAI (SHOULDER));

        COMP_THETA3.NEW_THETA3;
        COMP_THETA3.RESULT3 (THETAI (ELBOW));

        FLOAT_IO.WRITE (C2, FLOAT(THETAI(SHOULDER)));
        FLOAT_IO.WRITE (C2, FLOAT(THETAI(ELBOW)));
        FLOAT_IO.READ (C, RESULT);
        THETAI(WRIST_SWING):=LONG_FLOAT(RESULT);

        COMP_THETA5.NEW_THETA5 (THETAI (SHOULDER), THETAI (ELBOW), THETAI
            (WRIST_SWING));
        COMP_THETA5.RESULT5 (THETAI (WRIST_TILT));

        COMP_THETA6.NEW_THETA6 (THETAI (SHOULDER), THETAI (ELBOW), THETAI
            (WRIST_SWING), THETAI (WRIST_TILT));
        COMP_THETA6.RESULT6 (THETAI (ROBOT_END));

        -- below is the parallel program ---
    else

        COMP_THETA2.NEW_THETA2;
        COMP_THETA3.NEW_THETA3;

        FLOAT_IO.WRITE (C2, FLOAT(THETAI_1(SHOULDER)));
        FLOAT_IO.WRITE (C2, FLOAT(THETAI_1(ELBOW)));
        COMP_THETA5.NEW_THETA5 (THETAI_1 (SHOULDER), THETAI_1 (ELBOW),
            THETAI_1 (WRIST_SWING));
        COMP_THETA6.NEW_THETA6 (THETAI_1 (SHOULDER), THETAI_1 (ELBOW),
            THETAI_1 (WRIST_SWING), THETAI_1 (WRIST_TILT));

        -- results from parallel process
        COMP_THETA2.RESULT2 (THETAI (SHOULDER));
        COMP_THETA3.RESULT3 (THETAI (ELBOW));

        FLOAT_IO.READ (C, RESULT);
            THETAI(WRIST_SWING):=LONG_FLOAT(RESULT);

        COMP_THETA5.RESULT5 (THETAI (WRIST_TILT));
        COMP_THETA6.RESULT6 (THETAI (ROBOT_END));

    abort COMP_THETA2, COMP_THETA3,  COMP_THETA5, COMP_THETA6;

end RTXCHAN;
```

Program 2: The second Ada partition: RTXT4.ADA

```
-- This program implements the algorithm in the paper
-- INVERSE KINEMATICS OF THE RTX ROBOT :geometric approach & the solution
-- of non-uniqueness.

with  INTEGER_TEXT_IO, float_text_IO, long_float_TEXT_IO, TEXT_IO,
long_float_MATH_LIB, CALENDAR, CHANNELS, FLOAT_IO, INTEGER_IO;
use  INTEGER_TEXT_IO, float_text_io, long_float_TEXT_IO, TEXT_IO,
long_float_MATH_LIB, CALENDAR;
```

```
procedure RTXT4 is

pi: constant long_float := 3.141592654;
convd: constant long_float := 180.0/pi;
convr: constant long_float := pi/180.0;

got_result, coord_error, arm_error, changed_arm, parallel: boolean;
addc, ERROR4: character;
  COUNT:INTEGER;
  RESULT, NORESULT    : float;
  C2: CHANNELS.CHANNEL_REF := CHANNELS.IN_PARAMETERS(3);
  C : CHANNELS.CHANNEL_REF := CHANNELS.OUT_PARAMETERS (3);

  AX, AY, ax3, ay3, alpha, angle23, theta4, k1: long_float;
  sin23, cos23, correct4, x: long_float;
  ANGLE2, ANGLE3:float;

  begin

  INTEGER_IO.READ(C2, COUNT); -- Read number  to loop

for I in 1..COUNT loop

  FLOAT_IO.READ (C2, ANGLE2); -- read from partition 1
  FLOAT_IO.READ (C2, ANGLE3);

  angle23:= LONG_FLOAT(ANGLE2 + ANGLE3);
  correct4:=0.0;
  error4:='f';
  sin23:= sin(angle23*(pi/180.0));
  cos23:= cos(angle23*(pi/180.0));
  AX:=0.0; AY:=1.0;
  ax3:= ax*cos23 + ay*sin23;
  ay3:= -ax*sin23 + ay*cos23;

  If ax3=0.0 then if ay3>0.0 then theta4:= pi/2.0;
             elsif ay3=0.0 then theta4:=0.0;
             elsif ay3<0.0 then theta4:=-pi/2.0; end if;

    else
      x:=ay3/ax3;
      if parallel=true  and addc='y'
        then correct4:= (1.0/((ax3**2)*(1.0+x**2)))*
                   ( dax*((-ax3)*sin23-ay3*cos23)
                     + day*(ax3*cos23-ay3*sin23))
                        +dtheta4; -- put(correct4);
                          end if;
      alpha:= arctan(x);

    If ax3 >0.0 then k1:=0.0;
      elsif ax3<0.0 then if ay3 >= 0.0 then k1:=1.0; end if;
               else k1:=-1.0; end if;

    theta4:= pi*k1 + alpha + correct4;
  end if;

  if theta4 < -1.919 or theta4 > 1.919 then error4:='o';
       TEXT_IO.WRITE(C, ERROR4); -- an error flag
    arm_error:=true;
```

```
      end if;
        FLOAT_IO.WRITE (C, FLOAT(THETA4)); -- output result
   end loop;

   end RTXT4;
```

Program 3: The dummy Occam harness

```
#OPTION "AEV"
PROC rtxt4.program ([]INT ws1, in, out, ws2,
            INT32 program.result, VAL [6]INT stack.params)
  [1000] INT d:
  SEQ
   SKIP
:
```

Program 4: The Occam mini harness for the second Ada partition: RTXT$H.OCC

```
OPTION "AGNVW"
#INCLUDE "hostio.inc"

PROC rtxt4.harness (CHAN OF INT AdaChannel, AdaChannel2,
            []INT FreeMemory)

  #IMPORT "rtxt4.tax"

  [1]INT dummy.ws:
  ws1 IS FreeMemory:
  [4]INT in.program:
  [4]INT out.program:
  INT32 program.result: -- The exit status will actually be ignored.

  -- Use the stack options supplied when the program was bound.
  VAL [6]INT stack.params IS [-1, -1, -1, -1, -1, -1]:

  SEQ
    -- Set up vector of pointers to channels. in.program[0], in.program[1],
    -- out.program[0] and out.program[1] are not used.
    LOAD.INPUT.CHANNEL  (in.program[3], AdaChannel2)
    LOAD.OUTPUT.CHANNEL (out.program[3], AdaChannel)

    -- Invoke the Ada program.
    -- Assumes the entry point name has been changed to "rtxt4.program".
    rtxt4.program (ws1, in.program, out.program, dummy.ws,
            program.result, stack.params)
```

Program 5: Main Occam harness: (a) MAIN2.OCC, (b) MAIN2H.OCC

(a) MAIN2.OCC

```
#OPTION "AGNVW"
#INCLUDE "hostio.inc"

PROC MAIN2.ENTRY (CHAN OF SP FromFiler, ToFiler, []INT FreeMemory, StackMemory)
```

```
#USE "hostio.lib"

#USE "harness.lib"
#USE "rtxt4h.t8s"
#USE "rtxchanh.t8s"

BYTE b:
CHAN OF ANY Debug:
CHAN OF INT AdaChannel, AdaChannel2:
[2]CHAN OF SP FromAda, ToAda:
CHAN OF BOOL StopDebug, StopMultiplexor:
WHILE TRUE
  SEQ

    PAR

      -- A multiplexor to combine the debug and normal output.
      so.multiplexor (FromFiler, ToFiler, FromAda, ToAda, StopMultiplexor)

      -- A debug channel merger.
      alsys.single.collector (ToAda[0], FromAda[0], Debug, StopDebug)

      -- A process to invoke the Ada programs.
      SEQ
        PAR
          [125000] INT ws1:
          rtxt4.harness (AdaChannel, AdaChannel2, ws1)
          [125000] INT ws2:
          rtxchan.harness (FromAda[1], ToAda[1], Debug, AdaChannel,
                                        AdaChannel2, ws2)
        StopDebug ! FALSE
        StopMultiplexor ! FALSE

    so.exit (FromFiler, ToFiler, sps.success)
:
```

(b) MAIN2H.OCC

```
#OPTION "AGNVW"
#INCLUDE "hostio.inc"

PROC main2.harness (CHAN OF SP  FromFiler, ToFiler,
          CHAN OF INT AdaChannel,
          []INT FreeMemory)

  #USE "hostio.lib"

  #USE "rtxchanh.t8s"
  #USE "harness.lib"

  BYTE b:
  CHAN OF ANY Debug:
  [2]CHAN OF SP FromAda, ToAda:
  CHAN OF BOOL StopDebug, StopMultiplexor:
  SEQ

    PAR
```

```
-- A multiplexor to combine the debug and normal output.
so.multiplexor (FromFiler, ToFiler, FromAda, ToAda, StopMultiplexor)

-- A debug channel merger.
alsys.single.collector (ToAda[0], FromAda[0], Debug, StopDebug)

-- A process to invoke the rtxchan program.
ws IS FreeMemory:
SEQ
  rtxchan.harness (FromAda[1], ToAda[1], Debug, AdaChannel, ws)
  StopDebug ! FALSE
  StopMultiplexor ! FALSE
so.exit (FromFiler, ToFiler, sps.success)
:
```

REFERENCES

1. Coifffet P.: "Modelling and control", Robot technology volume 1, Kogan Page Ltd, 1983.
2. V.J. Lumelsky: "Iterative coordinate transformation procedure for one class of robots," *IEEE Trans. Syst., Man, Cybern.*, vol. SMC_14, no. 3 p. 500-505. 1984.
3. A.A. Goldenberg, B. Benhabib, R.G. Fenton: "A complete generalized solution to the inverse kinematics of robots," *IEEE J. Robotics Automat.*, vol. RA-1, no.1, p. 14-20, Mar. 1985.
4. H. Zang, R.P. Paul: "A Parallel inverse Kinematics Solution for Robot Manipulators Based on Multiprocessing and Linear Extrapolation" , *Proc. 1990 IEEE International Conference on Robotics and Automation*, 13-18 May 1990, p. 468-474 vol.1.
5. INMOS Limited, Occam 2 reference manual, Prentice Hall International, 1988.
6. C. S. G. Lee, P.R. Chang: "A Maximum pipelined architecture for inverse kinematics position computation," *IEEE J. Robotics Automat.*, vol. RA-3, p. 445-458, October, 1987.
7. R. Harber, J. Li, X. Hu, S. Bass: "The application of bit serial cordiac computational units to the design of inverse kinematics processors," *Proc. 1988 IEEE international conference on Robotics and Automation*, Philadelphia, Pennsylvania, 1988, p. 1152-1157.
8. H. Zang, R.P. Paul: "A Parallel solution to Robot inverse Kinematics", *Proc. 1988 IEEE International Conference on Robotics and Automation*, 24-29 April 1988, p. 1140-1145 vol 2.
9. Y. Song, R.M.C. De Keyser: "Inverse Kinematics of the RTX Robot. Geometric approach and the solution of non-uniqueness", *SO Proceedings of the 1990 American Control Conference*, San Diego, CA, USA, 23-25 May 1990. p 1780-1785 vol 2.
10. Alsys Ltd.: Ada Compilation System for the Transputer, Version 5, Application Developer's Guide.

Towards Ada 9X
A. Burns, Ed.
IOS Press, 1992

RECENT INITIATIVES OF THE ADA JOINT PROGRAM OFFICE

JOHN P. SOLOMOND
Director
Ada Joint Program Office
Room 3E114, The Pentagon
Washington, DC 22202
703/614-0210
E-mail: solomond@ajpo.sei.cmu.edu

ABSTRACT

Within the Department of Defense, the Ada Joint Program office (AJPO) is responsible for managing the effort to implement, introduce, and provide lifecycle support for the Ada programming language. Over the course of its history, the AJPO has been involved in numerous projects related to this mission. This paper describes four of the current initiatives of the AJPO.

I. INTRODUCTION

In addition to enforcing the mandate for Ada within the US Department of Defense, the Ada Joint Program Office (AJPO) has instituted a number of initiatives to enhance and improve the state of the practice in software engineering using Ada as a high-order language. AJPO initiatives have worldwide impact and are not just limited to the military sector, but include many commercial applications as well.

This paper provides details about four AJPO initiatives that will strengthen the technical aspects of the Ada language:

1.   the Portable Common Interface Set (PCIS) Programme;

2.   the merger of the Ada Compiler Evaluation Capability (ACEC) with the Ada Evaluation System (AES);

3.   the AJPO's Ada Technology Insertion Program (ATIP); and

4.   the AJPO endorsement of an Ada Style Guide.

2. PORTABLE COMMON INTERFACE SET (PCIS)

The PCIS Programme is an initiative of the Special Working Group on Ada Programming Support Environments (SWG on APSE). The PCIS Programme includes the development of requirements and specification based on interface technology for a NATO integrated project support environment. Originally, this program was to satisfy military requirements only. Today the PCIS Programme has evolved to one emphasizing a viable commercial interface that meets the needs of both the civilian and military community. The PCIS will be an evolutionary interface specification that includes that functionality necessary to be embraced as a successful commercial standard [1,2,3,4].

The SWG on APSE operates under a formal Memorandum of Understanding among the following NATO nations and official NATO representatives: Canada, Denmark, France, Germany, Italy, the Netherlands, Norway, Spain, the United Kingdom, the United States, and the NATO Communications and Information Systems Agency (NACISA).

The SWG on APSE tasked the International PCIS Programme Manager (John P. Solomond, AJPO Director) to accomplish the following during the initial PCIS Requirements Validation Phase (Jan 91-Dec 91):

a. Validate the NATO Requirements and Design Criteria (NRAC) and include civil (commercial) requirements. Alternatively, this equates to producing an International Requirements and Design Criteria (IRAC) document, which includes civil requirements for interface technology [1,2,5];

b. Investigate the present technology in interface requirements and assess the emerging technology over the next five years [1];

c. Compare the results of what industry is providing [1];

d. Analyze the differences, assign priorities, and cost the work [1].

PCIS is more than an interface set. The primary focus of the PCIS Programme is to bring interface technology to the environment user. This will provide the user with the capability to develop and maintain high quality applications at reduced cost. This benefit will be achieved through integrated tools, integrated processes, and the portability of tools, databases, and personnel in the software-engineering environment.

The IRAC contains the detailed requirement for the Portable Common Interface Set (PCIS) [5].

3.   MERGER OF Ada EVALUATION SYSTEM (AES) AND Ada COMPILER EVALUATION CAPABILITY(ACEC)

The purpose of merging the US ACEC with the UK AES was to capitalize on technology that existed both in the UK and the US. Importantly, the merged test suite would be publicly available and designated: "Approved for Public Release, Distribution is Unlimited" [6].

One possible approach for effecting this merger is to incorporate compiler performance and usability tests into the ACEC. These performance tests include both compile-time tests and execution-time tests, while the usability tests include tests related to the program library manager, diagnostic messages, and the symbolic debugger. Next, these candidate tests would be reviewed for redundancy with ACEC tests. If no redundancy was found, then the test objectives would be assessed to determine if they were valid; if necessary, test code and documentation would be revised. While the AES contains many non-compiler related assessment features, the merged suite will primarily address the Ada compilation system; besides the compiler, this includes the linker/loader, the symbolic debugger, the program library manager, and the diagnostic messages.

This merger will yield a more comprehensive evaluation test suite and benefit the Ada community as a whole. In order to effect the merger, the UK Ministry of Defence granted to the US Department of Defense a "worldwide, nontransferable, irrevocable, non-exclusive, royalty-free license to make, use, or transfer the Ada Evaluation System (AES) and unlimited use and reproduction rights in its technical information." (Ref: Acknowledgement of License of Ada Evaluation System)

Figure 1 contains the official acknowledgement of the referenced license.

Figures 2 and 3 describe a possible scenario for incorporating the AES performance and usability tests into the ACEC. Note that this is only one option and the actual merger may ultimately be accomplished technically in a different fashion.

**OFFICE OF THE DIRECTOR OF
DEFENSE RESEARCH AND ENGINEERING**

WASHINGTON, DC 20301-3030

ACKNOWLEDGEMENT OF LICENSE OF Ada EVALUATION SYSTEM

1. Purpose.

This document acknowledges the transfer of Ada Evaluation System rights from the Ministry of Defence of the Government of the United Kingdom of Great Britain and Northern Ireland to the Department of Defense of the United States of America.

2. Background.

The Department of Defense of the United States of America (US DoD), under the auspices of the Ada Joint Program Office (AJPO), has developed an Ada compiler performance and usability test suite known as the Ada Compiler Evaluation Capability (ACEC). The Ministry of Defence of the United Kingdom of Great Britain and Northern Ireland (UK MOD) has developed a suite of tests, known as the Ada Evaluation System (AES), to examine Ada compilers and other aspects of an Ada Programming Support Environment. An examination of both ACEC and AES suites by the Department of Defense has shown that there are certain user benefits to be gained through a merger of the subject suites into a single suite.

As the office responsible for the ACEC, the Ada Joint Program Office desires to merge the ACEC and the AES for the benefit of the US DoD, and ultimately, through wide-spread distribution, for the benefit of the Ada user community as a whole, including the UK MOD. To that end, the AJPO desires to implement an ACEC merger with the AES, and upon completion make this merged suite available to anyone who requests it. To accomplish this, the merged suite will be categorized as "Approved for Public Release, Distribution Is Unlimited". The AJPO will solely fund and manage this effort.

3. License.

In order to effect the subject merger, the UK MOD hereby grants the US DoD a worldwide, nontransferable, irrevocable, non-exclusive, royalty-free license to practice (make, use or transfer) the Ada Evaluation System and unlimited use and reproduction rights in its technical information.

G. M. M. stucs	*John P. Solomond*
For the Ministry of Defence of the Government of the United Kingdom of Great Britain and Northern Ireland	For the Department of Defense of the United States of America
19th June 1991	*17 Jun 91*
Date	Date

Figure 1. Acknowledgement of License of Ada Evaluation System.

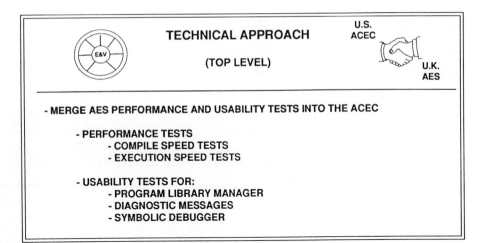

Figure 2.   Top Level Technical Approach for Incorporating AES Tests Into the ACEC.

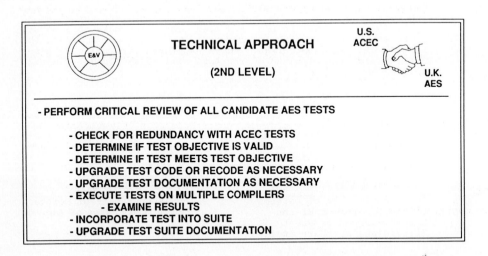

Figure 3.   Second Level Technical Approach for Incorporating AES Tests Into the ACEC.

4.   Ada TECHNOLOGY INSERTION PROGRAM

Another AJPO initiative is the Ada Technology Insertion Program (ATIP).   Under ATIP, the AJPO funds projects that will provide risk reduction for the insertion of Ada technology into US Department of Defense systems, or that accelerate Ada usage in currently developing systems.

ATIP provides funding support in areas where there may be particular technological barriers to the successful insertion of Ada; it also aids the effort to use Ada in the modification or upgrade of currently existing packages that were originally written in other languages.

This year's ATIP funding is dispersed among 14 projects, which are described below.   These projects will improve the support Ada can provide in education, bindings to other standards, and technologies such as engineering environments, prototyping, reuse, and security.

4.1   ATIP Education Projects

4.1.1   Undergraduate Curriculum and Course Development in Software Engineering

This project is intended to advance the capability of US post-secondary educational institutions to help provide a highly qualified software engineering work force.

The principle goals of this project are: to support the development of educational materials using Ada that will be widely distributed to and used by educators; to enhance the software-engineering content of courses and course sequences in computer-science curricula; and to demonstrate, though pilot implementations, the feasibility and viability of a comprehensive undergraduate curriculum in software engineering using Ada.

4.2   ATIP Projects for Bindings to Associated Standards

4.2.1   POSIX/Ada Realtime Bindings

The Portable Operating System Interface for Computer Environments (POSIX) is a Unix-compatible system environment. POSIX is intended to promote portability of application programs across the various Unix-derived environments.   It is a standard of the Institute of

Electrical and Electronics Engineers (IEEE).

This project will develop draft Ada bindings for the POSIX 1003.4 and 1003.4a standards; it will work with the IEEE standards organization to promote the use of these drafts as a starting point for development of standard Ada bindings; and it will develop and test a prototype implementation of Ada tasking using the 1003.4 (real-time) and 1003.4a (threads) services.

4.2.2   A SAMeDL Pilot Project on SIDPERS-3

The US Army is developing a military-personnel system called the Standard Installation/Division Personnel System (SIDPERS-3). This system is a Standard Army Management Information System (STAMIS) that automates 36 personnel work categories. The area of Ada bindings has presented significant challenges, and it was felt that the necessary Ada/DBMS binding layer could be provided the SAMeDL -- provided there were an appropriate SAMeDL support toolset.

This project will develop a SAMeDL toolset including a SAMeDL Module Manager and SAMeDL compiler.

These tools will target a designated database running on an Everex PC under Unix. Both an existing application and a new application will be developed utilizing this toolset. This effort is to provide concrete proof that the SAMeDL toolset has the robustness, maturity, and potential for reusability to be employed as the Ada/SQL binding of choice on any large, DoD Ada management-information system.

4.2.3   An Interactive Ada/X-Windows User Interface Generator

X-Windows is a network-based windowing system. Created at MIT, it provides a tool kit for building screens, a set of software packages that define the user interface, and a way to build icons.

This project will develop a general-purpose Ada/X-Windows User Interface Generator that will automatically generate Ada source code. Using this tool, a developer will be able to interactively develop a functioning user interface by selecting user interface primitives and arranging them on the screen. This tool is intended to reduce the bottleneck imposed upon Ada systems developers when developing window-based user interfaces based on the X-Windows system and Motif tool kit.

4.2.4 Common Ada/X-Windows Interface (CAXI)

Within the X-Windows community, two major environments currently available are the Open Window environment (with the X+ toolkit) and the Motif environment (with the Motif toolkit).

This project will design and produce a common interface to both the Xt+ and Motif tool kits. This interface will be written in Ada and allow application programs to interchangeably utilize either tool kit without requiring any modifications to the application program.

4.2.5 Ada Decimal Arithmetic Capability

Ada lacks a standard mechanism for decimal arithmetic and associated functions. Currently, organizations moving from COBOL to Ada must address the decimal-arithmetic problem in an ad hoc fashion, which has resulted in duplication of effort and non-portability.

This project will provide a mechanism for realizing COBOL-style exact decimal arithmetic in Ada 83. It will provide sufficient functionality to handle financial application with at least 18 digits of precision. It will offer early availability with Ada83 compilers, notational convenience, ease of transition to Ada 9X, and run-time efficiency.

4.2.6 ATLAS/Ada-Based Environment for Test (ABET)

In the field of Automatic Test Systems (ATS), the Abbreviated Test Language for All Systems (ATLAS) is used for programming the Test Program Set (TPS) for a Unit Under Test (UUT). ATLAS was originally designed as a test description language for testing UUTs. Although not necessarily a programming language, ATLAS does have some characteristics of a language (looping and some math functions). Technology has outpaced the ability of ATLAS by itself to test the more sophisticated UUTs.

ABET is an IEEE effort to provide an international standard for this environment. Ada is the language to be used for implementation of this standard. ATLAS would be one of many standards to be incorporated into ABET.

4.2.7   Ada Application Program Interface to GOSIP Network Services

Currently, there is no standard interface to GOSIP network services. Presently a significant number of automatic data processing efforts are separately developing their own GOSIP network services interfaces. This will become increasingly costly as more applications implement the DoD Standard Protocol and replicate functionality in a variety of ways.

This project will develop an Ada/GOSIP binding and standardize the interface of Ada applications to GOSIP network services. Once developed, this technology can be reused for environments that have already been developed, and it can be ported to other hardware suites, as well.

4.2.8   Ada SQL Interface Standardization

The Structured Query Language (SQL) has become a de facto standard for relational database management systems. Although many Ada bindings exist for commercial SQL products, a standard binding to SQL database is important to support portable Ada and reuse for MIS applications.

The Software Engineering Institute has been developing an interface technology for Ada applications that access SQL database management systems. One result is the SQL Ada Module Description Language (SAMeDL), which has been accepted by the International Standards Organization Working Group on Ada (ISO/JTC1/SC22/WG9) as a Committee Draft, the first step in the standardization process.

This project will fully document the SAMeDL as a language and its supporting methodology. The project will respond to the needs of the standardization process, coordinate efforts of potential vendors of SAMeDL processors, and respond to the needs of potential SAMeDL customers so as to assist the transition to practice of the SAMeDL.

4.3   ATIP Projects Focusing on Software Engineering Environments, Prototyping, Reuse, and Security

4.3.1   AdaSAGE Enhancements

AdaSAGE is an Ada development environment designed to facilitate rapid and professional construction of systems in Ada by application developers working with the end users. Applications may vary from small to large multi-program systems utilizing special capabilities. These capabilities include database storage and retrieval (SQL compliant), graphics, communications, formatted windows, on-line help, sorting, editing, and more. It was developed by the Department of Energy. It is currently used by all three services, and operates on various systems - including MD-DOS platforms, Unix System V, and OS/2. AdaSAGE applications can be run in the stand-alone mode or in a multi-user environment.

This project will provide data-field-by-data field validation capabilities as well as a user-friendly interface to the tool; it will enhance AdaSAGE's capability to import/export data from commercial file formats; and it will port AdaSAGE to the Unix operating system on the US Army's Small Multi-user Computer contract.

4.3.2   Reusable Ada Products for Information Systems Development (RAPID)

The mission of the US Army's RAPID effort is to develop, implement, maintain, and administer a total reuse program supporting the entire software development lifecycle. RAPID includes an automated library tool used for the configuration, identification, and retrieval of reusable Ada software components; it also has a staff supporting and training developers in reusability and sound software-engineering principles.

The RAPID center library (itself written in 30,000 lines of Ada code) now contains over 800 reusable software components (RSCs), consisting of over 550,000 lines of Ada code. The RSCs are derived from a variety of sources -- including existing US Army applications, commercial vendors, and existing repositories.

RAPID is now in Phase 3, a 12-month period during which the use of RAPID will be expanded to all of DoD as needed and allowed by funding. During this phase, one of RAPID's highest priorities is to continue to populate the library with quality RSCs.

4.3.3   Generic Avionics Data Bus Tool Kit

There is a need for a standard software interface that can be reused for various military-standard multiplex data busses and over multiple simulations with minimal changes. Also, such an interface should contain an integral set of monitoring and debugging tools to aid in the development and testing of data interfaces.

This project will offer a time-critical, multi-platform, multiplex databus interface designed and written in Ada. The initial software will focus on the MIL-STD-1553 protocol since it is the most prevalent, but it will be designed to be configured for future expansion to other types of data busses.

4.3.4   A Computer Aided Prototyping System for Real-Time Software

Major requirements for modern embedded software systems include the capability to respond in real-time to data inputs from multiple interfaces -- such as commands from end users, multiple weapons interfaces, and multiple tactical data link systems. Development costs have been increased by demands for efficient computations, lucid display, strict real-time deadlines, and the need to deal with sporadic input data and hardware interrupts in such sophisticated systems.

A prototype is an executable model of a proposed software system that reflects chosen aspects of the system, such as display formats, values computed, or response times. Rapid prototyping uses prototypes to help both developers and their customers visualize the proposed system and predict its properties in an iterative process.

The program will design and develop a computer-aided prototyping system (CAPS). This is to demonstrate a high-technology and low-cost approach to providing state-of-the-art software prototyping tools for real time Ada programs. It also provides the opportunity to utilize the thesis efforts of students at the Naval Post Graduate School, who are DoD personnel familiar with Ada and its embedded applications.

4.3.5   Ada Reuse in a Trusted Message Processing System

Extensive reuse of code written for other systems has raised questions in the minds of those concerned with the security of the resulting system. This project is a trusted message-processing system employing Ada reuse and a commercial operating system. It must achieve the B2 level of trust described in the Orange Book of the National Computer Security Center.

The system will be fielded as the Submarine Message Buffer (SMB) System, supporting personnel with two levels of security clearance. Among other elements, this project when completed in Ada is to provide a cost effective, non-developmental set of bindings suitable for many applications including automated information systems.

5.   Ada STYLE GUIDE

On August 12, 1991, the AJPO and the Software Productivity Consortium (SPC) signed a Memorandum of Understanding aimed at meeting the need of the Ada Community and the US Department of Defense for a freely available Ada style guide.

The AJPO is now advising defense and military agencies that *Ada Quality and Style: Guidelines for Professional Programmers* is "the suggested Ada style guide for use in DOD programs".

For some time now, there has been discussion in the Ada community and in the DOD about the need for a generally accepted Ada style guide. The need for a style guide arises because, while the Language Reference Manual provides a thorough definition of the Ada language, it was not intended to provide complete guidance on the appropriate use of Ada's powerful features. *Ada Quality and Style: Guidelines for Professional Programmers* was repeatedly mentioned as striking a good balance between general and organization-specific approaches to Ada programming. After receiving these comments, the AJPO initiated inquiries into methods by which *Ada Quality and Style* could be made freely available to the DoD and the Ada Community.

5.1   Guidebook Features

Ada Quality and Style: Guidelines for Professional Programmers was published by the Consortium in 1989. Since then, it has become a standard guidebook for Ada programming at many organizations. It offers Ada programmers a set of specific guidelines for using the powerful features of Ada in a disciplined manner in order to develop Ada code with high degrees of readability, portability, and reusability. The guidebook, however, is not being made into a standard MIL-HDBK. Instead, it is the AJPO's *suggested* guide. This allows more flexibility for future change in the guide than we would have been able to obtain had it been published as a MIL-HDBK.

5.2   Copyright

Although *Ada Quality and Style: Guidelines for Professional Programmers* will be freely available for downloading, etc., the SPC still retains copyrights. They have granted permission to use, copy, modify, and distribute copies -- but no fee may be charged, and all copies must include the copyright notice and the permission notice.

Furthermore, the name Software Productivity Consortium, Inc., cannot be used in advertising or publicity pertaining to distribution of the guidelines without specific, written prior permission. Neither the AJPO nor the SPC make any representations about the suitability of the guidelines for any purpose. It is provided "as is" without express or implied warranty.

5.3   Obtaining Copies

In the very near future, electronic copies will be made available on the Defense Data Network (DDN) and on the Ada Information Clearinghouse (AdaIC) Bulletin Board. Sessions on the AdaIC Bulletin Board are limited to 90 minutes. The following US access phone numbers are appropriate: Data: (+1) (703) 614-0215, or (+1) (301) 459-3865. Users should set their telecommunications parameters to: 300/1200/2400 baud; No Parity; 8 data bits; 1 stop bit.

For information on obtaining a hardcopy version, contact the Ada Information Clearinghouse via mail or phone: Phone: (+1) (703) 685-1477
                            Ada Information Clearinghouse
                            c/o IIT Research Institute
                            4600 Forbes Boulevard
                            Lanham, MD., USA 20706-4320

Also, glossy soft-back copies may be purchased through Van Nostrand Reinhart Publishing Company or through the Software Productivity Consortium.

6. REFERENCES

[1]   Solomond, John P., PCIS Requirements Validation Activity Work Plan, March 1991.

[2]   NATO Requirements and Design Criteria (NRAC) for the NATO Standard Interface Specification (NSIS) on Ada Programming Support Environments (APSEs), Version 2.1, December 6, 1988.

[3]   Military Standard Common Ada Programming Support Environment (APSE) Interface Set (CAIS), Revision A, MIL-STD-1838A, 6 April 1989.

[4]   Standard ECMA-149 Portable Common Tool Environment (PCTE) Abstract Specifications.

[5]   International Requirements and Design Criteria for the PCIS, Draft, 4 July 1991 (Draft document)

[6]   Solomond, J.P., Masters, G., "Acknowledgement of License of Ada Evaluation System, June 1991."